Three Fearful Days

Three days, three nights, three fearful days
Of death, of flame, of dynamite,
Of God's house thrown a thousand ways;
Blown east by day, blown west by night—
By night? There was no night. Nay, Nay.
The ghoulish flame lit nights that lay
Crouched down between this first, last day!
I say those nights were burned away!

"San Francisco,"
by Joaquin Miller
Sunset Magazine, June-July 1906

Three Fearful Days

San Francisco Memoirs
of the 1906 earthquake & fire

Compiled and introduced by
Malcolm E. Barker

LONDONBORN PUBLICATIONS
SAN FRANCISCO 1998

Londonborn Publications acknowledges the following for granting permission to reprint items as indicated:

Bedford Modern School, Bedford, England: "Like wind through a cornfield." Excerpted from *The Eagle*, July 1906.

The British Library, London: "Geary Street, at Powell" ("5:12:05 A.M."). Excerpted from letter, ADD MD 59.652.ff.82-9.

California Historical Society: "My dear Elise ..." Excerpted from letter, MS.3512. Also "A letter from a National Guardsman." Excerpted from letter, MS.3474.

Chinese Historical Society of San Diego: "Hugh Kwong Liang's story." Excerpted from "The Life Story of Hugh K. Liang," *Newsletter*, Spring 1996.

Dutton Signet, a division of Penguin Books USA Inc.: "The day before ... ," "Picturing the city," "Newshounds raid mayor's cellar," and "At the feet of a goddess." All excerpted from *Give Us a Little Smile, Baby*, by Harry J. Coleman. Copyright 1943 by E.P. Dutton & Company, Inc.; renewed 1971 by Henry J. Coleman.

The Menninger Clinic, Topeka, Kansas: "A 'subjective' view." Excerpted from *Menninger Perspective* Number 1, 1990.

Library of Congress Cataloging-in-Publication Data
Three fearful days : San Francisco memoirs of the 1906 earthquake & fire / compiled and introduced by Malcolm E. Barker
  p.   cm.
Includes bibliographical references (p.   ) and index.
ISBN 0-930235-06-1
1. Earthquakes--California--San Francisco--History--20th century--Sources.
2. Fires--California--San Francisco--History--20th century--Sources.
3. San Francisco (Calif.)--History--Sources.
I. Barker, Malcolm E., 1933- .
F869.S357T48   1998
979.4'61--DC21   98-13704
                                                           CIP

First printed May 1998

10 9 8 7 6 5 4 3 2

LONDONBORN PUBLICATIONS
P.O. Box 77246, San Francisco, CA 94107-0246

Remembering
the more than 3,000 men, women, and children
who did not survive the San Francisco
1906 earthquake and fire.

Acknowledgments

To those people who offered stories of their own families for this volume, I am truly grateful. Similarly appreciated are the people who lent items from private collections. Each of these letters and diary entries, no matter how brief, is a very personal bridge back to those terrifying days of earthquake and fire in April 1906. Combined with the hundreds of other accounts I read, they helped me more fully appreciate the human drama of the catastrophe, and guided my efforts to evoke that drama in the book. Sadly, space limitations prevented me from using all of the pieces submitted.

My thanks in this respect to James S. Browne, Robert J. Chandler, Pamela J. Fenner, Joanne W. Lafler, Shirley S. Levine, Bill Pickelhaupt, Patsy Pinkus, Ron Ross, Maria Sakovich, Sue Anne Sanders, Mike Smith, Mrs. James T. Watkins, and Nancy Weston.

Gary Sterling eased my initial research by allowing me to use his collection of California history books and ephemera without the restraints normally imposed by public libraries. His collection of earthquake postcards inspired the idea of reproducing specific cards *as cards*, complete with shadows and worn edges.

I am fortunate in having had Jackie Pels and David R. Johnson of Hardscratch Press work with me on the production of the *San Francisco Memoirs* trilogy. Each has added distinctive expertise: Jackie as editor of my text, and David as designer and creator of the covers. Jackie's encouragement with—and perceptive editing of—my writing in recent years has been invaluable. David skillfully added the three-dimensional effect to the postcard images, and removed scratches from the Hotaling advertisement and Mabel Coxe portrait, which I had taken from microfilm.

John Boring, another friend whose careful attention to accuracy and detail is much appreciated, reconstructed a portion of the official 1906 map of the burnt area. He then identified many of the locations referred to in the stories.

No research into the 1906 earthquake and fire is complete without studying the files of Gladys Hansen. During her 18 years as city archivist at the San Francisco Public Library, Gladys undertook the task of tracking down the identities of all the people killed in the catastrophe. It is owing to her efforts that we now have a more accurate count of fatalities. Today, she is curator of the Museum of the City of San Francisco, which holds an unparalleled collection of earthquake artifacts. I thank her for her help and encouragement in this project. The museum's website (http://www.sfmuseum.org) was also a valuable tool.

At the California Historical Society I thank in particular Patricia Keats and Emily Wolff, library director and photo collection manager respectively, for their help in locating earthquake ephemera and photographs.

And at the Golden Gate National Recreation Area Park Archives and Records Center I thank the archivist technician Mary L. Gentry, in particular for her help during my frantic last-minute photo search.

I could not have completed this book without the unstinting help of librarians and their assistants (including the many whose names I do not know) at the following facilities:

Bancroft Library at the University of California, Berkeley (Peter Hanff, Susan Snyder, Jack Von Euw); Judah L. Magnes Museum, Berkeley; National Archives and Records Administration, San Bruno (Kathleen M. O'Connor, archivist); the newspaper room at the University of California, Berkeley; Northern Regional Library Facility (NRLF) of the University of California, in Richmond; *San Francisco Examiner* library (Judy Canter, head librarian); San Francisco History Center at the San Francisco Public Library (Susan Goldstein, city archivist, Patricia Akre, photograph curator, and Tom Carey); San Francisco Performing Arts Library (Lee Cox, librarian); Sutro Library, San Francisco; and the United States Geological Survey, Menlo Park (Susan Garcia, information assistant for earthquake hazards). Also, the staff of The British Library in London for locating a copy of the letter to Miss Maria Mansell from "Harry."

In seeking a copy of Hugh Kwong Liang's account I was helped by Murray K. Lee and Dorothy Hom of the Chinese Historical Society of San Diego; Phil Choy, Him Mark Lai, and Jeannie Woo of the Chinese Historical Society of America; and also Mrs. Gwen Benjamin of Arlington, Virginia.

Constance Reid helped me with the account by Eric Bell, and Janet Bell, widow of his only son, Taine, sent me his photograph.

J.R. (Dick) Monaco let me use photographs made by his grandfather, J.B. Monaco, after the earthquake.

Jerome M. Garchik and Leah Garchik provided me with a copy of the original letter written by Mabel Coxe.

Thanks also to David J. Wald, seismologist at the United States Geological Survey in Pasadena, California, for setting me straight on specific earthquake details.

Last, but not least, I am grateful for the assistance, encouragement, and support of the following people during this project:

Peter Browning, Edward L. Crossley, Jack Fiske, Lynn Ludlow, Glen Millward, Susan Moore, Kevin J. Mullen, the late Mary Grace Paquette, Werner Pels, Rand Richards, Albert Shumate, Deke Sonnichsen, Walter and Margaret Swarthout, Margaret Viera, Jim Welter, and Peter Booth Wiley.

M.E.B.

Contents

Illustrations

For sources of these illustrations, see page 320.

The postcards
Enterprising printers and publishers wasted little time in producing
hundreds of books, postcards, and collections of stereoscopic cards
depicting the devasted city. These were eagerly sought after by survivors and sightseers alike. However, they did have their detractors. An
editorial in the *San Francisco Call* on May 20, 1906, warned that,

although they might be good for souvenirs and "the edification of our grandchildren," they could also harm the city.

Are we not damaging the city by every one of these views we send away? The whole world is familiar with our calamity, but is it necessary to harp on the subject after it is all over? Why not forget it as soon as possible and cease to keep the fire alive by fanning the dying embers? ... If we want to frighten people away from us this is about as good a way as any other.

This appeared under the headline "Pernicious advertising."

In 1906, postcards were called "postal cards" or "postals," and their backs were reserved solely for the address and a one-cent postage stamp. People sending them wrote their messages on the front, either around or across the illustrations. Many of the images appearing on the cards are available today as photographs, but these lack the sense of immediacy—of actually having been handled and inscribed by the people of 1906—that the cards have. Furthermore, the messages are themselves valid and very personal eyewitness accounts, which is why you'll see a few reproduced in this book *as* cards, complete with creases and crinkled edges.

San Francisco was not the only town devastated by the earthquake on April 18, 1906. Santa Rosa was almost demolished. San Jose and Santa Cruz were severely damaged. On the campus of Stanford University the library, gymnasium, and church were reduced to ruins. The earth split for a distance of approximately 290 miles extending from Mendocino in the north to Hollister, 100 miles southeast of San Francisco. The movement was felt by people as far north as Oregon, as far south as Los Angeles, and as far inland as central Nevada.

Yet it is called "the San Francisco earthquake."

Although devastation from the quake was widespread in the city, an even greater tragedy followed. Fires ran rampant for three days until almost five square miles of the downtown area lay charred and desolate.

Early estimates of the number of people killed in the city have recently been revised from the official 478 to more than 3,000. The number of people killed elsewhere has been estimated at 189.

The magnitude of the tremor has also been revised. Seismologist Charles F. Richter published the familiar 8.3 figure in 1958 after working from values recorded only in Europe, none being available locally. With recent California earthquakes—including the one in 1989 centered near Mount Loma Prieta in Santa Cruz County—stations in Europe have shown a relative bias of about ½ magnitude unit. Two independent studies using different approaches have redetermined the magnitude of the 1906 quake: in one instance to 7.7 and in the other to 7.9. As a consequence, seismologists now agree that it had a magnitude of 7.8 rather than 8.3.

This reconstruction of the official 1906 map of the fire-ravaged area identifies most locations mentioned in these stories. Not shown is the area extending south of Market Street to 20th Street between Dolores and Howard. Five hundred city blocks—approximately 4.7 square miles—burned. A few isolated spots survived.

For clarity, only streets mentioned are identified.

The stretch of Embarcadero running north from the Ferry Building was known as East Street North, while the southern portion was East Street South. Columbus Avenue was Montgomery Avenue. Grant Avenue had two names: North of Bush Street it was Dupont Street, and from Bush to Market it was Grant Avenue. The Western Addition extended west from Van Ness Avenue to Lone Mountain, and north from Market Street to the Marina.

Key:
 1. Fort Mason.
 2. James Stetson's home at 1801 Van Ness Avenue.
 3. Portsmouth Square (and Hall of Justice).
 4. A.P. Hotaling & Co. at Jackson and Montgomery.
 5. Montgomery Block (and Coppa's) at Montgomery and Washington.
 6. Appraisers' Building at Sansome between Jackson and Washington.
 7. Fairmont Hotel at California and Powell.
 8. Old St. Mary's Church at California and Grant.
 9. Ferry Building.
10. St. Mary's Cathedral at Van Ness and O'Farrell.
11. Origin of Hayes Valley Fire.
12. St. Francis Hotel at Powell and Geary.
13. Union Square.
14. Chronicle building (and Lotta's Fountain) at Kearny and Market.
15. City Hall at McAllister and Larkin, on City Hall Avenue.
16. Mechanics' Pavilion at Grove and Larkin.
17. Hotel St. Nicholas at Market between Polk and Larkin.
18. Post Office at Seventh and Mission.
19. Nevada House at Sixth and Howard.
20. U.S. Mint at Fifth and Mission.
21. Grand Opera House at Mission between Third and Fourth.
22. Call building (Claus Spreckels Building) at Third and Market.
23. Examiner building at Third and Market.
24. Palace Hotel at Market and New Montgomery.
25. Grand Hotel at Market and New Montgomery.
26. Fremont and Mission streets.
27. Railway station at Third and Townsend.

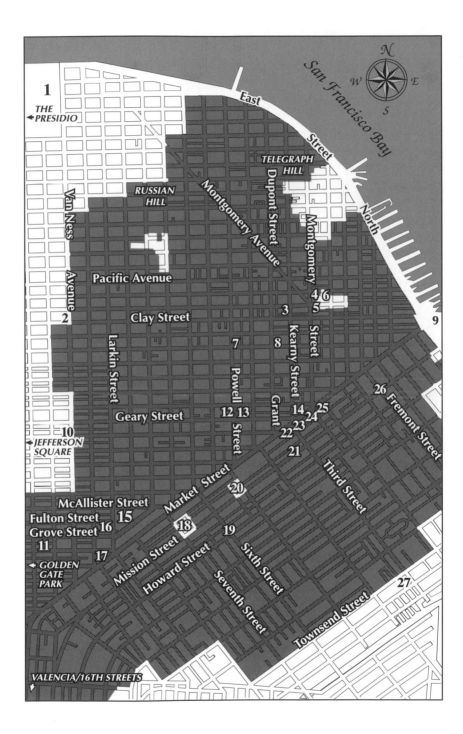

One half of a stereoscopic view from the Ferry Building, looking up Market Street. Barely visible at the top of Nob Hill behind the still-rising smoke is the Fairmont Hotel (extreme right).

Adding human interest

K NOWING I WAS WORKING on this third volume of the *San Francisco Memoirs* trilogy, people asked me, "What period does it cover?" When I answered, "The 1906 earthquake and its aftermath," their response, though suitably polite, often caused me to imagine them thinking, "Oh, dear, *another* earthquake book!"

I admit such exchanges sometimes gave me pause. Was I right in devoting an entire volume to this one event, which has already been the topic of several books, countless articles and many television programs, as well as the classic 1936 movie "San Francisco." But then I would look through the material I was gathering and my excitement over the project would return. After all, I reasoned, most of those other books limit themselves to the story of the earthquake; mine tells the story of *the people who endured it*. And whereas other books quote only a few lines or paragraphs of what various people said, I allow them several pages and, wherever possible, add extra information about them—who they were, where they lived, what became of them.

This attention to behind-the-scenes detail required an extra level of research, and while it was sometimes arduous it was also exhilarating. First I hunted down the stories. Then I sought out what I could about each individual. Thumbing through city directories often told me in what part of town they lived (reactions to the quake varied according to how severely a particular neighborhood was affected). The California Information File and the San Francisco Newspapers Index sometimes led me to people's birth dates—and therefore their age at the time of the quake—and what might have happened to them subsequent to April 1906. In a few cases, I found this information in the census records for 1900 and 1910.

For example, I suspected that "Annie Laurie" was not one writer's real name and felt vindicated when I discovered that it was the pseudonym of Winifred Black Bonfils. To learn of this woman's subsequent involvement with social work and charities adds a new dimension to her story of the refugee camps. (See "The real San Francisco.")

Two of my favorite stories are by Mary Edith Griswold and Edwin Emerson Jr. Imagine my delight when I came across an item in the *San Francisco Call* announcing their marriage exactly one month after the earthquake! When I re-read Emerson's story I saw that the wedding he describes matches his own, although he does not identify it as such. (See "Three days adrift" and "A joyous renaissance.")

The primary research was in *finding* these first-hand accounts. I read hundreds of letters, journal entries, and miscellaneous documents at the University of California's Bancroft Library, the California Historical Society, and the San Francisco History Center at the San Francisco Public Library. I looked through every earthquake book I could find. In this I was fortunate in my friendship with Gary Sterling, who offered me access to his impressive library of California history.

I soon realized that, for me, the Holy Grail would be the vast— yet mysteriously missing—collection of documents gathered by the Earthquake History Committee immediately after the quake. Even though this important source is often referred to by researchers, its exact whereabouts is not known. According to a report in the *San Francisco Examiner* on April 19, 1908, the committee had by then gathered hundreds of official documents, clippings from 36,000 newspapers—and "about 3,000 narratives of personal experiences ... all of them written before the story had become entirely untrustworthy."

The *Examiner* story, written by Henry Morse Stephens, professor of history at the University of California, added that the task of filing, indexing, and cross-referencing all this material was proceeding, though slowly. Sadly, little else has been heard about the work since then.

These comments by Professor Stephens helped sustain me:

[The committee] members realized from the beginning that it was their duty not only to relate facts, but also to render faithfully the atmosphere of the time. They desired further not only to record events and to reflect the pressing flavor of a critical time, but to bring out the human interest in their story. For while the events of April and May, 1906, in San Francisco are of surpassing interest from the way in which the community as a whole met its problems, the part of the individual in seeing and feeling what was going on around him was not to be neglected. … Particularly interesting were the personal experiences of the actual shock of earthquake, which, as collated, show not only the various ways in which the shock affected different buildings and different parts of the city, but also its psychological effect upon individuals of varying age and temperament.

It was this *psychological effect upon individuals* that intrigued me as I read through the hundreds of accounts I eventually gathered, and it is a continuing thread in this volume.

As with each of the previous volumes of memoirs, I went back as far as possible in seeking the original versions of all accounts, rather than rely on them as printed in more recently published books. This not only gave me an interesting look at any editing that might have been done but sometimes provided me with longer accounts and considerably more material. One such search led, if not to the Holy Grail itself, then certainly as close as anyone might expect to get.

From my friend Gary Sterling I borrowed a little book that had been printed privately in 1927—*Recollections of the Fire*, by James W. Byrne. According to the book's foreword, this was a reprint of Byrne's account that first appeared in *The Argonaut*, a San Francisco weekly journal, in November and December 1926. I went to *The Argonaut*, and—Bingo!—found 70 full-page articles that ran for 16 months, from May 1926 through August 1927, under the general title, "The Great Fire of 1906."

I doubt I would have unearthed this cache had I not sought beyond Byrne's little book.

Reading through the series, I realized that here perhaps is the most comprehensive history of the earthquake and fire to be found anywhere. It includes numerous official reports and documents, and well over 100 in-depth first-person accounts, many of which I have not seen reprinted anywhere. In several instances reference is made to the Earthquake History Committee resources, which leads me to surmise that those files were used to compile the series.

For other "new" accounts I continued my search elsewhere. At the British Library in London I found the letter from "Harry" to Maria Mansell. (See "5:12:05 A.M.") And thanks to Constance Reid (author of *The Search for E.T. Bell, also known as John Taine*), I obtained a copy of a letter that appeared in the magazine of a boys' school in England. (See "Like wind through a cornfield.")

For further stories and background material I read every issue of *The San Francisco Chronicle, The San Francisco Examiner, The San Francisco Call*, and *The Bulletin* from April through the end of 1906, in addition to many issues of *The New York Times* and *The Los Angeles Times* for the same period.

With this latest volume of memoirs I have not found the confusion of obsolete words that teased the readers in the earlier volumes so do not feel a glossary is warranted. However, it may not be amiss to remind today's younger readers that the the word "gay" as used frequently in these pieces originally meant merely "lively," "high spirited," or "fun loving."

As was my practice in the first and second volumes, I have not tampered with the original spelling and punctuation within the pieces except where necessary to clarify the text. I have, however, abbreviated some of the originals, deleting passages that repeat material already given by other writers. All such deletions within the text are indicated with an elipsis (...).

For the benefit of students and historians, I list resources by page number in "Resource notes" at the back of the book. I use brackets ([ ]) to interject immediate clarification of text, and to provide missing first names wherever possible. Parenthetical notations in the pieces were made by the original writers. All headings, with the exception of "Three days adrift," are my originals.

I do not claim that this volume replaces the missing record compiled by the Earthquake History Committee. However, I sincerely hope that, at the least, it fulfills the expressed aims of Professor Stephens by relating facts and rendering the atmosphere of those three fearful days of April 1906 and their immediate aftermath.

Malcolm E. Barker
San Rafael, California
February 1998

A city is shaken

W HEN THE 20TH CENTURY OPENED, San Francisco was experiencing an economic boom that began with the Yukon gold rush and was strengthened by the Spanish-American War. Its geographic location made it a vital embarkation point for thousands of gold seekers on their way to the Klondike and for troops going to the Philippines. Then, after the war, expanded trade with the Orient boosted the American economy—and firmly established San Francisco as the Gateway to the East.

The city was the center and distribution point for California's vast agricultural and canned goods industries. Passenger liners and cargo tramps from around the world berthed at wharves skirting its waterfront, alongside five-masted schooners laden with lumber from Puget Sound. Ferries criss-crossed the bay, connecting with the railway terminus at Oakland that served all major cities and regions to the east and those to the north, in Oregon and Washington. From a station at Third and Townsend streets trains served Los Angeles and other Southern California towns.

San Francisco's reputation for elegant hotels was acknowledged around the world and was about to be augmented by the addition of the St. Francis (1904) and the Fairmont (due to open in 1906). Similarly renowned were its restaurants: Zinkand's, Marchand's, Tait's, the Poodle Dog, and the Palace Hotel's Palm Garden, whose tables were central to the social whirl of the city's elite. Oysters and champagne were de rigueur.

The fun-loving spirit of the Gay Nineties spilled into the new century as San Francisco acquired a sobriquet: "the city that never sleeps." Theaters—from bawdy and vaudeville to drama and grand opera—attracted internationally acclaimed performers. Tourists came to wander the intriguing alleyways of Chinatown, to bathe in the sprawling salt- and fresh-water pools at the Sutro Baths, or simply to gaze at the Pacific Ocean from the gingerbread Cliff House perched on its rocky plinth at the very edge of the continent.

Spurred by this sudden prominence in the eyes of the world, San Franciscans began to re-evaluate their city's appearance. The hodge-podge of architectural styles that had evolved since the pioneer days of the 1840s and '50s was no longer appropriate. If San Francisco was truly to be the Paris of the West, as some people proclaimed, then it should have wide avenues and imposing plazas such as those in the French capital. In newspapers and magazines people debated how best to "beautify" San Francisco.

In January 1904 the Association for the Improvement and Adornment of San Francisco was formed. A few months later, Chicago architect Daniel Burnham, founder of the City Beautiful movement, was invited to submit a master plan. In a rare display of unanimity the press, politicians, and the citizenry approved the move, and the outcome was awaited enthusiastically.

In the meantime another idea gained popularity: that of hosting an exposition to honor the anticipated opening of the Panama Canal. What better way to show off San Francisco's assets than by a world trade fair? It was still too early to put in a bid, but at least the seed was planted in many people's minds.

When the Burnham Plan was finally submitted in September 1905, enthusiasm was not so widespread. Burnham's ideas were so extensive they would need decades to implement, during which time entire neighborhoods would have to be uprooted. New avenues would be cut diagonally across existing blocks. Streets on the steeper hills would be re-routed to follow the contour of the hills. The summits of Telegraph Hill and Twin Peaks would be leveled to make room for elaborate monuments reminiscent of ancient Rome. An area extending from the top of Twin Peaks to Lake Merced would become one huge park, displacing any homes within its perimeter. And the Panhandle would be extended across town, slicing through several blocks before terminating at the Pacific Mail Steamship docks near China Basin.

Principal opponents of the plan were traders and business operators who felt that San Francisco was primarily a commercial city and that its advancement as such should not be impeded by extravagant schemes of beautification.

The downtown skyline was already changing. Two- and three-story buildings were demolished to make way for steel-reinforced structures rising eight, nine, or even 10 stories. A huge clock tower topped the 10-story *Chronicle* building at Market and Kearny streets. And at Market and Third stood the tallest building on the West Coast, rising 16 stories above the street—the Claus Spreckels building where the San Francisco *Call* had its office and plant. Beneath its domed roof was a restaurant with an unprecedented view of the city.

Simmering beneath this air of confidence, however, was a nagging sense of unease, of foreboding. Earthquakes! Many older San Franciscans had vivid memories of the quake of 1868, in which 30 people in the Bay Area had been killed. Three years before that the City Hall had been severely damaged and water mains had burst in a less violent quake. In the decades that followed many if not most San Franciscans had come to accept the numerous smaller temblors as part of life in the city. Nevertheless, there was always the thought that "one day ..."

The San Andreas Fault, which marks the separation of two tectonic plates, lies for more than 650 miles along the westerly edge of California, extends to a depth of at least 10 miles beneath the surface, and runs directly through the Bay Area. The Pacific Plate extends to the west of the fault and encompasses not only the California coastline but most of the Pacific Ocean floor. To the east, the North America Plate extends over the entire width of the continent and parts of the Atlantic Ocean floor. The Hayward Fault that runs along the eastern side of San Francisco Bay and the San Jacinto Fault in Southern California are extensions of the San Andreas Fault system.

The plates are constantly shifting, each adapting to the other's movement. Occasionally, stress builds up and is then relieved by a sudden, violent movement—an earthquake. According to the National Earthquake Information Center, in the world there have been on average 18 "major" earthquakes (7.0 - 7.9 magnitude) and one "great" earthquake (8.0 or above) a year since 1900.

In San Francisco, along with the fear of a major earthquake was the lingering dread of fire, though for many people the fact that San Francisco had been almost completely destroyed by six separate fires between December 1849 and June 1851 was *history*. Strict codes introduced since then regulating construction methods and materials had led people to believe that their buildings were now fireproof. And the knowledge that the city had a well-equipped and efficient fire department gave them a further sense of security.

Dennis Sullivan, the Fire Department's chief, was not so confident. In 26 years with the department, he had seen first-hand the sorts of hazards that threatened disaster. He warned city officials and offered several proposals—repairing and reactivating underground cisterns that had been built in the 1860s, purchasing high explosives to be used in creating fire breaks, more training for his men—but was rebuffed. There was not enough money to pay for such schemes, he was told.

In his 1905 annual report Sullivan repeated a recommendation he had made earlier for replacing small and inadequate water mains in many of the city's streets, and he urged the decision makers not to delay any longer a Twin Peaks auxiliary salt water system, which had already been approved and budgeted for. He also stressed the importance of acquiring a light draft, high-power fire boat to protect the rapidly expanding docking facilities along the waterfront.

Eugene Schmitz was virtually unknown in November 1901 when he ran for and won the office of mayor of San Francisco. He had been persuaded to join the race by Abraham Ruef, a brilliant, ambitious young lawyer who saw this as his opportunity to gain a political foothold, not as frontman but as the power behind the scene.

Although lacking political know-how, Schmitz was tall and charming, with a compelling voice and good looks. He was a Catholic, born in San Francisco of Irish and German parents and respected as a model husband and father. He played the violin and was leader of a local theater orchestra. And his courtly manner and bearing belied his working-class background and enabled him to mix comfortably in all strata of the city's social scale.

Ruef seemed content to be the ventriloquist who manipulated the candidate. He brushed aside Schmitz's arguments that the latter had no experience in politics and no funds to run for office. These were matters he, Ruef, would take care of. And when Schmitz won the election Ruef became his attorney, the man to whom contractors and business executives would be referred. In time, Ruef became the city's most powerful political boss, and one of the suavest of any in the country. He easily outshone his predecessor Christopher Buckley, the notorious "Blind Boss of San Francisco" who manipulated municipal politics in the late 1880s and early '90s.

Graft in municipal politics was neither new nor unique to San Francisco. Many major cities across the country were plagued with corruption during this period. Graft was so commonplace that Ruef did not have to seek it himself. Corporations and municipal utilities seeking favors from the mayor and Board of Supervisors volunteered to pay him monthly *retainers* of $250, $500, or more. Cash. No receipt. These, of course, were to be considered *attorney fees* which, Ruef rationalized, were perfectly legal and could not be confused with bribes.

One lucrative business for the Ruef-Schmitz partnership was the issuance and renewal of liquor licenses for what were termed "French restaurants." The ground floors of these establishments were occupied by some of the finest and most elegant restaurants in the city— popular venues for dining with client, business associate, or wife. On the second floors, the dining areas were more intimate, catering to couples who desired privacy with their dinner. On the upper floors, the distinction between dining area and sex salon was less subtle. And, since champagne was a staple of dining out in San Francisco, a restaurant—especially a "French restaurant"—without the required liquor license could die a sudden death.

But protection rackets were not limited to the wealthy champagne set. Nor to sleazy Barbary Coast businesses around Pacific Street. Brothels and liquor dens thrived throughout the town, often under the noses of police officers who might look one way while extending their hands another.

So although San Francisco in those early years of the 20th century may on the surface have seemed far removed from the bawdy, riotous days of its youth half a century earlier, in some respects it was still the same wide-open town where, for a price, almost anything was possible.

Early in Schmitz's tenure, Fremont Older, editor of the San Francisco *Bulletin*, began a campaign to uncover graft at City Hall. The task proved long and tedious, and the results were often tenuous. For years Older's newspaper maintained a constant barrage of attacks, but the lack of hard evidence, and the increasing popularity of Mayor Schmitz and Boss Ruef, invalidated many of his charges.

After the 1905 election, Older initiated a high-level investigation with the aid of some very influential people. He went to President Theodore Roosevelt in Washington, seeking the services of the federal government's special prosecutor Francis J. Heney (born and raised in San Francisco) and Secret Service detective William J. Burns. For financial backing, he went to Rudolph Spreckels (the youngest son of sugar millionaire Claus Spreckels) and former mayor James Phelan. Both agreed to help. He also gained the confidence and support of the district attorney, William H. Langdon—a Schmitz appointee.

By April of 1906 this team was already at work covertly gathering evidence in preparation for the trial that would expose graft and corruption in the Ruef-Schmitz administration. On the 17th, the mayor learned of Spreckels' involvement—a sign that the matter now extended far beyond mere nit-picking in the newspapers. That knowledge must surely have played on his mind as he spent the evening quietly at home with his family.

Downtown that same Tuesday evening, on Mission Street between Third and Fourth streets, the city's elite flaunted their best formal wear at the Grand Opera House for the second night of the opera season. Critics had panned the opening night performance of *Queen of Sheba*, but that did not dampen the enthusiasm and excitement of the second-night audience as Enrico Caruso sang the role of Don José opposite Olive Fremstad in Bizet's *Carmen*.

This is how Charles S. Aiken, editor of *Sunset Magazine*, remembered that night:

> All society—with a big S—was out in force. Beautiful women gorgeously gowned, with opera cloaks trimmed with ermine, and diamonds on hands and hair; men with pop hats and the conventional cast-iron sort of clothes that mean joyous discomfort;

here were wondrous bunches of orchids and roses; the singing and acting that charmed and the deafening applause; then came the hoarse shouts of carriage numbers, the strange melody of automobiles, the clang of electric cars; then tuneful orchestras at the Palace palm garden, or at Tait's, or the Fiesta, or Techau's, and oysters poulette and Liebfraumilch, Welsh rarebit and steins of Muenchenbrau or terrapin Maryland and Asti tipo chianti. And after all came the home-going in the early hours, with down-town streets still crowded, and the dazzling electric signs swinging wide over welcoming portals, making the garish city night shame the modest moonlight.

At approximately 12 minutes past five the next morning—Wednesday, April 18, 1906—the first earthquake hit San Francisco, waking most of its residents and interrupting those already at work. It lasted only a few seconds and momentarily left everyone in suspense. Then came the second and most severe jolt, and for 45 to 60 seconds the entire city was relentlessly shaken and twisted.

Eyewitnesses described the movement as a violent to-and-fro interspersed with sudden jolts and terrifying circular swings. Standing or walking was impossible. Many people were thrown from their beds. Those who were standing were tossed to the ground. And all the while they heard a cacophony of rumbling, crashing, sliding, and wrenching. No human sounds were heard during that terrifying three-quarters of a minute. No screams. No crying out. It was as if every man, woman, and child was stunned into silence.

Several roads split open, propelling streetcar tracks upward into hideous shapes and revealing gaping chasms beneath. Loosened cobblestones danced about like popcorn in a pan. Power cables snapped and fell to the ground, "writhing and hissing like reptiles" in the words of one eyewitness. Gas connections broke and kitchen stoves overturned, releasing fumes that soon started fires. Underground mains ruptured, spilling water that could have put out those fires. And, at the Civic Center, three tiers of columns peeled away from the brand new City Hall rotunda and reduced to rubble a structure that had taken 26 years and six million dollars to build.

The ship *Wellington*, entering the bay, "shivered and shook like a springless wagon on a corduroy road," according to Captain

McCullough, the harbor pilot. Yet the sea "was as smooth as glass and showed not a ripple."

At The Chutes—an amusement park on Haight Street—lions cowered and trembled, tigers behaved like frightened kittens, and monkeys "ceased their chattering and crowded in a wriggling mass in the corner of their cage," according to a report in the *Call*.

For most people, the terror was heightened by their stupor upon being awakened so mercilessly. They had no warning of what was happening. As they struggled to regain their sensibilities in that trance-like state between sleeping and waking, many imagined themselves in a nightmare. Some were alert enough to jump out of bed. Others found themselves so numbed they could not move at all, and they watched in bewilderment as their furniture and other belongings bounced, slid, or smashed around them.

And all of this happened in less than one minute.

The greatest immediate tragedies were in the crowded wood-frame hotels and rooming houses in the working-class neighborhood south of Market Street. Buildings clustered around Sixth and Howard streets collapsed upon themselves, burying more than a hundred tenants on the lower floors. Rescuers scrambled among the ruins to untangle the victims but were soon driven back by flames. None ever forgot the anguished cries of the people still trapped. The four-story Valencia Street Hotel also collapsed upon itself, leaving barely one floor standing at street level. As many as 100 people may have perished there either in the collapse or in the fire that wiped out the entire block two days later.

The Valencia had been built on the site of the lake beside which, on June 29, 1776, Spanish Franciscan fathers had celebrated Mass—the event which, according to some historians, signified the birth of San Francisco. The Spaniards named the lake *Nuestra Señora de los Dolores*.

Throughout the first day smaller shocks continued to startle everyone, the most severe of these being at about 8:15 A.M.

Nobody knows for sure where or how the first fire broke out. What is known is that 52 fires started a few minutes after 5:12 on Wednesday morning. Ominous clouds of smoke were soon seen spiraling above the city. Unhindered, those blazes billowed and converged until they were raging furnaces devouring block after block. For three days and nights they taunted the hapless firefighters. Glaring flames turned nights into days. Smoke irritated eyes. And an almost constant shower of cinders pestered the skin like so many mosquito bites.

When the fires were finally extinguished on Saturday, 4.7 square miles of downtown San Francisco—approximately 500 city blocks, from Van Ness Avenue to the Ferry Building and from the southern slopes of Russian Hill to Townsend Street—was a wasteland littered with the gutted shells of once imposing buildings. Only the waterfront structures and a handful of isolated buildings escaped annihilation.

According to the United States Geological Survey, an estimated 28,188 buildings in San Francisco were destroyed, with property damage set at $400 million in 1906 dollars—a fifth of it caused by the earthquake. More than half of the city's residents—225,000 of 400,000 people—were left homeless. The number of people killed was originally said to be 478, but recent research by Gladys Hansen (formerly San Francisco city archivist) and Frank R. Quinn (formerly Registrar of Voters) indicates that the figure was closer to 3,000.

Ironically, Fire Chief Dennis Sullivan—the man who had tried so earnestly to alert city officials to this very possibility, the man who had more experience and knowledge of fire-fighting than any other in town—was one of the quake's first victims. He and his wife slept in separate rooms on the top floor of the fire station at Bush and Kearny streets. Towering above the three-story station was the eight-story California Hotel, topped by a cupola. During the quake the cupola and a large section of hotel wall toppled onto the smaller building. The weight of this mass sent it crashing through the roof and each successive floor of the station until it finally buried itself in a confusion of ruins in the basement. Mrs. Sullivan narrowly missed being struck by the falling cupola, but she and her bed slid down into the vortex behind it. Her husband rushed into the room and, temporarily blinded by the rising cloud of dust, fell through the hole and was buried beneath the still-falling rubble. Although Mrs. Sullivan survived her injuries, the fire chief succumbed several days later.

From his home on Washington Street, Brigadier General Frederick Funston walked to the top of Nob Hill, and then down

"Sept 16, 1906 8.30 P.M. This is the way this building looked before Apl 18. The city is still almost in total darkness, and an awful sight. We have visited most of it today. And the glorious sunset. Lovingly Sunshine."

"Why should we want to visit Rome? This shows what the big wiggle did to the City Hall. Lovingly Bess."

Jones and California to Sansome Street. The scenes he saw along the way convinced him of the gravity of the situation. Obviously, the city's Fire Department could not contain the blazes; many of the water mains had broken. And the police force would need help in maintaining order throughout the vast devastated area. With Major General Adolphus Greely on leave in Washington, Funston had been placed in command of the U.S. Army's Pacific Division. It was up to him to take charge.

He hailed passing automobiles, but the drivers ignored him. Cursing, the brigadier general half-ran, half-walked uphill from Sansome to the army stable on Pine Street near Hyde, some 10 steep blocks. There he ordered one of his men to prepare a saddle-horse while he sent messages to Colonel Charles Morris, commanding officer at the Presidio, and Captain Meriweather Walker, commanding officer at Fort Mason, ordering them to report with their troops to the Hall of Justice at Portsmouth Square. On his way from Sansome Street, Funston had been told by a patrolling policeman that, with City Hall in ruins, both the mayor and the chief of police would probably use the Hall of Justice as their headquarters.

Fifteen minutes after the earthquake, John Williams and Myrtile Cerf, two men from the city attorney's office, arrived at the devastated City Hall and were surprised when the mayor failed to show up. They drove to his house at 2849 Fillmore Street, between Vallejo and Green streets, arriving at about six o'clock. Apart from downed chimneys and cracked walls, they saw very little damage in that neighborhood. Mayor Schmitz was stunned to hear of what was happening elsewhere in the city, and immediately he climbed into their automobile. They drove down Van Ness Avenue to see the City Hall, and then along Market Street. At Kearny Street they turned and went to the Hall of Justice.

The moment he arrived, Schmitz began issuing orders as if he were a seasoned military commander. The severity of some of his orders, and the sincerity with which he issued them, astonished many people who, in the beginning, questioned his ability to handle such a catastrophe. Particularly surprising to many was the fact that he took these decisive actions without consulting Abe Ruef.

He ordered troops from the Presidio to patrol the burning districts and keep people away from the ruined and collapsing buildings. He sent a special detachment to guard the treasurer's office at City Hall, the vaults of which contained six million dollars. In his drive across town he had seen several instances of looting. This prompted his boldest order: that looters be shot dead on the spot. Lighted candles were forbidden in any building in the city. He also ordered that all saloons be closed immediately, and the sale of liquors banned. Any establishment caught selling liquor would have its stock spilled in the street. This liquor ban lasted about 10 weeks.

A Mission District printer whose shop had survived the quake printed 5,000 copies of this proclamation, which were then distributed around town and posted on telegraph poles, lamp posts, and other visible surfaces. Because there was no electricity, soldiers commandeered passers-by to take turns at the treadle operating the press.

Realizing that the situation presented problems that normal channels of city government would not be able to handle, Schmitz made a list of people he felt could be more effective. He called them The Committee of Fifty, and sent for them to meet with him at three o'clock that afternoon. At the meeting, other names were added until the Fifty numbered closer to 100. These were then broken down into 22 subcommittees ranging from Resumption of Civil Government to Organization of the Wholesalers. Included were separate subcommittees to deal with the resumption of the judiciary and transportation; restoring water, lighting, and telephones; and providing food and housing for those who needed it. There was a Citizens Police Committee, an Auxiliary Fire Committee, and a Committee of History and Statistics, which later became the Earthquake History Committee assigned the task of compiling a complete history of the disaster.

In selecting these people, Schmitz included men who had opposed him on occasion, as well as men who had been participating in the investigation against him and Ruef. James Phelan and Rudolph Spreckels were on the original list, but Abe Ruef, surprisingly, was not, although he was added later. One indication of the times is that no women's names appeared on the first list, and the only subcommittee that had women as officers was one called Relief of Sick and Wounded.

Schmitz opened the meeting by announcing, "Let it be given out that three men have already been shot down without mercy for looting. Let it be also understood that the order has been given to all soldiers and policemen to do likewise without hesitation in the cases of any and all miscreants who may seek to take advantage of the city's awful misfortune."

The meeting was interrupted when the windows of the Hall of Justice shattered and masonry fell as dynamite blasted a building a block away. The mayor and his committee members left the hall and continued their discussions in the center of Portsmouth Square. They agreed to convene twice a day as long as the emergency lasted. This they did, although they had to keep changing venues as the fires advanced through the town.

The sight of armed troops patrolling the streets, together with the draconian tone of Schmitz's proclamation, led some people to assume that martial law had been imposed. But it had not been, nor was it ever. Nevertheless, even local newspapers continued under the impression that it was.

The mayor later wrote, "While the orders issued at that time were perhaps without legal authority, and were extraordinary, they were accepted by the people with good nature and good will, and there was a general desire to carry out the suggestions made in my written and verbal messages."

The degree of damage from the quake was not immediately apparent to many people, depending upon what part of town they were in at the time. The farther they were from the downtown area built on land fill, and the sturdier their homes, the less overall damage they first noticed, or suspected, as had been the case with Mayor Schmitz.

Some survivors told of sweeping up fallen plaster and broken ornaments, then preparing to carry on as if nothing had happened. After all, San Franciscans were used to earthquakes! Others told of getting dressed and walking in the direction of the rising columns of smoke, curious to see what was happening. A few even wandered downtown expecting to get breakfast in one of the restaurants or hotels there.

Fleeing from the burning City April 18, 1906. San Francisco, California.

207 Charles Weidner, Photographer, San Francisco Printed in Germany.

Sightseers soon found themselves passing an ever-growing stream of people going in the opposite direction, toward the parks, away from the approaching fires. These were families and others whose homes had been severely damaged or were now threatened by fire. Their numbers grew as the day wore on, until streets leading to Golden Gate Park, the Presidio, and numerous smaller parks around the city became conduits of human flotsam.

While one stream of refugees was moving toward the parks, another was weaving a circuitous route to the Ferry Building, hoping to get a boat for Oakland—or anywhere away from the city. Fires at the foot of Market Street forced detours through side streets. But many of these were also blocked, which added miles to the journey. People who succeeded in hauling weighty belongings all the way to the waterfront were horrified to be told that there was room on the ferries for people only—no baggage.

The first troops arrived downtown from Fort Mason at approximately 7:45 A.M. and were posted two to a block in an effort to keep looters and sightseers away. More troops arrived throughout the morning from the Presidio, Angel Island, and Fort Miley. These were scattered throughout the city, with special units guarding the U.S. Mint on Fifth Street, the new main Post Office on Mission and Seventh streets, and the Appraisers' Building on Sansome at Jackson— three of the few downtown buildings that eventually survived the conflagration.

Units of the California National Guard began assembling downtown without waiting for direct orders from their commander, Brigadier General John A. Koster, who was in Ukiah and beyond communication.

The U.S. Navy also came to the aid of the city. The destroyer *Preble*, the fire boat *Leslie*, and the tug *Active* all sailed down the bay from the Mare Island Navy Yard and anchored along the Embarcadero in company with the tug *Sotomoyo* from Yerba Buena Island. The *Preble* brought all available surgeons and nurses from Mare Island.

And so, within a few hours of the early morning earthquake and outbreak of fire, the battle to save San Francisco was being waged by six agencies: the city's police and fire departments, the National Guard of California, the U.S. Army, the U.S. Navy, and a group of citizens' committees. For the most part—certainly during the first couple of days—they all worked more or less in harmony. Politics were put aside. Suspicions and personal animosities were forgotten for the time being. Funston managed to curtail his distrust of and dislike for the mayor, while the mayor seemed to take on a whole new persona. Even his staunchest critics acknowledged his sudden emergence as the man of the hour.

Although many early accounts spoke in glowing terms of the heroic effort to save the city, the battle was not without its controversies. One was the manner in which dynamite was used—ostensibly to create breaks in the fire lines, although in many cases it resulted in spreading the fires. Another was the shooting of civilians suspected of looting. And then there was the officious manner in which many home owners were prevented from trying to save their own buildings and possessions.

Funston later shielded his men from much of the criticism by stating that the army had consulted with the city's police and fire departments "and complied with their wishes in every way." Furthermore, he stated, nobody had been shot by troops for looting. Similar assertions were made by Funston's superior, Major General Adolphus Greely, who re-assumed active command of the Pacific Division when he returned to the city on April 23. In a report to the Secretary of War, Greely wrote that aside from victims of the quake and fire only nine people, all men, were killed.

"Of these nine victims, two were killed by members of the National Guard of California," he wrote, "one was shot by members of a so-called citizens' vigilance committee, one by a police officer for looting, and one through the combined action of a special police officer and a marine. The remaining four deaths of unknown parties occurred at places not occupied by the Regular Army."

In retrospect, these figures seem as unrealistic as do the figures at the other extreme bandied about by sensation mongers. The mayor's proclamation had sanctioned the killing of looters, and reports of shootings can be found in private letters and journals as well as in newspaper stories. The two examples included in this book ("A letter from a National Guardsman" and "The shooting of Cadet Aten") identify the shooters as regular soldiers. And Cadet Irvine

Aten states that he was only one of three patients being treated at the Presidio Hospital for gunshot wounds inflicted by soldiers.

A report in the *Call* on May 6, 1906, stated that of the 358 bodies examined by the coroner's office only one appeared to have gunshot wounds. The coroner was quoted as saying, "In the time of great excitement we heard of many cases of shooting, but the fact that we never received the bodies convinces me that the stories were false." Curiously, this fails to take into consideration that the heat generated by the fires was so intense—estimated to have reached 2700 degrees Fahrenheit—that it cremated bodies where they fell and, consequently, no true tally could be made of casualties, nor of whether they died from gunshot wounds.

The use of dynamite was a much-debated issue before the final fuse was set. One factor rarely mentioned in post-1906 accounts is that dynamite per se was not the only explosive used. Stick dynamite, granulated dynamite, black powder, and gun cotton all were used, regardless of their suitability under the prevailing conditions. Strict laws then, as today, prohibited storing large quantities of high explosives in or near large cities, and the closest supply was across the bay, at the California Powder Works at Pinole. Getting dynamite from there took time, and meanwhile the only significant amount of explosive available was gunpowder stored at the Presidio.

In the beginning, a small supply of stick dynamite was obtained from Angel Island. Lieutenant Raymond W. Briggs of the Artillery Corps was given some of this, but he soon exhausted the supply. In his report he said that he then received "a number of wagons ... loaded with giant powder—dynamite in granular form."

He hesitated, knowing that its combustion would set fire to any building it destroyed. But, "urged as a last resort," he used it on two buildings at the corner of Kearny and Clay streets. The result was as he had anticipated. Both buildings immediately caught fire, and burning material blew across the street and set another block ablaze.

The use of dynamite might have been successful if water had been available to wet down the resultant ruins. As it was, sparks from the explosions started fires in the woodwork and other combustible materials within the blasted buildings.

General Funston later admitted that gunpowder was "ill suited to the work" and "all that portion of the city where gunpowder was used ... could have been saved only by the use of carloads of dynamite."

The army's strongest critic was Henry Anderson Lafler, a journalist and assistant editor of *The Argonaut*. When Funston wrote an article for *Cosmopolitan* magazine entitled "How the Army Worked to Save San Francisco," Lafler responded in a small book using the same title but giving his version of what happened. He said that the army "captured" the city like an "alien foe" in a war, and that ordinary citizens were "cowed by careless men with guns" who prevented them from going to the aid of exhausted firemen.

Such drastic measures were not necessary to prevent looting, Lafler said, and he asked rhetorically, "Is there any thief worse than fire; is there any robber more to be dreaded than flame?"

"We were strangers in our own streets," he wrote, "driven from our own houses; gray-haired men, our foremost citizens, the sport of the whims of young boys, whose knowledge of the city was confined to its dance-halls, its brothels, its saloons."

Lafler was not alone in commenting on the youth of the soldiers. Some of the writers included in this book make similar comments. This raises a question for historians and other researchers trying to sort out the conflicting accounts that have been bequeathed to us. In addition to the U.S. Army and the National Guard, three battalions of cadets from the University of California patrolled the city's streets for the first two nights and days. All of these groups wore uniforms and carried guns. In the eyes of many people, these uniforms signified "soldier," meaning a member of the U.S. Army. Very few accounts make distinctions among regular soldier, National Guardsman, and cadet. How many of those "young soldiers" were, in fact, militia from the state's Guard or students from Berkeley?

To add to the confusion, other young men donned clothing that resembled uniforms and tried to pass themselves off as soldiers.

Just as it is incorrect to place all the blame for the spate of fires on "dynamite," so it surely is to blame "the army" for all the shootings.

In subsequent investigations and court trials, neither the guardsmen nor the army or navy escaped with clean slates. No serious charges were brought against the cadets who, in an editorial in the *Call*, were praised for carrying out their patrols with "the precision, coolness and courage of veterans."

During the first few days nobody was allowed into the city without a pass. This particular pass was issued on April 23 to Benjamin Frank Weston, a Berkeley resident who had an office in San Francisco. Without the "Do not impress" rider, he would have been forced—as were most able-bodied men—to help clear the streets of rubble.

In the days immediately after the fire all men and youths who happened to be downtown were forced to help clear the streets of rubble. No one was immune from impressment unless he had a special pass—neither wealth nor position was sufficient to avoid the duty. There are a number of accounts of the city's more prominent residents being forced at bayonet point to clear debris from the streets so that emergency vehicles might pass. According to one of these accounts, Secretary of State Charles Curry was forced by "a martinet of a corporal" to spend an hour and a half tossing bricks and other debris into carts on lower Market Street.

This issue of impressment was another source of discord between civilians and the military. After a particularly strong complaint from bakers who were forced to sweep streets in the early mornings after their shifts baking bread, the mayor and the governor ordered the army and the National Guard to stop the practice.

The Fire Department suffered greatly from the loss of its chief, Sullivan. His temporary replacement, John Dougherty, who was about to retire, was not able to provide the leadership and strategy required at such a time. The difficulty was compounded by the loss of telephone and alarm systems that normally linked the stations, and the constant stream of refugees and sightseers crowding the streets. In a number of instances fire hoses were burst and couplings broken by the wheels of speeding vehicles, or the heavy hand-trucks of the refugees.

But the most perilous was the lack of any pre-arranged course of action. Sullivan is reported to have once told a friend that if the city's water mains were broken by an earthquake he would concentrate all of his men and equipment on saving the downtown business section. He would use his engines to pump salt water from the bay, and, if necessary, he would dynamite buildings south of Market Street to create a break. Furthermore, he would not make any effort to save the residential areas until after the business section was out of danger.

As it happened, many firemen remained with their equipment in their own districts, assisting neighborhood people and property. Consequently, most of the fires that broke out in residential areas away from downtown were brought under control before they could spread, while the entire business area was destroyed.

The major exception to this was the Hayes Valley Fire, or, as it is better known, the Ham and Eggs Fire. This broke out in a building on Hayes Street between Franklin and Gough at about 10:30 on the morning of the 18th. It is believed to have been caused by a defective chimney attached to a stove on which a woman was cooking breakfast. According to one eyewitness, "It was just a tiny flame that shot up from the roof of a two-story structure and it looked to me as if a little bucket of water would subdue it."

By the time overworked firefighting equipment arrived, the "tiny flame" had become an inferno that burned for 24 hours and wiped out most of a 30-block area stretching from Octavia Street to Van Ness Avenue and from Golden Gate Avenue to Market Street. It set ablaze the ruins of City Hall, which burned slowly for three days, and also forced evacuation of the temporary hospital that had been hurriedly set up in the Mechanics' Pavilion. It was finally stopped at 20th Street and Mission early Friday morning.

Meanwhile, other major fires swept uptown from the Ferry Building and were not checked until they reached the east side of Van Ness Avenue where buildings, including many elegant mansions, had been dynamited to create a fire break.

The popular theory was—and has continued to be—that the sheer width of the avenue defeated the flames. But this was challenged by the architect Burnham. Back in San Francisco to revitalize his beautification plan, Burnham said that the fire stopped because of a change in the wind direction, not because of the width of the thoroughfare. He recalled the 1871 fire in Chicago when flames crossed wide streets and continued to burn until there was nothing left to burn.

"A great conflagration sweeping with the wind cannot be stopped by human energies," he said. "No matter how wide the barriers are the wind will drive the fire across them. ... It was that wind from the west that saved the remainder of the city, not the width of Van Ness Avenue."

His theory was supported by Professor Alexander McAdie of the U.S. Weather Bureau, who said that when the light north wind died away, the west-northwest wind turned the fire back on itself.

"Like the Warder of the Marches, it kept the bounds, 'Thus far and no farther,'" he wrote in the June 1931 *Harvard Alumni Bulletin*.

Credit for saving the waterfront rests with the navy. From Thursday morning until Saturday sailors and officers worked alongside, or independently of, the local firefighters. The full significance of this concerted effort can be better appreciated when we realize that, in 1906, 90 percent of all people entering or leaving San Francisco passed through the Ferry Building, and the city's economy depended upon goods imported and exported via the embarcadero wharves.

The governor of California, George C. Pardee, arrived in the Bay Area on one of the first trains from Sacramento. When he realized that all telegraph and telephone lines in the city were inoperable, he established his headquarters in the office of Oakland Mayor Frank K. Mott. He immediately arranged for more telegraphic equipment to be installed, and for two days he sent a constant stream of messages around the United States asking for help.

The response was immediate. All across the country, relief committees were formed. Great quantities of food, clothing, medical supplies, and other items were sent by rail or steamer. Schoolchildren helped with the packaging. Many of the country's top entertainers took part in charity concerts and performances. Businesses large and small contributed to seemingly limitless funds. Municipalities joined in, adding hundreds of thousands of dollars in cash and supplies.

President Roosevelt instructed the Secretary of War to send all available tents and bedding. And in Ogden, Utah, the local people were not able to buy fresh bread—every loaf that came out of the ovens was shipped to San Francisco.

Refugees gathered in all the parks and public squares of the city. On the first nights most people slept outdoors. Even those who still had homes chose not to sleep in them, but instead huddled in back yards or on front doorsteps. Social barriers were obliterated, and men and women from the city's wealthiest mansions found themselves standing in line with those from the poorest neighborhoods to get their share of food and water at the relief stations.

With banks destroyed or closed, few people had any ready cash. Ferries and trains carried passengers without asking for fares. And the U.S. postal service accepted all mail from the city without postage.

Because of the shortage of stationery, people wrote their messages on whatever they could find—shingles, scraps of old newspapers, pieces of cardboard, and, in at least one instance, a detachable collar.

Circulars were posted throughout the town warning people to boil water at least 30 minutes before drinking it, and to wash all fresh vegetables.

The army took responsibility for feeding people and establishing camps around town. Buildings and tents on the Presidio grounds housed 16,000 refugees. The tents were laid out in numbered streets, and a directory kept of who was living where. A strict regimen was enforced, with daily inspections of all tents, kitchens, and toilet facilities.

Colonel G.H. Torney, who had the duty of overseeing sanitary conditions throughout the city, explained in a *Call* article on May 7, 1906, that these measures were necessary to prevent the spread of infectious diseases. Of particular concern, he said, were refugees who had been "willfully violating sanitary laws at every opportunity" before they became charges of the government. He added that the battle against infection had hardly begun.

Apart from regular military inspections of sanitary conditions, life in most of the city's parks and vacant lots was less orderly than at Presidio camps. These refugees were left to their own devices in setting up tents, or whatever shelter they could contrive from the materials at hand. Families and groups of friends cooked meals on their own jerry-rigged stoves. There was no privacy, and little protection from fog and rain.

The earthquake and fire had scattered not only humans but rats. Bubonic plague-carrying rodents scampered among the ruins. Some were seen eating dead bodies. Prevailing conditions left the city vulnerable to an outbreak of the plague, and only stringent enforcement of the army's precautionary methods prevented that disaster from becoming a reality.

There were a number of cases of typhoid and smallpox in the parks and camps, but these were isolated as soon as discovered and a full-blown epidemic was averted.

Despite the lack of home comforts, refugee life was not without its brighter moments. A sense of camaraderie prevailed as social and cultural barriers were replaced by a common effort to survive.

James Jones wrote this letter on a detachable collar and mailed it, as is, without postage, to his son and daughter-in-law in New York:

Dear Wayland and Gussie: All safe but awfully scared. Frisco and hell went into partnership and hell came out winner—got away with the sack. Draw a line from Ft Mason along Van Ness Ave. to Market St., out Market to Dolores to Twentieth, thence to Harrison, 16th & Potrero Ave. R.R. Ave. to Channel St. and bay. Nearly everything east and north of this boundary line gone, and several blocks west of it, especially in Hayes Valley as far as Octavia St. from Golden Gate Ave. east. Fire is still burning on the northside but is checked in the Mission. I and a band of 40 or 50 volunteers formed a rope and bucket brigade, back-fired Dolores from Market to 19th, pulled down houses and blanketed westside Dolores and won a great [?] victory. More with paper & stamps. James G. Jones. April 21st, 1906.

Some accounts actually suggest that, for many people, the outdoor life was not without its benefits. As a report from the London Hospital printed in *The Argonaut* on September 8, 1906, had it:

These people were fortunately deprived of their trams, alcohol and luxuries; they had nothing but simple food, and they were compelled to take exercise in the open air to get it. The men have found it possible to live without cigars or whiskey and the ladies without candy. They have cooked their simple meals in the streets, to the better ventilation of their houses; for lack of light they have gone to bed early, with the compensation that they have risen with the lark. They have had the enforced benefits of a sanitarium, and good health is the result.

And Cupid was busy. The number of marriage licenses issued during April and May far exceeded the number for any preceding two-month period.

Within hours of the quake, the world's telegraphic wires were buzzing with reports that San Francisco had been completely destroyed. Many read like elegies for the dead, referring to San Francisco in the past tense and implying the city was gone, never to return.

Newspapers elaborated upon the skimpy details that were coming across the wires. What they didn't know, they made up. Within a few weeks hastily prepared books, filled with gory details to satisfy the most sensation-seeking reader, were for sale everywhere. These told of looters cutting fingers from dead bodies to retrieve rings, of soldiers shooting civilians scavenging for food among the ruins, and of refugees rushing hysterically through the streets.

In their efforts to scoop competitors, some publishers faked illustrations by cutting existing photographs and rearranging pieces of buildings to imply their collapse, and then adding flames and clouds of smoke.

Many of the wildest stories that appeared in the nation's newspapers during those first few days were later attributed to men and women who left the city on the first available trains and embellished their accounts for the benefit of reporters who greeted them at each station where they stopped across the country.

The *New York Times* sent its own reporter to gather an eyewitness account. He compared the terror of the fleeing refugees he met along the way with the attitude of those he met in San Francisco and

The illustration, below, reveals the extent to which at least one art department went to obtain an "action shot" of the earthquake—apparently in the hope their readers would not see the original, above. The hands on one clock face were changed to read 5:30, although those on the other face were not. Even allowing for San Francisco's fame as "the city that never sleeps," there are alot of people on the streets for so early in the morning!

concluded, "The cowards have fled and the brave remain." Arriving at Oakland, he saw refugees who had spent the night in tents, or who had slept on the sidewalks with only concrete steps as pillows. "They were reading newspapers, laughing and joking," he wrote. "Hardly one appeared wretched or even depressed."

This echoes a common thread that runs through the accounts of writers (professional and amateur) who visited the city immediately after the quake—a genuine admiration for the people who had lived through the catastrophe yet who displayed little or no sense of tragedy. "Heroic" was a word constantly used. Newspapers across the country told of the "Spirit of San Francisco" and implied that this loyalty to one's city and determination not to be cowed by disaster was unique to San Franciscans.

William James, the psychologist and philosopher brother of Henry James, was at Stanford University during the quake. After visiting the city he, too, noted an almost total lack of expressed self-pity. "Not a single whine or plaintive word did I hear from the hundreds of losers whom I spoke to," he later wrote. Instead, everybody seemed to be helping everyone else.

But rather than label this as uniquely San Franciscan, or Californian, or even American, James saw it as a normal human reaction. In any such "heavy action" situation where many people are involved together, "healthy animal insensibility and heartiness" override mental pathos and anguish, he said.

Photographer Arnold Genthe saw it differently. In his autobiography, *As I Remember*, he wrote:

> The attitude of calmness ... the apparent indifference of the people who had lost everything, was perhaps not so much a proof of stoic philosophy that accepts whatever fate brings. I rather believe that the shock of the disaster had completely numbed our sensibilities. I know from my own experience that it was many weeks before I could feel sure that my mind reacted and functioned in a normal manner. If I had shown any sense, I might easily have saved some of the things I valued most ... which I could have carried away in a suitcase. As it was, practically everything I possessed had gone up in smoke.

The idealistic view of selfless and heroic San Franciscans during those three fearful days persisted for many years. Writer after writer eulogized it while admitting that there were occasional instances of looting. But a contrasting view was revealed in a closely typed, 11-page report found in the National Archives in 1975. The report, written by Lieutenant Frederick Newton Freeman, described in detail how the navy fought to save the city's waterfront. It also painted a grim picture of drunkenness and selfishness among people in that neighborhood:

> Throughout this day [April 18] constant trouble had been experienced owing to the large number of drunken people along the waterfront. ... The crowds rushed saloon after saloon and looted the stocks, becoming intoxicated early in the day. In my opinion great loss of life resulted from men and women becoming stupefied by liquor and being too tired and exhausted to get out of the way of the fire. During this whole day we needed unarmed men to rescue women and children in the neighborhood of Rincon Hill, the fire having made a clean sweep of this poor residence district in about an hour's time. The most heartrending sights were witnessed in this neighborhood, but with my handful of men we could not do as much for the helpless as we wished. Able-bodied men refused to work with the fire department, stating that they would not work for less than forty cents an hour, etc. Men refused to aid old and crippled men and women out of the way of the fire and only thought of themselves.

Freeman also criticized the "thousands of sightseers" who crossed the bay from Oakland and created further problems for his fire-fighting teams. Incensed, he ordered the Southern Pacific Company—operators of the ferry service—not to let anybody enter the city by ferry until General Funston gave permission.

Some writers have dwelt on the "declassified" status of Freeman's report and speculated as to why it was classified in the first place. But according to Kathleen O'Connor, archivist at the San Bruno office of the National Archives, it was simply a case of mis-filing. (See "Resource notes" for details.)

Another account of less-than-heroic San Franciscans appeared in the *Call* on May 12, 1906. Apparently, a group of "dissolute males" and women "painted and dressed in their gaudiest finery" fled from the saloons and brothels of the Barbary Coast and gathered on the steps of the Mint as the fires approached. There they waylaid a passing wagon, stole its cargo of champagne "and other fine liquors," and engaged in "a wilder, fiercer orgie than the red light district had ever known."

Eventually, troops and police arrived. "A bedraggled, writhing, cursing, disheveled swarm of men and women, some so drunk that they had to be carried by companions little more able to stand, was forced from the steps," the report added. "Shouting, yelling, shrieking, singing, they moved on before the bayonet and the club. The Tenderloin had drunk its farewell to old San Francisco."

The ashes of San Francisco had scarcely cooled when Ruef resumed his machinations. Thanks to his *fees*, United Railroads was able to install permanent overhead trolley wires for the city's streetcars instead of underground cables, even though the general public strongly opposed the overhead construction. Also, thanks to him, the Home Telephone Company of Los Angeles snagged the lucrative telephone franchise without opposition.

In October 1906, Ruef was charged with bribing the supervisors, who were subsequently granted immunity from prosecution in return for full confessions. But it was not until May of the next year that he implicated Schmitz in the French restaurant cases. In June, the mayor was sentenced to five years in San Quentin and removed from office, but the conviction and prison sentence were overturned seven months later by the state Court of Appeal.

Ruef's trial continued until December 1908, when he was sentenced to 14 years in San Quentin. He served only 4½ years before being paroled.

In 1921 Schmitz was voted back into City Hall as a supervisor.

Boosters of the Burnham Plan proclaimed that nature had provided the perfect opportunity to implement its proposals. But reality demanded otherwise. If San Francisco was to retain its position as a world economic leader, and not lose it to Los Angeles or Portland, it would have to be rebuilt as quickly as possible. Even in those days before environmental reports, such grandiose redevelopment would require raising millions of dollars in municipal funds and conducting lengthy negotiations over property lines. Consequently, the city was rebuilt on the same basic grid that Jasper O'Farrell had laid out in 1847.

Fillmore Street between Sutter and Pine, where most buildings had escaped with minimal damage, became the temporary hub of San

Francisco. There, the major newspapers and business houses rented space while grand new skyscrapers rose from the ruins downtown. The city's government moved into Franklin Hall, at the corner of Fillmore and Bush streets.

The residential districts took longer to rebuild, and hundreds of people were still living in refugee camps two years later. With the approach of the winter of 1906, the Army erected more than 5,000 wooden shacks at camps throughout the city. Many large single-family homes were converted into boarding houses. Along Van Ness Avenue, dynamited and burned-out mansions were replaced by hastily built retail stores, while others that had survived the catastrophe were converted to restaurants, clubs, or stores—thus signaling the end of an era for one of the city's more opulent residential neighborhoods.

Within a couple of weeks, streetcars were running—without fares—along Market Street from the Ferry Building, and along Turk and Eddy to Fillmore. The Post Office resumed mail delivery. Telegraph and telephone services began operating again. And banks were able to open their now-cooled safes and resume business.

On May 12 the streets of San Francisco were illuminated as 23,000 lamps were turned on for the first time since the morning of April 18. That same week, thousands of homes were able again to use their gas fires, stoves, and lamps. And the sounds of reconstruction reverberated as the downtown business section rose to heights and glories it had not known before.

According to a report by the city's Chief Engineer Marsden Manson, $90 million was spent on reconstruction during the 19-month period ending January 1, 1908. This averaged out to $104 every minute—and completion of a building every hour and 45 minutes.

Once the city had risen from the ashes, talk of hosting a world's exposition to commemorate the opening of the Panama Canal was revived. It would be an excellent opportunity to quash rumors of San Francisco's demise, and to rid it of the tarnish of graft trials. But San Diego and New Orleans also wanted the exposition, and San Francisco found itself part of a bitter rivalry until Congress named the city the official venue in 1911.

A sparsely developed area facing the entrance to the bay and known as Harbor View—now the Marina District—was selected as the site. The uneven shoreline was filled in, and a magical mini-city of pastel-colored pavilions, exhibit halls, and amusement arcades soon spread over 635 acres. The world was at war, and some countries eventually pulled out of the fair, but nevertheless 25 countries and 43 states and territories participated. From its opening on February 20, 1915, until its closing 10 months later, the fair attracted more than 19 million people.

Although the Burnham Plan was rejected in detail, it did inspire a grandiose scheme for a Civic Center that has since developed into one of the finest examples of architectural complexes in the country. The buildings, faced with California granite and recalling the classic lines of Roman architecture, are considered among the best of the Beaux-Arts style to be seen anywhere. The first to be completed was the Nourse Auditorium (now the Bill Graham Civic Auditorium) that opened on the site of the Mechanics' Pavilion in 1915, just in time to accommodate some of the fair's events. A new City Hall, sitting with regal splendor on two city blocks across the plaza from its predecessor, was dedicated a few days after the fair closed, its imperial dome rising higher than that of the Capitol in Washington, D.C. The library building at the eastern end of the plaza opened in 1917, and was open until 1995, when a new library opened beside it, on the site of the old City Hall.

The 7.1 Loma Prieta tremor in 1989 was a reminder that San Francisco is still at the mercy of earthquakes. It killed 11 people and injured hundreds in the city. Approximately 120 buildings either collapsed or were condemned and later demolished. Portions of the city remained without electricity for three days. The district most ravaged was the Marina, where homes collapsed upon themselves and broken gas mains ignited fires that lit up the night sky. The City Hall was damaged and subsequently closed for an extensive seismic retrofit. Throughout the city other buildings as well as freeways and bridges have since been similarly retrofitted in an effort to lessen their vulnerability in the event of another severe earthquake.

Harry J. Coleman joined the San Francisco *Examiner* as a photographer in 1905 after working in New York on William Randolph Hearst's *Journal*. This is the first of four extracts from his autobiography, *Give Us a Little Smile, Baby*, published in 1943 by E.P. Dutton & Company, Inc.

The day before . . .

ON THAT MEMORABLE TUESDAY I HAD two picture dates scheduled. One was with [Enrico] Caruso and his friend [Antonio] Scotti at the Mission Street Opera House, the other at Mechanics' Pavilion, where Jimmy Coffroth [sports promoter] was about to hand over a thousand-dollar prize to the winner of his colossal masked roller-skating carnival.

I spent most of the afternoon re-slicing the old publicity bologna with Caruso and Scotti, later repairing to the Palace Hotel Bar for bumpers of "Number Six" at two bits [25 cents] a slug. ("Number Six" was Colonel Fitzpatrick's code designation for a particularly violent concoction.) The Palace's bar, bounded by a spotless brass footrail and offering a tempting free lunch, was not only a good place to drink but it was the center of political plotting for the whole West Coast. Report said that the State of California was run by the boys who gathered around the Palace Bar—much the same kind of situation that the Empire State endured at the hands of patrons of New York's Hoffman House.

That night it seemed to me that the fun-loving San Franciscans were merrier than ever, although I suppose it is only a melodramatic heightening of my memory, thinking of it now in retrospect. But the glittering mob of skaters in their gay costumes rolled by my camera around the Pavilion floor like a mad carnival.

After Coffroth had parted with his thousand dollars, I wandered around the city. Crowds packed the tables at Tait's, Zinkand's, Marchand's, Techau's, Delmonico's, Sanguinetti's, Lucchetti's, the Pup,

Tortoni's and the old Poodle Dog. Audiences filled the city's theatres, from the Columbia, Majestic, Alcazar, Alhambra, Valencia, Fischer's and the Orpheum, down the line to McCullough and Barret's burlesque houses, and the old Central, where gallery gods and melodrama held forth.

The Palm Garden adjoined a drive-in courtyard at the Palace Hotel and was a popular rendezvous for the city's social elite.

At the Palace Hotel, loungers sprawled in the lobby's luxury and outside silk-robed Chinese porters with plush-coated manure scoops followed horse cabs through the vast drive-in Palm Court. Guests at the Palace looked down upon a lovely patio from their balconied rooms, while those at the new Fairmont atop Nob Hill could view the Golden Gate, and St. Francis patrons contemplated verdant Union Square. Lesser views could be had at the Manx, the Lick House, St. Nicholas and a hundred other hostelries.

With an empty late evening on my schedule, I strolled through the fog to Pratt and Tierney's backroom beer lounge. There all hands were weeping copiously in their brew as a hard-boiled nightingale warbled the unexpurgated lyrics of "Frankie and Johnnie" and "Sam,

Sam, the Lavatory Man." I wasn't in the mood for this pastime and moved back to the Pavilion, where the icebox was heavy with brew and my press badge and credit rating were equally honored.

The skating carnival still hadn't reached its peak as the first hour of Wednesday passed. I strolled across Larkin Street and bummed around the Central Emergency Hospital, where the boys of the lobster shift always had a pint salted away and a crap game going in the basement of the new City Hall. That was our "late watch" headquarters, nerve center for news and key spot for pictures after dark.

Dr. Arthur McGinty was there that early morning, wearied from his night-long siege of splinter pulling, in which a large portion of the Pavilion floor had been carted across in minute slivers from the unhappy landings at Coffroth's party. The good doctor did not know it, but he was only a few hours away from the biggest emergency job of his career. Head nurse Margaret Sheehy and steward Jimmy O'Dea frowned as an ambulance call rang in, but I winked at police officer Ed Parquette when I noted that it originated in the neighborhood of my house. That meant a fast and free ride home for me. Later, I waved goodnight to driver Jack Flynn and his panting team. They had only a few more calls to answer that night before the bricks and mortar crashed down upon them.

The following is a brief excerpt from Marcelle Assan's *Episodes of the San Francisco Catastrophe as told by an Eyewitness,* a book published in Paris in 1908. The translation is by the late Dr. Mary Grace Paquette, specialist in Franco-California history. The Grand Opera House was on Mission Street, between Third and Fourth streets.

A night at the opera

THE SKY WAS SO PURE AND SO BLUE. It was even a warm day! Therefore, everyone seemed to be celebrating and talking animatedly about that evening's great event: the Italian opera. At exactly 7 P.M., I met my friends at their exquisitely furnished little apartment on Bush Street. We were all dressed for the occasion, and we made quite an impression on one another in the small living room, but later on it would not be the case when we appeared in the midst of so much lavishness. Even as we approached the portal of the Opera House, we observed a long line of cars extending into the darkness of the surrounding streets. From these cars into the half-light first emerged delicate profiles. Next we caught sight of marvelous brocades and sparkling diamonds. At last, stepping out onto the street were beautiful men and women in evening wear. The street filled with the essences of perfumes and powders. After greeting people and shaking hands on all sides, we took our places in our box.

The spectacle of the room was wonderful. One would have to recall a similar evening at the Paris Opera during the Empire to equal such beauty and majesty: everywhere were diamonds, white shoulders, magnificent eyes, sylph-waisted women wrapped in lace worthy of a queen, with lustrous Oriental pearls wrapped around lovely throats. It was all breathtakingly beautiful. In front of the audience, Caruso, the Italian tenor, inspired by the glinting eyes of his rich American admirers, sang as he never had before, his acting imbued with Italian ardor, and elevated the enthusiasm of his public to the point of delirium. People applauded wildly, threw flowers, acclaimed

Bizet, the great composer of Carmen; Caruso, the Don José who met so well the expectations of the spectators in attendance; Marcel Journet, a Frenchman, who played the toreador, and all the other singers who were part of such a highly talented troupe. Then, at the last note from the bowstrings, the ladies stood and wrapped themselves in their gold lamé or pearl-encrusted, satin-brocaded cloaks, in their gauze and flowered ruffs.

"Are we going home now?"

"Oh, of course not! It's not yet time to sleep in Frisco."

And various animated clusters of theatergoers set out for different parts of Market Street to parade their fancy dress, their diamonds and their beauty. We joined our friends, while different groups went in the direction of high-priced restaurants of varying nationalities. As for us, we opted for Del Monico's, famous for its elegance and the many mysterious events which have occurred there, making it even more alluring for San Franciscans. In its great gilded and mirrored rooms, in its thickly carpeted stairwells, by the light of its electric candelabras, through the crack of the heavy doors left ajar, only joyous parties of men and women could be glimpsed and overheard enjoying themselves.

Champagne corks popped amid bursts of laughter and both sibilant and animated voices. The restaurant was filled on every floor, and everyone was playing all the most exciting games while tipsy from champagne or cocktails. Husbands and wives no longer knew each other, nor did they want to: it was merriment totally free and American. However, people had to think about going home through the darkened streets, with their heads on fire and tired of so much laughter, in carriages rented for the night at impossible prices, and so we, along with everyone else, headed for our homes. As arranged, I stayed with my friends. We went to bed and fell into a deep sleep that only such a long and active evening could induce.

This photograph was taken shortly before the curtain was raised at the
Grand Opera House on the night of April 17, 1906.

James Marie Hopper's article "Our San Francisco" that appeared in the June 1906 issue of *Everybody's Magazine* has been acclaimed as one of the best contemporary pieces written about the earthquake and fire. He was born in Paris and, at the age of 10, was taken to California. While at the University of California, Berkeley, he became legendary as a football quarterback and coach, and he was one of the trio that first stole the Stanford Axe in 1898. He studied law, but chose instead a career as a writer. At the time he wrote "Our San Francisco," Hopper was a reporter on the San Francisco *Call*. This is the first of four episodes from that article.

The portrait was made by Arnold Genthe.

Restless horses

AT MIDNIGHT I WAS AT THE Grand Opera House, where the Conried company was giving "Carmen." I still can see Caruso striking open the gates of the arena with his long catalan. I see him stab, I hear [Olive] Fremstadt's scream, Caruso's wail of remorse, glutted passion and remorse commingled; I see his magnificent crawling movement to her as the curtain comes down. I see myself walking back slowly to my paper, the *Call*, a few steps away, and I am saying to myself: "Surely, what I have felt to-night is the summit of human emotion." And now when I think of that, I almost laugh.

After turning in my copy, I went up Post Street to my room in the Neptune Hotel, six blocks away. It was two o'clock in the morning, and that is San Francisco's fairest hour. The blustering sea-breeze has ceased at that time; from the land comes a breath of air already dawn-scented. From the slope I was climbing I could see the dark loom of the big buildings below, the bay beyond with the red and green lights and the long silhouettes of ships at anchor, and still farther, the familiar hearthlike glow of the mainland towns. The night struck me as particularly peaceful. As I passed a livery-stable on Post Street between Powell and Mason Streets, a horse screamed with a sudden, shrill cry. I asked a stableman lolling in the darkened doorway what was the matter. "Restless to-night; don't know why," he answered. And then, with my head poked in, I heard the thunder of a score of hoofs crashing in tattoo against the stalls.

I went up to my room. "Fine night," said the elevator-boy. "Beautiful," I answered.

The earthquake struck at 5:12:05 on the morning of Wednesday, April 18, 1906. For thousands of people, that precise moment became an indelible flash of memory that would remain with them for the rest of their lives. Here are a few of the many accounts that were recorded shortly afterward. Of particular interest (and value) are those by police officers who, being alert and on duty, actually SAW the earthquake tear the city apart.

First, James Hopper continues his recollections. Then, from different parts of the city, other people recall their experiences during those same few minutes.

Some of these stories continue as separate pieces following this chapter. For resources, see "Resource notes."

5:12:05 A.M.

Post Street, at Taylor

> James Hopper got to bed at about three o'clock in the morning after filing his report of the opera for the *Call*. He was living at the Neptune Hotel, on Post Street.

I slept, but with a hot, restless slumber. I dreamed. I heard a scream, then another. It was the scream of Caruso before Carmen's prostrate form, and the strident cry of the horse in the stable. They mingled, rose interwoven in a fiendish crescendo—and then I awoke to the city's destruction.

Right away it was incredible—the violence of the quake. It started with a directness, a savage determination that left no doubt of its purpose. It pounced upon the earth as some sidereal* bulldog, with a rattle of hungry eagerness. The earth was a rat, shaken in the grinding teeth, shaken, shaken, shaken with periods of slight weariness followed by new bursts of vicious rage. As far as I can remember, my impressions were as follows: First, for a few seconds a feeling of incredulity, capped immediately with one of finality—of incredulity at the violence of the vibrations. "It's incredible, incredible"—I think I said it aloud. Then the feeling of finality. "It's the end—St. Pierre, Samoa, Vesuvius, Formosa, San Francisco—this is death." Simultaneously with that, a picture of the city swaying beneath the curl of a tidal wave foaming to the sky. Then incredulity again at the length of it, at the sullen violence of it. "It's incredible—vertical and rotary—look at

---

* Astral.

[69]

me in my bed—like a fish in a frying-pan." This last figure pleased me. "Just like a fish in a frying-pan," I repeated. Then an impulse to get out of the hideously grinding walls, mastered immediately, solely from a repugnance, as I remember it, to making a show of myself. "No, if I die, I die in bed, not with my legs bare to the skies." Incredulity again at the mere length of the thing, the fearful stubbornness of it. Then curiosity—"I must see it."

I got up and walked to the window. I started to open it, but the pane obligingly fell outward and I poked my head out, the floor like a geyser beneath my feet. Then I heard the roar of bricks coming down in cataracts and the groaning of twisted girders all over the city, and at the same time I saw the moon, a calm, pale crescent in the green sky of dawn. Below it the skeleton frame of an unfinished sky-scraper was swaying from side to side with a swing as exaggerated and absurd as that of a palm in a stage tempest.

Just then the quake, with a sound as of a snarl, rose to its climax of rage, and the back wall of my building for three stories above me fell. I saw the mass pass across my vision swift as a shadow. It struck some little wooden houses in the alley below. I saw them crash in like emptied eggs and the bricks pass through the roof as through tissue paper.

The vibrations ceased and I began to dress. Then I noted the great silence. Throughout the long quaking, in this great house full of people I had not heard a cry, not a sound, not a sob, not a whisper. And now, when the roar of crumbling buildings was over and only a brick was falling here and there like the trickle of a spent rain, this silence continued, and it was an awful thing. But now in the alley someone began to groan. It was a woman's groan, soft and low.

JAMES M. HOPPER

Washington Street, at Davis

Police Officer Jesse B. Cook was on duty in the Harbor District and standing at the corner of Washington and Davis streets.

I heard a rumble like the roar of the sea, and then the earth seemed to rise under me, and at the same time both Davis and Washington streets opened in several places and water came up out of these cracks.

The street seemed to settle under me, and did settle in some places from about one to three feet. The buildings around and about me began to tumble and fall and kept me pretty busy for awhile dodging bricks. I saw the top-story of the building at the southwest corner of Washington and Davis streets fall and kill Frank Bodwell of the firm of Bodwell & Co., commission merchants, and Harry Hanson, the entry clerk of the same firm. They were both buried under at least two tons of brick.

JESSE B. COOK

Market Street, at Grant

Police Officer Michael J. Brady had reached Market Street after patroling Grant Avenue from Chinatown.

At first I heard a low rumbling noise like thunder. Then the earth began to shake under me, and I realized that it was an earthquake. I ran to the middle of the thoroughfare, and felt like stumbling as I ran because the surface of Market Street was rising and falling like waves on the bay on a stormy day.

I thought I was gone when I saw the Phelan building suddenly lurch over Market Street. But it lurched back again, and as it set back in its place its foundations ripped and cracked and seemed to screech. The tall *Call* building rocked to and fro from north to south, while the Mutual Bank building on the opposite side of Market Street, near Geary, similarly lurched and dipped over the thoroughfare.

The shake ended with a violent twist or rotary motion that caused the stone cornices of the building on the south side of Market Street west of the *Call* building, and therefore much nearer me, to come crashing down on the sidewalk. At the same time the front of the Oberon building, on O'Farrell Street near Stockton, and parts of other buildings on the same side of that block came tumbling to the ground. These were all in plain sight of where I was standing.

On Grant Avenue the effects were not so startling; but nearly all the plate glass windows sprung and seemed to explode as they were bent and twisted by the force of the earthquake. These, as they burst, crashed into the street. ... While the cornices were crashing down from the structures west of the *Call* building, the steeple of St. Patrick's church on Mission Street toppled over, as did the tall chimney stack of the power house on Stevenson Street, midway between the *Call* building on its north and St. Patrick's church on its south.

MICHAEL J. BRADY

City Hall police station

> Police Officer Edward J. Plume was sitting at his desk in the police station situated on the ground floor of City Hall at Larkin and McAllister streets.

At 5:10 A.M. by the station clock I was seated at a desk in the office when I felt a slight trembling of the great building. This had lasted a few seconds when Officer [J. M.] Dwyer said, "That's an earthquake." Then the seemingly light temblor began to increase in violence, and all of a sudden I was thrown clear out of the chair. As I was then being tossed from one side to the other by the shocks, I tried to find something to hold on to and prevent myself from falling.

Meanwhile the noise from the outside became deafening. I could hear the massive pillars that upheld the cornices and cupola of the City Hall go cracking with reports like cannon, then falling with crashes like thunder. Huge stones and lumps of masonry came crashing down outside our doors; the large chandelier swung to and fro, then fell from the ceiling with a bang. In an instant the room was full of dust as well as soot and smoke from the fire-place. It seemed to be reeling like the cabin of a ship in a gale. Feeling sure that the building could never survive such shocks, and expecting every moment to be buried under a mass of ruins, I shouted to Officer Dwyer to get out. The lights were then out, and though the dawn had come outside, the station, owing to the dust and smoke inside, and the ruins and dust outside, was all in darkness.

Dwyer and I made a rush for the nearest door, stumbling over chairs and desks and other litter as we scrambled out to Larkin Street. It was dark in the street, and choking with dust. We ran across to a small alley. The dust from the buildings that were still falling made it impossible to see anything. As I reached the alley, the front walls of the Strathmore [Hotel] began to fall. There was a vacant lot about fifty feet away, and I ran there and stood alongside a high fence waiting for the ruin to become complete.

EDWARD J. PLUME

Central Emergency Hospital

> As part of his beat duty, Police Officer Edmond F. Parquette was visiting the Central Emergency Hospital, located in the basement of City Hall.

I was just stepping through the entrance of the office when the whole place began to shake, and in a few seconds the shaking became so severe that I had to hold on to the door to save myself from falling. During the next few seconds it seemed as though we were living through a whole lifetime. So many things were happening that there was no time to notice anything in particular. The building was shaking and rocking like a mad thing. The furniture was rolling and hopping about, the plaster and everything else on top was falling. Then there was the roaring of the earthquake itself, and the crashes and shocks and rumblings as we felt the walls and pillars of the City Hall bursting and breaking over our heads, and the [interior of the] dome came tumbling down in great lumps that crashed like new earthquakes and broke into pieces, bursting and banging against the doors and windows.

My idea was, when I could get hold of any idea, that the whole City Hall had fallen on top of us and we were buried for good and all. The lights had all gone out. It was black dark and smothering. Nobody could see his hand in front of his face; while the scattering bricks and plaster and mortar threw out a suffocating dust that filled wards and corridors and was choking me. Moreover, and to make matters worse, though I could see nothing, I had felt and heard the bricks and masonry that fell from the walls and dome, thundering down and banging against the lower walls and windows and burying the entrances. Every entrance to the hospital was thus blocked clean to the top of each doorway, or higher.

EDMOND F. PARQUETTE

Fremont Street, at Mission

> Patrolman Harry F. Walsh was on Fremont Street between
> Mission and Howard streets when he stopped in at Meese &
> Gottfried Company's machine shops for a cup of coffee with
> the watchman, William Beatty.

A couple of minutes after Beatty went out [taking coffee to the engineer], the first shock came, and the windows began to crackle and then to burst and fall. I jumped up and ran for the door. It was a big iron drop door, and it was shut. Two machinists who were working in the rear shop started running the same instant that I did. One ran for the front door. I don't know what became of the other, because, apart from the row and confusion of the earthquake shaking the building, the heavy machines on the floors above began crashing down through the ceiling and on top of the machinery in the ground floor shops, and were bumping like thunder as we were running through the smother of it.

I shouted to the man running for the open door with me: "Wait until we open the lock!" But he wouldn't wait. The machinery was flopping from on top so that it was a poor chance to go back looking for the key or anything else. But we found that we could drag the corner of the door inwards and upwards, bending it so that a man could crawl out underneath. I held it up for the machinist and he wiggled out. Then he bolted like a rabbit, the Lord knows what way, and I was left inside. But I got the key somehow, unlocked the door and hoisted it, and got out on the street.

Fremont Street was then rolling in waves. First it opened and closed in big cracks. At least I first noticed big cracks opening and shutting as I looked at them. Then I noticed that the street was moving in waves like the sea, and was lifting under me like the sea.

I ran for the alarm box on the corner, and before I reached it, the Meese & Gottfried Building and the power company's building crumpled up and fell flat.

The engineer to whom Beatty had carried the cup of coffee got out all right. So did the machinist. But Beatty, after giving the engineer his coffee, had started his rounds as watchman to ring the time clocks on the upper floor, and he was caught and killed. It was not until months later that his body was recovered, and identified by the special officer's uniform and badge.

HARRY F. WALSH

Palace Hotel Courtyard

> Frank Louis Ames had stepped into the Palace Hotel court-yard on his way to the Ferry Building after an early morning meal at Zinkand's restaurant.

Inside the Palace, the office lights were bright and inviting. Even as I was looking in at them the tall palms in the courtyard that was part of the hotel lobby began to sway. At first I thought it was an optical delusion. But then the ground felt as if it were sinking under my feet. … I turned instinctively to the tall buildings of the *Chronicle* and *Call*. The clock in the *Chronicle* tower seemed to waver, and the *Call's* skyscraper, anchored as it was hundreds of feet in the ground, simply rocked. Cornices and bricks came tumbling around me. The team [of horses] in the *porte cochere* of the Palace ran, and as the horses passed me I could not help noticing that the beasts' eyes were big with terror, and foam was coming from their nostrils. I stepped into an alcove for safety. It seemed as if the very earth were reeling. … As I stepped from the alcove, the pavement simply went in waves under my feet. I ran for the *Chronicle* building because, judging from the way the bricks were falling from the Palace I believed that it was about to fall. The quake ran from east to west and the cobblestones of Market Street seemed alive. Every one of them was moving and the street car rails were twisted from their places.

FRANK LOUIS AMES

Upstairs in the Palace Hotel

> James W. Byrne and his mother were staying in adjoining suites on the top floor of the Palace Hotel.

I got out of bed and found that the rocking floor made walking rather wobbly; but I was able to get into my overcoat and slippers, and run out into the corridor to go to my mother's room. When I reached her

door she was in the act of opening it; her intention being to go to my room to find me. She had hurriedly thrown on a wrapper, but was scarcely better clad than I was in my overcoat and pajamas. Some other guests of the hotel were popping out of their rooms at this time, and most of them were attired more airily than we were. But the earthquake seemed to have ceased, and my mother decided to remain in her room and complete her toilette before going downstairs.

JAMES W. BYRNE

Grand Hotel

> William Cushing, visiting from Nevada, had a room on the fourth floor of the Grand Hotel, the Palace's annex across New Montgomery Street.

My first intimation of trouble came when I was thrown out of bed and found myself sprawling in the middle of the floor. Simultaneously my ears were assailed by a chorus of terrifying noises, the creaking and cracking of timber, the crashes of falling plaster and breaking glass. For a moment I thought I had been suffering from a nightmare and had leaped out of bed. But the plaster showering down from the walls and ceiling quickly banished this idea, and I got a notion that the hotel was on fire. I rose to my feet. No sooner had I come up standing than the floor seemed to be jerked up under me and I was pitched violently across the room, through the door of my bathroom, and into the bath itself.

WILLIAM CUSHING

Geary Street, at Powell

> The following is from a letter addressed to Maria Mansell in England and signed "Your loving nephew, Harry." The writer was staying at the News Building Hotel on Geary Street, next to the St. Francis Hotel and its still-under-construction annex.

The noise made by the rattling of the doors, windows and sash weights and the metallic clanging of the new steel frame of the hotel [and] the creaking and groaning of the building was deafening and appalling. The shocks were vicious and terrific in the extreme and I was thrown violently up and down in my bed. My bed laid with the building north and south, my head against the south wall, the bureau was against the north wall and faced the foot of the bed. On the right of the bureau was a square fancy table and on that I kept my leather suit case laid flat, across which I used to lay my shirt and underclothes for the night.

I must have been laying on my back when I woke for I just raised myself up on my elbows and remained in that position without moving until it was all over. I had no thought of getting out of bed for like a flash I realized the utter helplessness of getting down stairs and out into the square before the building fell, if it was to fall, and instinctively I felt that it was safer to stay where I was. So I laid there looking at the ceiling which was cracking all over, it being light enough to see distinctly, and thinking of the two buildings towering above and half expecting a thousand tons of masonry to burst through the roof and blot all our lives out. And still I did not feel afraid, the suspense was too great, there was no room for fear.

The utter helplessness, the knowledge that there was no human hand at the helm or at the throttle looking after our safety or trying to avert any disaster, that we were in the hands of an irresponsible power, a power that ignores the existence of mankind and his works, that Nature was at work and was obeying her fixed laws and that she would obey them and accomplish her purpose even if it involved the destruction of the whole earth, seemed to give one the courage of despair. The dominant thought was "How long can it last, will it never, never end?" Then with a terrific twist and whirl, it did end. My window was open, my ears were keyed to the highest tension and from the St. Francis came the screams of women and children and the O Lordy! O Lordy! with the deep southern intonation of the negro waiters.

I thought that it was all over but the cessation lasted for about ten seconds only, for after a slight, ominous tremble and rattle we were in the midst of a shock as severe if not severer than the first one. I was more awake now, my faculties were clearer, and having survived one shock though the interval was so short, I felt calmer and had more confidence in the outcome. But the swaying increased. I saw my bureau move up and down, saw it tilt backwards and forwards, saw it travelling towards the foot of my bed. Then my attention was attracted to my underclothes. They danced up and down slipping on the smooth surface of the leather and finally fell on the floor. Then my valise followed them. The plaster like coarse salt came sifting down on my head through the cracks in the ceiling. And the shock continued but the buildings still stood. It did not seem possible that any building ever built could stand such treatment for any length of time.

HARRY (MANSELL?)

Pacific Avenue, at Fillmore

Jacob Bertha Levison, a director of Fireman's Fund, lived with his family at 2420 Pacific Avenue.

I leaped out of bed but could not retain my footing because the house was still jumping. This can be better understood when I say that it took two or three attempts or lunges before I could get hold of the knob of the door leading to the room occupied by my sons John and Robert, nine and seven years of age who were terrified beyond words.

By this time the earthquake had ceased, but expecting another momentarily, I got the boys in bed with their mother and went for Charlie, a baby of fifteen months, who was in the rear of the house with his nurse. It was then that I appreciated more than I had before how terrifying the earthquake had been, for the baby was screaming and frightened almost into convulsions. He did not calm down until I got him into bed with his mother.

I am frequently asked whether I was badly frightened by the shaking, to which I invariably reply that I had passed the point of being frightened, exactly as one might on a sinking vessel in mid-ocean when fully alive to the inevitable. My only thought was to get the family together so that when the house went down we should all go together.

JACOB B. LEVISON

The Valencia Street Hotel

> On his regular beat, Police Lieutenant Henry N. Powell looked into the cafe of this hotel—a popular rendezvous for night workers living in the Mission district.

I just peeped in and walked out again through the lobby. Then, as I was going out of the door, the earthquake came and I hurried my paces. The first quiver was strong enough, but it was not terrifying. As I stepped out to reach the middle of the street and safety from the falling glass and stuff that accompanies all earthquakes, the twister came, and for a few moments it baffled me.

Valencia Street not only began to dance and rear and roll in waves like a rough sea in a squall; but it sank in places and then vomited up its car tracks and the tunnels that carried the cables. These lifted themselves out of the pavement, and bent and snapped. It was impossible for a man to stand, or to realize just where he was trying to keep standing. Houses were cracking and bending and breaking the same as the street itself and the car tracks. In my wake, out of the Valencia Hotel, the night clerk came scampering and tripping over the waves and iron obstacles of the pavement. Close behind him followed the remittance man. I caught the remittance man, who was unsteady on his legs, and ran with him toward Nineteenth Street. As we ran we heard the hotel creak and roar and crash. I turned to look at it. It was then daylight and the dust of the falling buildings had not had time to rise. The hotel lurched forward as if the foundation were dragged backward from under it, and crumpled down over Valencia Street. It did not fall to pieces and spray itself all over the place, but telescoped down on itself like a concertina. This took only a few seconds.

Before we got to Nineteenth Street I halted. When the dust and tumult subsided, and I could find my feet amid the crumpled ruins of the street, I made my way back to the Valencia as best I could. In the first gasp of recovery from the shock it did not occur to one that the tragedy was so complete. Everything seemed to be burst up. The Valencia Hotel looked no worse than the street. Later—a second or so later—one realized that the crumpled four-story building was full of living people.

The four-story Valencia Street Hotel on Valencia between 18th and 19th streets collapsed within itself during the quake. Two days later the entire block was destroyed by fire.

In the southeast corner room on the top floor lived a Jewish tailor and his wife. I knew them quite well. When I got to the place these good people were at their window practically on a level with the street, very uneasy and very anxious to escape, but unwilling to leave before they had dressed and saved some things. Near them, on the top floor, lived an old painter who was very fond of birds and had his room full of canaries in cages. The wall in the front of his room fell out, but he and his canaries were all safe on a level with the street, unhurt but frightened.

As well as I could ascertain comparatively few persons on the top floor had been hurt or killed, and everybody in the lobby and cafe on the main floor escaped before the building collapsed. It was on the floors in between that the havoc occurred, and heart-rending scenes were witnessed while some of the residents on these floors were being taken out, most of them dead or injured.

Mr. William P. Bock, the proprietor, was never found. His wife was taken out comparatively uninjured. His two sons, William H. and Albert C. Bock, also lived in the hotel. When the rescuers dug down to where William H. Bock was buried, they found him dead, but his wife in the bed beside him was scarcely injured. The other son, Albert Bock, was found to have a broken shoulder. Neither his wife nor baby were hurt. The baby, when rescued, was contentedly sucking at its bottle.

HENRY N. POWELL

Sixth Street, at Howard

> The area most devastated during the initial earthquake was a cluster of inexpensive hotels and rooming houses in the South of Market area. William Stehr lived on the top floor of the Nevada House at 132 Sixth Street.

It came into my head to jump out of the window on to the roof below; but while I was waiting to make up my mind the house I was looking at collapsed with a deafening roar and spilled down in a cloud of dust from which I could plainly hear the agonizing screams of the inmates. The dust then came spurting up in so thick a cloud that I could neither see nor breathe. It choked me. So I hurried back from the window to the other end of the room and began to dress myself.

I had just got on my trousers and shoes when I heard another crash. Looking out again through the window I saw that the Brunswick House, the second building south of us, on the corner of Sixth and Howard Streets, had also collapsed, and was tumbling into a heap of ruins in a smother of dust. This building was said to have been occupied by 150 people, of whom only fifty escaped with their lives.

I did not put on any more clothes, but jumped up and tried to open the door of my room and get out. But I found that I could not open it. The earthquake had jammed the door, and every jerk of the quake made it faster and tighter. As I was tugging at it I felt the floor tilting and sinking under me, and I knew that the house was going down like the others. So I hung on instinctively to the door handle while the whole floor dropped. As it sank I felt three distinct bumps as the lower floors collapsed in turn under the weight of the roof and the top story. With each bump came a frightful crash and cracking of timbers and glass and the cries of other people in the house who were being destroyed.

There were about fifty people in the Nevada at that moment, and of these only seven escaped, including myself. The landlord, Mr. Lee, his wife and daughter were among those that perished, but his young son Frank was among those saved.*

The cries of these people who were being killed, especially the women, were dreadful to hear; even to me, in my own peril, thinking every instant that I would be crushed, they were the most dreadful part of the experience.

Then came another bump, very sudden and very severe. The place fell in on top of me, the breath seemed to be knocked out of my body and I went unconscious.

When my senses came back I was buried and in complete darkness. I tried to feel myself all over, working my limbs as best I could, to find out if any bones were broken. But though I could feel that I was painfully bruised all over, I guessed that all my bones were intact.

Then I tried to raise myself, because when I came to I was lying flat; but the weight of the debris that covered my body was more than I could lift. My feet were pinned fast, so I ceased struggling and rested for a minute or so. While I was gasping for more breath for a second

* At the inquest, Frank Lee testified that 13 residents of the Nevada House survived and 23 were killed—many of them by the fire.

struggle I heard somebody running over the debris over me, so I shouted for help as loudly as I could.

No attention was paid to my calls; so I began to struggle again, and presently managed to release my feet. But I lost my left shoe. It was wedged in too tight, and it was by pulling my foot out of it that I escaped. After that I began to grope and feel about me to find some way of escape. Then I began to hear other agonizing screams for help, and screams of "Fire!" And soon after I began to smell smoke, and I fancied I could hear flames crackling sharply.

This made me struggle desperately, and soon I got my arms out over my head, and could feel an opening that led upwards on a slope. I worked my way along till I could see a little glimmer of light. I got to the crack in the debris and could see out; but I was in a very tight place and was very tired from the exertion, so I had to stop for a while. But I got a breath of fresh air which revived me, and I began to cough violently and spit out the dust and plaster with which my mouth and lungs seemed to be filled.

After resting for a minute or so, as well as I could judge, I began to pull away the laths and plaster that blocked the passage. It was hard work doing it in such a tight and narrow passage. But after a while I made a hole large enough to crawl through, and then I found that I was not at the end of my trouble. I had to turn on my back and crawl upward through a sort of chimney that was bristling with nails and splinters of laths and plaster that tore my sides and my clothes. But eventually I squeezed through and found myself sitting amid the ruins nearly on a level with the street, and all around me was ruin and debris.

I was too exhausted to mind much, and I was bleeding badly from a cut over the scalp. As the blood was running into my eyes, the first thing I did was to sit on the debris and tie my handkerchief around the cut on my head to staunch it. Then I looked at my watch, which was still going. It was 5:45 o'clock. As I was sitting there, trembling and trying to collect my scattered senses, a man that I don't think I ever saw before or since climbed up beside me with a bottle of whisky and told me to take a drink. I took it and thanked him. It made me feel much better. Then he went off with the bottle to give a drink to somebody else.

Soon I began to take enough interest in things to look about me. On all sides, where the Nevada, the Ohio, the Brunswick and other lodging houses had been, there was nothing but a big pile of debris. On this pile a number of men were working desperately trying to rescue people that were buried. Some of these men were armed with axes and hatchets, but the majority had nothing but their bare hands to work with.

For some time I was too exhausted to stand up, much less try to help them. I just watched while they dragged at the broken timbers and things, while smoke kept puffing up among them from the fires that had started underneath. Then I began to hear again the cries and shrieks that I had ceased for a time to notice. It was very dreadful when someone gave a long agonized scream when the fire caught him, and then ceased.

But the rescuers kept on working in each spot until the fire drove them back. Wherever they heard a voice or a cry they started to dig down to it; but in most cases the victims were too deeply buried, and the flames drove away the rescuers while the victim perished.

WILLIAM F. STEHR

Post Street, at Taylor

Edward M. Lind worked late and had not returned to his bachelor apartment on the corner of Post and Taylor streets until 4 o'clock in the morning.

When the big shock came at about 5:15 A.M. it shook the place badly. I had a high bookcase in my bedroom which held a number of volumes that I particularly treasured, including a number of autographed books by Jack London. This piece of furniture fell forward with a bang that awakened me. I sat up, saw the bookcase was down and the place was tossed generally. But I did not feel like tidying it up again just then. So I lay down and fell fast asleep again.

EDWARD M. LIND

(He was awakened about 7 o'clock when a friend knocked on his door.)

After the collapse of City Hall trapped him in the basement emergency hospital, Police Officer Parquette helped the staff and patients escape. The hospital included a separate ward for mentally ill patients. The following is reprinted from *The Argonaut*, September 25, 1926, and is part of Parquette's official report submitted to Chief of Police Jeremiah Dinan shortly after the event. The *Argonaut* spelled his name "Parquet," although police records spell it with an additional "te."

EDMOND F. PARQUETTE (b. 1877)

Escape from Central Emergency Hospital

Even when the quaking and twisting ceased, the lumps of masonry still kept falling; and above all these noises of crashing and breaking, and the bellowing and thundering of the quake itself and the thuds of the pillars and cornices as they hit the ground, there were the shrieks and yells of the lunatics, and the moans and cries of the other patients. Everybody seemed to be yelling and shrieking at the top of his voice.

Very quickly after the shocks ceased, the dust began to clear away or settle down, and stopped choking me. The cries died down too, though many of the poor creatures kept on shrieking from terror or moaning from hurts and apprehensions. As soon as these howls and cries had quieted down a little, and I could see a bit through the gloom—the dawn light was able to filter the chinks in the fallen masonry, and so through some of the upper parts of the windows—I made my way as best I could to the room of the matron, Mrs. Rose Kane, whom I found safe and unhurt.

Neither of us then knew what damage was done in the hospital itself; but I told her to stay where she was, as it seemed a safe place, while I went to look for the nurse [Margaret Sheehy] who I knew was in the Female Ward on the other side of the Hospital. I found her quite safe and uninjured, and together we went upstairs to the main floor of the City Hall, where the doctors had their quarters, and found the doctor was also unhurt. This was Dr. Arthur McGinty.

Only one doctor had slept there that night. The room was a very long one with a bed at each end. The bed at one end had been mashed and driven through the floor to the basement by a lump of masonry from the dome or some cornice. Fortunately nobody was sleeping in it. The bed at the other end, where the doctor on duty that night was sleeping, was practically untouched except for some falling plaster and the like. But I saw we were all hemmed in, and the windows were blocked by iron bars as well as masonry. So I took out my gun and fired a shot through the top of a window to let people outside know we were alive.

We then all went back to the Matrons' room downstairs, and on the way we met the chief steward ["Jack" Flynn] of the hospital, who also had escaped injury. Nobody in the hospital or in all the City Hall had been hurt, except some that were injured in the scramble to escape after the earthquake.

Then with the help of all the hospital staff I started to clear away a portion of the pile of bricks and debris that blocked the entrance to the Detention Ward. When we cleared off enough from the top we crawled out through an opening. Then realizing the danger of leaving the insane patients confined in their cells, I crawled back again with Mrs. Kane and helped her release these patients.

In the meantime Officer O.R. Harrell, who had been sent by Captain [Bernard] McManus to help us, had managed to effect an entrance through the Larkin Street side of the hospital. The hospital extended from City Hall Avenue on the south along Larkin Street to McAllister Street on the west side of the City Hall. He helped the rest of us in getting out the patients and removing them to the Mechanics Pavilion.

Captain McManus had meanwhile come out from the Police Station House and surveyed the situation, and had seen how the ruins had cluttered up the Emergency Hospital. Thereupon he had run over to the Mechanics Pavilion which was only half a block south of the City Hall on Larkin street, and had asked the superintendent, Mr. [Matthew G.] Buckley, to open that building as a temporary hospital of refuge. This Buckley did in less than a minute; so as soon as we could get the patients out they were carried to the Pavilion, and by this time, though it was only a few minutes after the earthquake had ceased there was quite a crowd of people about and all these, with the men of the Underwriters Fire Patrol, were ready and anxious to help in every way they could.

Meanwhile Dr. Charles B. Pinkham, now [1926] Secretary of the California State Board of Medical Examiners, and Dr. Tilton E. Tillman, who were then both surgeons to the Emergency Hospital, had arrived on the scene. This was about 6 o'clock or earlier. When Dr. Pinkham saw that all access to the hospital was buried under the debris of the fallen dome and cornices, he ran to the Underwriters Fire Patrol Station on City Hall Avenue nearby and got the company to come to the rescue. These men came over and quickly dug away the obstructing masonry. Then they tore the iron bars from the windows of the hospital along Larkin Street, and thus established a feasible means of exit for the imprisoned staff and the more or less helpless patients. Thus, despite the obstacles over which they had to be carried, all the patients, including the insane, were quickly got out of the place.

.   .   .

We returned to the hospital, and everybody helped to collect and remove the operating tables, cots, medicine chests, instruments and every other accessory that we could carry out of the place. All these were taken to the Pavilion, as well as the gurneys, or hand wagons, on which patients were transferred from the operating tables to their cots, and so forth. These gurneys were already in great demand, as injured persons were already beginning to arrive from all parts of the city, and I was detailed with several other officers to receive these victims and carry them into the Pavilion.

Dr. Charles Miller, Chief Surgeon of the Emergency Hospital, was in charge by this time; and he ordered Officer Thomas F. Reagan and myself to go off and gather all the bandages, cotton, lint and other necessary medical supplies that we could find in the nearest drug stores. We took a wagon and went to the Owl Drug Store on Market Street between Mason and Taylor streets and cleared it out of all such supplies. These we took back to the Pavilion.

> Dr. Tillman, who had worked late on April 17 as a relief surgeon, had intended to sleep that night at the Emergency Hospital but instead went home. The bed he would have slept on at the hospital was the one that was "mashed and driven through the floor to the basement." No people were killed in the collapsing City Hall. However, in his report Dr. Tillman told of one fatality: Bob, an ambulance horse that broke out of its stable, ran across the street, and was crushed by the crumbling cupola.

The Mechanics' Pavilion was a large wooden building at Grove and Larkin streets, where the Bill Graham Civic Auditorium is today. Only a few hours after Harry Coleman was there photographing the roller-skating carnival for the *Examiner*, it was hurriedly converted into an emergency hospital. Nurse Lucy B. Fisher gives us a glimpse of conditions in this account, which is excerpted from her article "A Nurse's Earthquake Experience" in *The American Journal of Nursing*, November 1906.

A nurse's story

WE FOUND ON OUR APPROACH to the Pavilion that its entrance was surrounded by a cordon which was guarded by a force of policemen. We asked to be passed through the line but were refused until we said we were nurses. Instantly at the mention of the word "nurse" we were directed to the entrance. What a scene that huge building presented as we entered it; a building of such large dimensions that its area covered an entire block! The floor was strew with mattresses, which were nearly all occupied by patients even at that early hour. Near the entrance to the building, where the patients were received, an improvised surgery had been established; it was surprisingly well equipped under the circumstances and seemed to lack nothing in the way of operating-room tables, dressings, instruments, enamel pans and basins, and even quantities of hot and cold sterilized water. Some days later I learned that most of this outfit had been carried over from the Central Emergency at the City Hall opposite, immediately after the earthquake, when Dr. [Arthur] McGinty, the surgeon on duty that night, had ordered the policemen to open the Pavilion for the new emergency hospital; the rest of the supplies had been appropriated from the surrounding drug-stores.

Patients were being brought in constantly and rapidly moving groups of physicians and uniformed nurses were gathered around the operating-room tables. In the body of the building there was a large number of people waiting on the patients; among this number were not only physicians and nurses, but men and women from other professions—lawyers, ministers, priests, Sisters of Charity, and many more not belonging to any profession. All were hurrying back and forth eagerly trying to help the poor sufferers in the way that seemed to them the best, for supervision in so much confusion was impossible.

My friend and I quickly took off our wraps and asked to be assigned to duty. "Pitch in," was our only order, and we followed it explicitly.

I lost sight of my friend immediately in the confusion and the bigness of the place, but caught glimpses of her later, once with a pillow-case pinned to her waist, in which she was carrying dressings (a plan which I copied as it was a time-saver and consequently a valuable suggestion), and later when the word was passed that appalled us and made all the rest of the morning's experience insignificant in comparison to the new disaster that threatened us.

I saw that at the surgery there were plenty of nurses and decided instantly to work in the body of the building. I feared that in the confusion some of the many critical cases might be overlooked, so I hurried around among the thickly-strewn mattresses with an extra blanket and a hot-water bottle bag or cup of hot coffee for those with feeble pulses and blue lips.

That hot coffee completed my surprise over the adequate hospital equipment. I have since learned that the many gallons of coffee and quantities of milk and bread that were brought in came from hotels in the neighborhood (the St. Nicholas was one) and the restaurants. The mattresses and beds not supplied by the Emergency Hospital came also from the hotels. There were of course dressings to be done and hypodermics to be given for stimulation and anaesthesia. There was great danger in the confusion that the drugs administered would be duplicated, so as a precaution each one who gave a hypodermic injection pinned a tag on to the patient on which was written the quantity of the drug and time when it was given.

Considerable perplexity and delay was caused in losing the location of patients. The arrangement in itself was confusing—mattresses lying without any attempt at regularity all over the floor and constantly being rearranged by kindly-disposed people. I would go off for a basin of sterilized water to do a dressing and come back to the place where I supposed my patient to be and be unable to find him without a great deal of trouble.

Naturally in the eagerness of so many to help there was duplication of work. I recollect receiving the answer from one man to whom I offered coffee that he had already taken three cups.

.　　.　　.

A horse-drawn ambulance delivers another injured person to the makeshift emergency hospital at the Mechanics' Pavilion where, the night before, a masked carnival and roller-skating contest had been held.

As in a bad dream when out of a confused mass of memories but one or two definite incidents can be recalled, so out of my experience in the Pavilion only a few scenes are pictured clearly in my memory.

One of these pictures is of a group standing around a cot on which lay the unconscious and mangled form of a woman. In the group were physicians and nurses and the injured woman's sister, a Salvation Army lassie. I held the woman's poor crushed leg while the surgeon put on a temporary bandage after deciding that an amputation was necessary. The surgeon told me later in the week that the woman had at that time I saw her a chance of recovery, but she was moved twice on account of the fire and subsequently died from shock.

Time seems to go much more slowly when it is crowded with events than when the hours pass in comparative uneventfulness. I remember one of the physicians in the Pavilion asking of another the time of day. "Half past eight," was the answer. "Great heavens," the surgeon exclaimed, "I thought it was at least twelve o'clock."

An earthquake heavy enough to be terrifying occurred in the middle of the morning. A number of people started to run out of the building, but were prevented by the policemen at the door and by Dr. [Charles] Miller, Surgeon-in-Chief of the Central Emergency, who called out, "Stay where you are!" The words were no sooner completed than the shock was over.

It must have been almost noon or a little after when I was making an attempt to systematically pass from one patient to another with a pitcher of coffee and some bread, when my companion came up to me and in a low excited voice said: "The building is on fire; the patients are to be removed as quickly as possible at the rear entrance." I looked around, expecting to see people rushing excitedly about rescuing patients, but evidently few then had been told of the fire, for groups of men were standing about who had undoubtedly come to help but did not know what to do. I went up to the men near me and passed the word on to them in a low voice and directed them to pull the patients on the mattresses to the rear entrance beginning with those nearest the exit, as there was no passage way to drag the further mattresses until those in front were removed. Others passed the word quickly and in an incredibly short space of time every one was at work and the three hundred and fifty-four patients were removed in ambulances and automobiles to the established hospitals. It was the wings of love that helped the hands and feet of the men and women to save those helpless ones who lay so patiently and uncomplainingly upon the floor waiting to be carried out. Not only then but during the entire morning the patients showed marvelous fortitude and complaints and cries of pain where almost unheard.

Dr. McGinty remained in the building until the entire equipment was removed, including not only the surgical supplies but all of the mattresses and bedding. A few people whose imaginations may have been abnormally developed by the reading of dime novels or attending the Central Theatre spread the most sensational reports regarding the fate of the patients. Some said they had been chloroformed, a report attributed to a nurse which on the face of it would appear false to anyone who knows the length of time it takes to produce complete anaesthesia; others said that the patients had been shot. Surely our calamity was tragical enough without it being necessary to add unnecessary horrors to it by such falsifications!

Dr. James W. Ward, President of the Board of Health, supervised the transferring of the patients and assigned my friend, another nurse and myself to the California Women's Hospital, and directed us to the automobile that was to carry us there. Paul Revere's Ride might justly be compared to ours but nothing less sensational. I thought to myself, "We have lived through the earthquake and fire, but this is the end surely." We whirled around corners so rapidly we had to clutch on to each other to save ourselves from being thrown out; we sped past other automobiles and just escaped running over numbers of people along the route. The "hell wagons," as they have so often been called, were converted in our disaster to "chariots of mercy." They were the salvation of hundreds of lives and redeemed their reputation so fully that few San Francisco people will ever again tolerate the abuse these vehicles so popular in the "Lighter Vein" of current periodicals.

At the California Women's Hospital Lucy Fisher and her friend were told there were already sufficient nurses. They went to a hospital in Golden Gate Park and helped tend its patients for the next few days.

After his escape from Meese & Gottfried's machine shop, Patrolman Harry F. Walsh tried to pull the alarm in the call box near Howard Street but found that the wires were down. His story, as reported in *The Argonaut*, May 15, 1926, continues.

HARRY F. WALSH (b. 1874)

Cattle stampede at Mission and Fremont

I THEN HURRIED UP FREMONT STREET to Mission, and on the way I met an old watchman named John Maguire, who was employed at W.T. Garratt & Company's foundry on the west side of Fremont Street, opposite Meese & Gottfried's.

"What is it?" he asked me quite earnestly. "It's an earthquake," said I, just as earnestly. But it really might have been anything, because the second shock seemed to me to feel more like the pull-back in the snap of a cracking whip than anything else. It just jerked the ground from under everything.

While John Maguire was talking to me, the cornices and chimneys were still dropping into the street every now and then from the places where they had been loosened. But I had hardly time to notice these when I saw a lot of wild cattle stampeding up from Mission Street, and charging at everything that came in their way.

Some vaqueros had been driving this herd of beef cattle up Mission Street from the water front, on their way to the stock yards at the Potrero, when the shock came and scared them. The cow-men simply disappeared. I never knew where they ran to; while the cattle went daft with terror and started running anywhere.

While a lot of them were running along the sidewalk of Mission Street, between Fremont and First Streets, a big warehouse toppled out into the thoroughfare and crushed most of them clean through the pavement into the basement, killing and burying them outright. The first that I saw of the bunch were two that were caught and crippled by falling cornices, or the like, on Fremont Street, near Mission, and they were in great misery. So I took out my gun and shot them. Then I had only six shots left, and I saw that more cattle were coming along, and that there was going to be big trouble.

At that moment I ran into John Moller, who owned the saloon at the southeast corner of Fremont and Mission streets, almost across the street from where we met. I asked him had he any ammunition in his place and if so to let me have some quick. He was very scared and excited over the earthquake and everything; and when he saw the cattle coming along, charging and bellowing, he seemed to lose more nerve.

Anyhow there was no time to think. Two of the steers were charging right at us while I was asking him to help, and he started to run for his saloon. I had to be quick about my part of the job, because, with only a revolver as a weapon, I had to wait till the animal was quite close before I dared fire. Otherwise I would not have killed or even stopped him.

Steers on their way to the stockyards on Potrero Hill were either crushed by collapsing buildings or shot as they ran wild along Mission Street.

As I shot down one of them, I saw the other charging after John Moller, who was then at the door of his saloon and apparently quite safe. But as I was looking at him and the steer, Moller turned, and seemed to become paralyzed with fear. He held out both hands as if beseeching the beast to go back. But it charged on and ripped him before I could get near enough to fire.

When I killed the animal it was too late to save the man. We got a hose wagon from a fire engine that came along and could do nothing in its own line of business for lack of water. It took Moller down to the Harbor Emergency Hospital, on the wharf at the foot of Mission Street, where he died very soon afterward.

Things were then moving very quickly. A dozen or more of the wild cattle came tearing into Fremont Street, and my revolver was empty.

Then a young fellow came running up to me carrying a rifle and a lot of cartridges. It was an old Springfield, and he knew how to use it. He was a cool shot, and he understood cattle, too. He told me that he came from Texas, but I don't think he told me anything else about himself. We were too busy with the cattle. We probably killed fifty or sixty out of that herd. Some of them were running wild, others crippled or wounded. We were going to shoot a horse that we saw standing up, half buried in masonry, on Mission Street between First and Fremont; but when we got near the poor creature we found it was already stone dead. It was near there that the big warehouse—Studebaker's wagon warehouse I think it was—had fallen out and crushed a number of the cattle clear through the sidewalk and into the basement.

We used the rifle alternately, the Texan and myself, and it was shortly after seeing the dead horse that I gave it back to him and turned up Fremont Street. I never saw the Texan again.

Eugene Schmitz's tenure as mayor of San Francisco had been plagued with rumors of graft and corruption since it began in 1901, yet his critics were unable to find any substantial evidence to unseat him. In spite of the rumors, he was very popular, and was voted back for a third term in 1905. That popularity reached a new high during the tragic days of April when even his staunchest critics admitted that he was one of the principal heroes of the catastrophe.

He lived with his family at 2849 Fillmore Street, between Vallejo and Green streets—an area that was not badly affected by the initial quake. At first, he wandered around his neighborhood checking damage to the buildings there and was totally unaware of the havoc being wreaked downtown.

The following is excerpted from a report he wrote prior to May 1 which was published in the *Argonaut* issues of January 15 and 22, 1927.

Mayor Schmitz takes control

At six o'clock Mr. Myrtile Cerf and Mr. John T. Williams of the City Attorney's office came to my house in an automobile and told me that the City Hall had been destroyed by the earthquake. At that time we could already see indications of a great fire somewhere in the down town district. I got into the automobile with Mr. Cerf and Mr. Williams and we drove down Green Street to Van Ness Avenue where we turned south toward the City Hall.

On Van Ness Avenue we met a company of soldiers under the command of a Captain whose name I do not know, and I asked him where they were going.* He said he had been sent by General Funston to report to the Mayor or the Chief of Police at the new City Hall. I then said to him: "I am the Mayor. The new City Hall is destroyed. I am now going to the Hall of Justice. Report with your company at the Hall of Justice where you will receive orders what to do."

We then drove down to the new City Hall where I saw that the dome had fallen in and the building was a complete wreck. We then drove down Market Street to Kearny Street, and thus to the Hall of Justice, where we arrived at about a quarter to seven o'clock.

All along Market and Kearny streets I saw signs of great destruction that had been caused by the earthquake shock of the early morning. Numbers of people were out in the street and the buildings presented a pitiful appearance. The Hall of Justice had also been badly damaged,

---

* Captain Meriweather Walker with companies C and D of the U.S. Engineers from Fort Mason.

and the Chief of Police [Jeremiah Dinan] informed me that the tower of the building was about to fall.

I got all the officers and officials together, and immediately established quarters in the basement of the Hall of Justice. A little while later Colonel [Charles] Morris of the Presidio reported to me for duty. My orders to him were that he should take his men and distribute them over the city, but especially in the district that was burning, and that they should drive the people back from the burning houses and keep them away from the ruins of houses that had collapsed or been burned. Also to place a special guard around the City Hall, and especially to guard the vaults of the Treasurer's office in that building, which contained about $6,000,000.

Anticipating that looting would take place—I had already seen some of it on my trip down town—and realizing that we would have no place in which to keep prisoners if we arrested any, and that it was time for firm and decisive action, I told Colonel Morris and also the Captain that reported to me from General Funston, to let the news be widely spread that anyone caught looting should not be arrested but should be shot.

Colonel Morris asked me if I would be responsible for that order and I told him Yes; that I would be responsible for that order; we could take no prisoners; we must stop looting, and therefore to shoot anyone caught looting. The same order was also issued to the Police Department.

The next order I issued to the police and military authorities was to close all places where liquor was sold and to notify those who sold liquor that they should discontinue the sale. Also that they were to close their establishments and keep them closed, and that if any man were found disobeying that order, the liquor in his place should be confiscated and spilled into the street.

That order went out immediately and was immediately acted upon by the military and civil authorities.

By this time the building known as the Morgue, across the alley at the rear and to the east of the Hall of Justice, had been destroyed by the earthquake. In the basement of the Hall of Justice, under the sidewalk, there was a place that was used as a shooting gallery by the Police Department. In this we then established a temporary Morgue, and the bodies of the men, women and children taken from the ruins of the old Morgue were brought there.

It should be mentioned that when I learned from Chief Dinan that the tower on the Hall of Justice was unsafe, and realized that the prisoners in the jail upstairs were in peril of their lives, I asked the Chief what was to be done with them. He did not know what to do with them so I had all the prisoners brought before me. The Chief separated those who were charged with misdemeanors from those that were charged with felonies.

To those who were charged with misdemeanors I administered a severe lecture, telling them I was going to give them their liberty, but if any of them were caught in any overt act he would not be subject to arrest but would be shot down. I then asked them to go and keep the peace, and thereupon released them. There were also three women prisoners that I lectured and then released. The prisoners charged with felonies I had handcuffed together and placed in cells in the basement some feet from where I was then issuing orders.

At this time I appointed a Committee of Fifty, and sent word to the men appointed that they should meet at three o'clock that afternoon in the basement of the Hall of Justice. In the selection of this Committee of Fifty I considered neither nationality, creed, nor political affiliations, but picked out the men of the community that I thought were best fitted for the task that then confronted them, and seemed by their abilities best equipped to solve the problems and carry into effect the propositions that would come before them. Irrespective of their politics or their social standing, these men all worked harmoniously and solely for the benefit of the public.

Meanwhile, pending the meeting of the Committee, the Chief of Police and myself were kept busy signing orders permitting responsible persons to pass through the lines in order to give aid where needed and so forth, and also in issuing special officers' stars to all those we knew to be really reliable, or that came to us recommended by responsible parties. I think we issued on that day, April 18, something like two thousand special officers' stars.

When fire threatened the Hall of Justice on the second afternoon the prisoners were marched in chains to Fort Mason. (See "A letter from a National Guardsman.")

Meanwhile, many of the guests at the Palace Hotel were still unaware of the horrific scenes that were being enacted in less secure buildings. According to this account by James Byrne, some guests dressed and went down into the Palm Court for coffee and rolls. This is the second extract from his privately printed book *Recollections of the Fire*, which was originally serialized in three issues of *The Argonaut* (November 27 and December 4 and 11, 1926).

JAMES W. BYRNE (1858-1930)

Breakfast in the Palace Palm Court

Looking out of the market street window I could see no building in the vicinity that had collapsed or seemed to be seriously damaged. Some bricks had fallen, chiefly from the cornices and fire walls at the top of buildings and were littered along the sidewalks. Practically none of this debris, however, spread out as far as the thoroughfare, and there was nothing in sight to convey the impression that the community had suffered a great catastrophe. The idea of a great fire did not occur to me, and I could see nothing of the collapses of buildings and similar calamities that had occurred in other sections of the city.

Having surveyed what I could see of the situation, I returned to my own quarters and dressed hurriedly. Some of the plaster had fallen in my mother's* room, and she was anxious to get downstairs and away from the hotel. In view of the fact that we were all prepared to start for Europe on the Saturday—three days later—she did not care to risk the chance of another earthquake in the Palace.

As soon as she was dressed, we went to the elevator which was then running and were taken downstairs in it. There is no mistake about the fact that the elevator was then in service or that Mrs. Irvine and myself and other people were taken up and down in it. For some reason that I did not learn, it was stopped a little while later; but at this period it was in service.

* Mrs. Margaret Irvine.

I took my mother into the court of the hotel where we took seats at one of the small tables. Numerous other people were about. In the kitchen, an old Irish woman was then preparing coffee and rolls for the help. It was too early for the dining room to be open. I went into the kitchen and got some rolls and a couple of cups of coffee which I took out to the table where my mother was sitting.

Two friends of ours, Mr. and Mrs. E.D. Beylard, of San Mateo, who had come up to town for the opera the night before, came and sat at the table adjoining ours. Mr. Beylard also went out to the kitchen and brought back coffee and rolls for Mrs. Beylard and himself.

While we were taking our coffee we were looking about, noting the effects of the earthquake, and the numerous people of whom many were in very light attire.

It will be remembered that the glass roof of the old Palace Court was part of the main roof of the hotel, eight stories above. The court measured 84 by 144 feet, an immense area. Looking up at it I noticed that only two of the panes of glass had fallen out during the shock, and I pointed them out to Mr. Beylard.

I was apprehensive on account of my mother and was very anxious to get her away from the hotel to the Golf Club or Burlingame or some other place outside the city, but no vehicle of any kind was available. All the street cars and telephones were out of service, but I believed I could get a carriage either at Conlan's on California Street or at Kelly's livery stables on Pine Street near Van Ness Avenue, and started out to try my luck. I went up by Post Street because I wanted to see how the shock had affected the Pacific Union Club on the corner of Post and Stockton streets. Therefore I did not see any of the tragedies and comedies that had resulted from the total collapse of some buildings and the facades falling out of others on Geary Street.

At the Pacific Union Club I found that the damage done by the earthquake was trifling. There was a little gap in the firewall of the lightwell on the eastern side of the building, and a red sandstone key-piece had been shaken out from the window of the room occupied by Mr. Horace Platt on the Stockton Street side. Some of the plaster on the main staircase also was cracked; but nothing had happened that would materially interfere with the regular routine of the establishment. The elevator was running, and was kept running most of the day; lunch and dinner were served as usual.

From the Club I continued my journey to the livery stables. When I got there I found that every available horse and vehicle had long since been hired by people that wanted to move from their houses or get out of the city. Therefore, I had to walk back again to the hotel.

On my way downtown I went by California Street, as far as the Fairmont Hotel on Nob Hill. There I stopped to take a survey of the city below. Then I saw that fires had broken out in all directions. I actually counted seventeen fires.

Then I hurried back downtown to the Palace. At Kearny and Market streets I found a cordon of police and soldiers, and I was not allowed to get through to cross over to the hotel. While I was trying to explain my emergency, Mr. Ernest Simpson of the *Chronicle*, who was inside the lines saw me and came to my help. Thanks to his intervention, I was allowed to pass through.

A lot happened to James Hopper—or, Jimmy Hopper, as he was better known—before he was able to reach his office at the *Call* building, as he relates in this continuation of his *Everybody's Magazine* article.

JAMES HOPPER (1876-1956)

A strange elation

I WENT DOWN THE STAIRS and into the streets, and they were full of people, half-clad, disheveled, but silent, absolutely silent, as if suddenly they had become speechless idiots. I went into the little alley at the back of the building, but it was deserted and the crushed houses seemed empty. I went down Post Street toward the center of town, and in the morning's garish light I saw many men and women with gray faces, but none spoke. All of them, they had a singular hurt expression, not one of physical pain, but rather one of injured sensibilities, as if some trusted friend, say, had suddenly wronged them, or as if some one had said something rude to them.

As for me I felt a strange elation. I was immensely proud of myself. I had gone through that hideous minute and a quarter with full command over myself, and now I was calm, absolutely calm. I threw my chest out and looked with amazement upon my dazed co-citizens. And yet when a few days after, I saw again a friend who had met me just at that time, he told me that I had been so excited I couldn't talk, that my arms trembled as I gesticulated, and that my eyes were an inch out of their sockets.

As I walked slowly down the street I was very busy taking notes—for the paper. "Such and such number, such and such street, cornice down; this building, roof down; that building crumbled." And then, "Good Lord!" I exclaimed to myself after a while, with childish peevishness, "I'm not going to take a list of all the buildings in the city!" I kept on going toward the paper. I thought that I was observing very carefully, but I wasn't. I remember now, for instance, seeing the roof of the Hotel Savoy caved into the building. And yet I did not try to find out if many had been hurt or killed. It was rather unimportant details that struck my eyes. In Union Square I remember a man in pink pajamas, a pink bath-robe, carrying a pink comforter under his arms, walking barefoot upon the gravel. In the center of the square an old man was with great concentration of purpose deciphering the inscription of the Dewey monument through spectacles of which the glasses had fallen out. I cut across through the Square and for the first time I heard some one speak. A man said to me, "Look!" I looked the way he was pointing, at a three-story wooden building called the Geary.

Union Square, looking toward Stockton and Geary streets. Notice the trunk near the base of the Dewey monument (left). A few hours after this photo was taken the entire area was devastated by fire.

It stood between an unfinished building at the corner of Stockton and Geary Streets and another tall building. The two sky-scrapers had shaken off their side walls upon the wooden one nestling between them, and only the façade of the latter stood, like cardboard scenery. At one of the windows was a man. He was trailing to the ground a long piece of cloth that looked no thicker than a ribbon, with the evident intention of sliding down by it. I shouted to him to wait a moment and ran to the door. I found the stairs still up, stuck along the front wall as with mucilage. I went up to the third floor over piles of plaster and laths, and there forgot about the man. For I came to a piece of room in which was a bed covered with débris, and out of the débris a slim white hand and wrist were sticking like an appeal. I threw off the stuff and a woman was beneath, still alive, a little, slender thing whom I had no trouble in carrying down to the sidewalk, where some one put her on an express wagon. I went back with another man and we found a second woman, whom we took down on a door. She seemed to be dying. There was another woman in another corner, but a pile of bricks was upon her and she was dead.

By this time the ruins were fairly swarming with rescuers, and a policeman had to drive away many of them with his club. All the time, however, I could hear a mysterious and insistent wailing somewhere in back. Finally I located it on the second floor. A strip of the hallway still remained along the right wall. I followed it till I came to a place where the whole hall was intact, and there, as upon a platform amid the ruins, a woman with long, disheveled hair was pacing to and fro, repeating in a long-drawn wail, over and over again, "Oh, my husband is dead, and a young man is dead, and a woman is dead; oh, my husband is dead, and a young man is dead, and a woman is dead!" "Where is your husband?" we roared in her ear, for she seemed unable to hear us. She pointed toward the back. We went toward the back and came to the abrupt end of the hall. Below us was a mound of bricks with the end of a bed-post emerging. Mechanically we began, three of us, to take up the bricks one by one, throwing them behind us. Above us towered the walls of the homicidal building. After a while a fireman joined us. He seemed stupefied, and like us began to take up bricks one by one. Finally another fireman came and called him. "Come on, Bill," he said, "there's fires." They went off and then after we had worked a time longer a red-headed youth who was digging with us said, "Wat's de use of digging out those that's dead?" This remark struck us all so profoundly true that without another word we all quit.

Photographer Arnold Genthe awoke to the sound of his priceless collection of Chinese porcelains crashing to the floor.
What happened next is recorded in this excerpt from his autobiography, *As I Remember* (1936). The above is a self-portrait.

Arnold Genthe (1869-1942)

Ludicrous sights

THE WHOLE HOUSE WAS CREAKING and shaking, the chandelier was swinging like a pendulum, and I felt as if I were on a ship tossed about by a rough sea. "This can't go on much longer," I said to myself. "When a house shakes like this, the ceiling is bound to collapse. As soon as the plaster begins to fall, I'll cover my head and accept what comes."

An ominous quiet followed. I was about to get up when I found Hamada, my Japanese servant, standing beside me. An earthquake was, of course, no new experience for him, but now he looked thoroughly frightened and was as pale as a Japanese can be. "Master," he said, "very bad earthquake—many days nothing to eat—I go, yes." Before I could say anything he was on his way downstairs. I looked at the clock; the time was a quarter past five. I looked out of the window and saw a number of men and women, half-dressed, rushing to the middle of the street for safety. Pushing his way through them, with a sack of flour over his shoulder and carrying a basket of provisions, was Hamada.

I went to the top floor to see what had happened to my studio. The chimney had fallen through the roof, most of the book shelves had collapsed and the books were buried under mounds of plaster from the wall and ceiling. A sixteenth-century wood sculpture of Buddha had landed right side up and stood unharmed and inscrutable in the midst of the debris—"serene, indifferent of fate."*

* See Bret Harte's poem at end of chapter.

The earth continued to indulge in periodic tremors, though less violently. I started to get dressed and decided that the most suitable "earthquake attire" would be my khaki riding things—I was to live in them for weeks.

The streets presented a weird appearance, mothers and children in their nightgowns, men in pajamas and dinner coats, women scantily dressed with evening wraps hastily thrown over them. Many ludicrous sights met the eye: an old lady carrying a large bird cage with four kittens inside, while the original occupant, the parrot, perched on her hand; a man tenderly holding a pot of calla lilies, muttering to himself; a scrub woman, in one hand a new broom and in the other a large black hat with ostrich plumes; a man in an old-fashioned nightshirt and swallow tails, being startled when a friendly policeman spoke to him, "Say, Mister, I guess you better put on some pants." … But there was no hysteria, no signs of real terror or despair. Nor did buildings show an alarming evidence of destruction; here and there parts of damaged walls had fallen into the streets, and most chimneys had collapsed. At Delmonico's, the front of one of the rooms on the third floor had fallen into the street. A chair with some clothes had been carried with it. The distressed owner called out to a passing workman, "Do you want to make $20?" "Sure," he replied, "what is it?" "See that suit there? I want you to bring it up to me here." Just then another shock occurred. "Ah, you better come and get it yourself."

After wandering about for a while, I went to the house of some dear friends of mine, Milton and Mabel Bremer (she is now married to my old friend Bertram Alanson). I found them calmly sitting on the front steps. The one thing that Mabel was apparently most anxious to save was a pair of evening slippers—a purchase of the day before—which she thrust into my large coat pockets. But it did not save them. I left them at my studio when I returned there later and they were burned with all my possessions.

We decided that it would be a good idea to have some breakfast and went to the St. Francis Hotel which had not been damaged. When we arrived we saw that we were not the only ones who had had the brilliant idea of breakfasting there. The lobby and the dining room were crowded. Near the entrance we saw Enrico Caruso with a fur coat over his pajamas, smoking a cigarette and muttering, "'Ell of a place! 'Ell of a place!" He had been through many earthquakes in his native Italy but this one was too much for him. It appeared that when he was awakened by the shock, he had tried his vocal cords without success. "'Ell of a place! I never come back here." And he never did.

Inside the hotel, people in all kinds of attire from evening clothes to nightgowns went milling about. There was no gas or electricity, but somehow hot coffee was available which, with bread and butter and fruit, made a satisfying breakfast. When I asked the waiter for a check he announced with a wave of his hand, "No charge today, sir. Everyone is welcome as long as things hold out."

After seeing my friends home, I went back to my studio to get a camera. The one thought uppermost in my mind was not to bring some of my possessions to a place of safety but to make photographs of the scenes I had been witnessing, the effects of the earthquake and the beginning of the conflagration that had started in various parts of the city. I found that my hand cameras had been so damaged by the falling plaster as to be rendered useless. I went to Montgomery Street to the shop of George Kahn, my dealer, and asked him to lend me a camera. "Take anything you want. This place is going to burn up anyway." I selected the best small camera, a 3A Kodak Special. I stuffed my pockets with films and started out. It was only then that I began to realize the extent of the disaster which had befallen the city. The fire had started simultaneously in many different places when the housewives had attempted to get breakfast for their families, not realizing what a menace the ruined chimneys were. All along the skyline as far as eye could see, clouds of smoke and flames were bursting forth. The work of the fire department was badly hampered, as the water mains had burst.

By this time the city had been put under martial law with General Funston in supreme command. He decided to check the progress of the conflagration by dynamiting a block in advance of the fire in order to create a breach over which the flames could not leap. All day and night the detonations resounded in one's ears and yet the fire continued to make headway. By noon the whole town was in flight. Thousands were moving toward the ferry hoping to get across the bay to Oakland or Alameda. On all streets leading to Golden Gate Park, there was a steady stream of men, women and children. Since all wagons or automobiles had been commandeered by the military authorities, only makeshift vehicles were available. Baby carriages and toy wagons, carts constructed out of boxes and wheels, were used to transport groceries, kitchen utensils, clothes and blankets; trunks mounted on roller skates or even without them were being dragged along by ropes. No one who witnessed these scenes can ever forget the rumbling noise of the trunks drawn along the sidewalks—a sound to which the detonations of the blasting furnished a fitting contrapuntal accompaniment.

Farther out on Geary and Sutter Streets, men and women cooked on improvised stoves on the sidewalks and as the crowds passed they called out invitations to stop for a rest and a cup of coffee. Up on the hill the wealthy were taking strangers into their homes, regardless of any risk they were running. I recall the picture of Henry J. Crocker laughing heartily as he carried the pails of water from the faucet in his garden to a little iron stove, probably one of his children's toys, set up by the curb in front of his red stone mansion.

I have often wondered, thinking back, what it is in the mind of the individual that so often makes him feel himself immune to the disaster that may be going on all around him. So many whom I met during the day seemed completely unconscious that the fire which was spreading through the city was bound to overtake their own homes and possessions. I know that this was so with me. All morning and through the early afternoon I wandered from one end of the city to the other, taking pictures without a thought that my studio was in danger.

As I was passing the home of some friends on Van Ness Avenue, they were on the porch and called out, "Come in and have a drink." While we were raising our glasses, there occurred another shock. Everyone but my hostess and I ran outside. "Let us finish anyway," she said.

"Sure," I said, giving her as a toast the line from Horace, "And even if the whole world should collapse, he will stand fearless among the falling ruins."

On my way to the Bohemian Club I met Charles K. Field. "You dummy," he said. "What are you doing here? Don't you know that your house is going to be blown up?" This was the first time I had thought of such a possibility. Turning back I hurried up Sutter Street to find a militiaman guarding the entrance of my studio.

"You can't get in here," he said, handling his rifle in an unpleasant manner.

"But it's my home," I said.

"I don't care whether it is or not. Orders are to clear all houses in the block. If you don't do as I say, I shoot, see?"

There were rumors that some of the militia, drunk with liquor and power, had been shooting people. I did not want to argue with him, but I did want to get inside, with the hope that I might save a few of my things.

"How about a little drink?" I asked.

"Well, all right," he replied eagerly.

In my cellar I had been keeping a precious bottle—Johannisberger Schloss 1868, which I had brought from the Bremer Rathskeller in 1904—reserving it for a special occasion worthy of it. There had been several gay events that might have justified its consumption, but now there was no doubt about it. The special occasion had arrived. I knew that to my unwelcome guest it would mean nothing, so I brought out for him a bottle of whiskey and while he poured himself drink after drink, I sipped the wine, if not with the leisurely enjoyment that it called for, at least getting some of its exquisite flavor without having to gulp it down with barbarous haste. When my militia friend had absorbed enough of his bottle, he pushed me through the door saying, "Now you have got to get out of here or I'll have to shoot you, see?"

From a safe distance I watched with others the dynamiting of the block of our homes. There was no expression of despair. ("Well, there it goes!" "That's that!" being the only comments heard.) That night I slept in Golden Gate Park together with thousands of others who were in the same plight. The crowd there suggested more a camping out than refugees from a disaster in which they had lost their homes and all their material possessions. A cheerful spirit seemed to prevail throughout and whatever one had was gladly shared.

Genthe quoted from this section of Bret Harte's poem, "San Francisco (From the Sea)":

Serene, indifferent of Fate,
Thou sittest at the Western Gate;
Upon thy height, so lately won,
Still slant the banners of the sun;
Thou seest the white seas strike their tents,
O Warder of two continents!

Here is a view of the earthquake from the perspective of a Chinese American teenager. Hugh Kwong Liang was born in San Francisco on February 7, 1891. In 1900 his mother took his sister and two brothers to China to escape the anti-Chinese sentiment then prevalent in the city. Hugh, as the oldest son, remained to help his father operate their grocery store. But his father died in November 1905, and Hugh was left in the care of his cousin, Lung Tin. The following is an excerpt from the reminiscences Liang recorded for his nieces and grand-nieces after seeing the film "Roots." The reminiscences were serialized in the newsletter of the Chinese Historical Society of Greater San Diego and Baja California, Inc., in 1995-96.

The Brenham Place referred to was a lane on the west side of Portsmouth Square. It is now Walter U. Lum Place.

Hugh Kwong Liang's story

DURING THE EARLY HOURS CHINATOWN seemed fairly safe. There was that big playground at Brenham Place above Kearny Street with Washington and Clay streets on each side. There were no buildings only trees. It seemed unlikely the flames could leap over the big playground to Chinatown. Besides, people had gone to the famous Kwong Chow Temple and consulted the revered Kwon Kong (warrior god) and Kwon Kong assured us that Chinatown was safe and no one should have to leave. So the merchants and everybody stood firm and hoped for the best.

However, it wasn't too long that the fire began to approach Chinatown on all sides. It was coming from Montgomery and Kearny streets toward the playground on Brenham Place. The wind was so strong that it just swept past the trees and everything and set fire to the buildings right in Chinatown. Now the panic was on!

Merchants hastily packed as much as they could of their most valuable merchandise on horse-drawn trucks to try to get out of the city. The trucks cost $100 per load and not many were available. Whatever was left in all the stores was burned later. Some trucks were also there to take passengers at $50 per person.

Cousin Lung Tin told me he was sorry that he could not take me along as he didn't have any more money. Before he left Cousin Lung Tin tried to console me with his meaningless advice. He said he was sure I could survive the ordeal since I was young and an American citizen and spoke the language and therefore should not be afraid of the future. So he hopped on the truck and went his way. I have never heard from Lung Tin to this day. That was certainly cruel and heart-less on Lung Tin's part. I was sure he had money, since he took every cent from father's store when he left. As the truck pulled away with Lung Tin, for the first time I broke down and cried. In my mind what was to become of me now that I was left penniless and all alone in this mess.

There was nothing I could do but take courage to carry on and follow the crowd of refugees up over the hills away from Chinatown to face the fate awaiting us. I dragged my father's trunk from block to block and up toward Nob Hill as the fire kept crowding towards us. As I looked down the hill and saw the whole of Chinatown burning including the building on Washington Street, where I was born, a feeling of great sadness and awe came over me. To think, even the sacred Kwong Chow Temple with the revered Kwon Kong (warrior god) was burned to ashes. It seemed that nothing was left of old Chinatown.

In the midst of that great disaster, there was one exception which could be termed a modern miracle. The St. Mary's Church at Dupont [Grant] Avenue and California Street somehow withstood the earthquake and fire and remained erect to the end. That is an historical fact.

The fire kept coming closer. I could hear the continued dyna-miting of buildings from distant parts of the city. There was no food or water even though I didn't feel hungry. What was I to do? Oh yes, carry on and on! So I turned away from my dear old Chinatown for the last time and joined the slow march with the other refugees. Pres-ently, city officials directing the refugees march approached us and told us to proceed toward the open grounds at the Presidio Army Post. We did as directed and dragged ourselves slowly toward the Presidio.

Upon our arrival at the Presidio about 6 P.M., soldiers rushed to help us. At first they distributed canvas tents to us and showed us how to put them up. Each tent must contain more than one person. I met a boy named Jimmy Ho, who was 16 and all alone like me, and asked him to share a tent with me. He did not have any baggage so my father's trunk was the only thing that we had in our tent. During this time the city continued to burn. The fire was so intense and the wind so strong that sparks came flying in from the flames and landed all over the top of our tent. Luckily water was now available and we had to spray water on the canvas top of our tent at intervals to prevent it from catching fire.

Suddenly, something was happening nearby. I heard a woman crying for help a few yards away from us and Ho and I rushed over to her tent. We found a young Chinese woman in her early twenties, who had just given birth to a baby. Several Chinese ladies were already there to help her. Her husband was frantically running around looking for a doctor. Then we noticed that her tent was very hot from the sparks, so we sprayed the tent for her and returned to our tent.

Now to my bitter surprise, my father's trunk had disappeared. Evidently some heartless person had stolen the trunk. So that for me was the last straw. Now for the first time I really felt completely hopeless and downhearted. My friend Jimmy Ho was so sorry for me and perhaps for himself too, that he broke down and sobbed. Jimmy said that he had relatives among the refugees and he would like to set out to find them. As there was nothing I could do to help Jimmy, I agreed with him that he should, by all means, try to locate his relatives and wished him success. So Jimmy Ho reluctantly bid me farewell and went on his way.

It was getting dark and the fire was still raging and edging closer. I had the feeling now that even the Presidio was not safe. I then made up my mind that eventually I must face death. Now at last, as strange as it may seem, I was not afraid any longer. The horrors of the day and my personal sufferings throughout the ordeal may have deadened my nerves. I was thinking even though my thoughts were wild and morbid, that I was willing to accept the cruel fate of death, but how to die was the question. My alternatives: (1) I will not burn to death. (2) I may starve to death, which cannot be helped. (3) Death by drowning seemed the easiest. So I chose number 3, but where can I find water? I was told there was a body of water some distance away. So while the other refugees remained in their tents praying and hoping that the fire somehow might be brought under control and not come to the Presidio, I set out to look for the waterfront. If I found it, I would stand by. If the fire should come close to me, I would jump into the water and drown. It was that simple.

I walked and walked in the darkness not knowing where I was going. Then suddenly something caught my attention. I thought I saw a light flashing at intervals from an object on the distant horizon. As I approached closer it looked like a boat. My heart was at once gladdened for that must be the waterfront I was seeking.

As I got closer I also saw two army trucks. Soldiers were unloading things to put on the boat. I crept quietly toward the boat and while the men were busy at the trucks, I quickly sneaked on the boat and hid under a table. Very soon I felt the boat start to move. I was really scared. I must have regained my nerves, although I was shaking all over wondering what they would do to me when I was found. Soon I heard footsteps coming near and the light was turned on. Then I knew I was in the kitchen (galley), since the men were talking about food.

Suddenly one man yelled out "look!". He reached under the table and pulled me out. They immediately called for the leader or captain. There was only six or eight men on that boat. They all came around and stared at me in surprise. The captain acted very stern and started to question me. I told the whole story of the earthquake and fire and terrible ordeal that I went through. To my surprise the captain and men were all very sympathetic and told me that everything would be all right and for me not to feel bad any longer. I then had my first food in over 24 hours. They gave me some meat, vegetables, and coffee and told me to help clean up things in the galley, to which I gladly complied.

The next morning, April 19th, we arrived at the town of Napa. No words can adequately describe my feelings that morning when I realized I was at last out of the nightmare of San Francisco. I was not brought up in religion. My folks only taught me to worship idols, but my miraculous escape from the San Francisco disaster set me to thinking that there must be a merciful God in Heaven who decides on our destiny and that he had shed his blessing on me. Who else could have directed me to that boat? From then on to this day I have believed in one God and Father.

Before I left the boat, the men took up a collection of coins and gave it to me with their best wishes. I shall never forget their kindness. I awoke to the fact that those men were the real Americans. They were so nice and considerate. It was a far cry from the race prejudice and harsh discrimination that I knew. Perhaps there is hope that things will get better with me.

As soon as I got off the boat, I went to the little Chinatown in Napa to inquire if some Liang cousins might be there. When they found that I was a refugee from the San Francisco earthquake, they all gathered around me to get the true story about the fire which was still going on. I found no Liang cousins, but they told me there was a very prominent Chinese person in the city of Vallejo who was a Liang. Vallejo was only a short way from Napa, so I got on the train and went there. As I was a refugee they did not collect train fare from me.

When I arrived in Vallejo I found very few Chinese there. I inquired about the Liang family and was told that a Mr. Liang Yoke Ping was a steward in the U.S. Navy Yard and had a large family. I went there at once and to my surprise, Mr. Liang Yoke Ping recognized me. He knew my father well and visited my family in San Francisco many times. I also recognized him as one I used to call Uncle Yoke Ping. So Uncle Yoke Ping took me in and treated me as one of the family.

Hugh Kwong Liang enrolled at the University of California at Berkeley but left early to begin a lifelong career in Chinese vaudeville. As part of the first all-Chinese barbershop quartet, he performed in theaters around the state and ultimately on Broadway in New York. He later became the featured soloist on the popular NBC radio show, the Major Bowes Amateur Hour. He died in Washington, D.C., in 1984 at the age of 93.

Mary Edith Griswold was an assistant editor of *Sunset Maga-zine*, and in the June-July 1906 issue of that periodical she had an article entitled, "Three Days Adrift: The Diary of a San Francisco Girl During the Earthquake and Fire." In it, she tells of sleeping in the park and on vacant lots, and of a brief "ex-ploring expedition" inside the fire lines. She also writes about her artist friend L. Maynard Dixon and his wife, Lilian, with whom she shared the house at 1443 Greenwich Street.

Three days adrift

APRIL 18.—EVENING. In a sand lot near foot of Van Ness avenue. I'm writing by the light of the burning city. The fire is still twenty blocks from my house, but we came out here to spend the night because we have been afraid since the first earthquake shock. Then, the house swayed and creaked and trembled; rose and fell like a ship in a tempest. I couldn't walk on the floor at all—had to crawl to the door on my hands and knees. Just as I opened the door my big plaster cast of "The Winged Victory" fell from her pedestal and smashed to the floor. She made a big heap of rubbish. I was too terrified to think.

I tried to call to the Dixons, but couldn't articulate. They didn't hear a sound from me throughout those terrible forty seconds. I thought it was the end—but neither the beautiful dreams nor the horrors that are supposed to panorama instant death came to me. My heart beat double quick somewhere up in my throat. I felt nauseated. But I managed to save my toppling mirror; saved it while all other breakable objects in my room went smash. I held on to it with one hand and braced myself against the door frame with the other and watched the crystal scent bottles slide off and spill their precious fragrance on the drunken floor; my statuette of Psyche fell from her shelf and broke her head off. But my little Aztec idol Huitzpochitle took his tumble like a valiant god-of-war without a scratch. He rolled about on the floor in an undignified way but he never changed expression. The final jerk almost upset the bureau on top of me, but after that my house rocked regularly for a while like a swing when you "let the old cat die." I felt the ease which followed the cessation of great pain. When I felt quite sure that the floor was firm under my feet again I went out on the balcony. A cloud of dust rose from the city as though a race of giants were shaking their great carpet. Almost all the chimneys were down. Almost instantly columns of smoke began to rise from the other side of town.

We dressed. When we wanted to wash we found there was no water. Next, we hurried down town to see if Maynard Dixon's studio* was all right. On Union street the cable slot looked as if it had been run through a Chinese wash house fluting machine.

We had to walk, there being no cars.

In the Latin Quarter the streets were full of terrified people all crowding to keep in the middle of the street. It was the quietest crowd I was ever in. Scarcely any one spoke. The children didn't cry. The fear of God was upon us all. Everyone was afraid of another shock.

Maynard's studio was in chaos. The canvases were uninjured but his Navajo pottery was sadly smashed and mingled on the floor with the rest of his studio litter. A box of matches had been ignited by the shock and extinguished again by a vase of water spilling over it.

From the studio we went down Montgomery street to the Palace Hotel. It was uninjured. Things inside seemed quiet and in order. There was no broken glass, no plaster—everything was quiet and in place. A Chinese servant in a white linen blouse was calmly dusting the furniture in the Palm Garden. Men were passing to and fro in the corridor, others were reading the newspapers in the office; the clerks were at the desk. The proud boast that the Palace was earthquake proof had been vindicated.

From there we went along Market street to Lotta's fountain. The old buildings east of Sansome street were blazing. We saw the cupola on the roof of the "Fly in the Pudding" restaurant turn into a beautiful "set piece" and other old wooden buildings of early days catch fire. People in the street were kept busy dodging the speeding automobiles. Suddenly there was another earthquake shock. The crowds scurried panic stricken to the middle of the street. There they waited breathlessly for another disaster. But it never came.

* 728 Montgomery Street.

By nine the fire had come up to the Grand Opera House. Third street was a mass of people from south of Market street trying to escape with their household goods. There were women pushing sewing machines in front of them, children carrying phonographs, men dragging trunks. The screeching sound of the trunks dragging on the cable slots went to my marrow. At the corner a fireman stood beside a hydrant from which trailed a string of empty hose. A woman darted out of the crowd and ran up to him.

"What's the matter, Tom?"

"There's no water."

Up to now we had only felt fear, now we knew fear. No water, and fires on every side! The fireman kissed the woman and told her to go back to the folks, assuring her that he was all right. The woman did not cry but her lips trembled. She realized better than we could the terrible import of these words.

We then started for the editorial rooms of the Sunset Magazine in the Sunset Press building at the other end of Market street. At every cross street streams of people from south of Market came, staggering under the weight of the burden of their loads. "San Francisco will burn," said somebody. Dixon thought he ought to try and save something from his studio—he and his wife turned back—I obstinately insisted upon going to Sunset office—insisted that I wasn't afraid to proceed alone. So soon as they left me I was sorry and tried to catch them, but they were lost in the confusion. There was much to see. Earthquakes uncover strange secrets. The ruins of our monster seven million dollar City Hall cried to heaven the shame of the men who built it. At Sunset Press the printers were gathered in the street. The front wall of the top story had fallen revealing the machinery of the engraving plant.

While I waited there feeling like a shipwrecked sailor on a drifting sea one of my fellow editors, Allan Dunn, hove in sight. I hailed him. He threw me a line, as it were, and towed me up to his house on the top of Hyde street hill. Mrs. Dunn was walking up and down in front of the house clad in her best tailor suit, her pretty new opera cloak on her arm. We went inside and burned up all the gas left in the pipes making coffee.

A slight temblor sent us helter-skelter into the street where the crowd going toward the fire caught us up and whirled us along to the top of the hill on Sacramento street. The fire was roaring over an immense territory. We wanted to get into the thick of things and went down to Union Square. It was full of refugees sitting on their household goods. There were gathered Chinamen, Italians, "muckers" from south of Market street, Grand Opera singers; painted women who blinked as though they had not seen daylight for months; and fashionable people in evening dress donned hurriedly when they were awakened by the earthquake—a succotash of civilization—I didn't see any policemen. There was no need of any—the crowd was perfectly quiet—it was this unearthly, unnatural calm which made me afraid to speak. I saw only one talkative person. She was a beautiful creature of stunning style who walked between two men, her hands in her muff. I believe she was the only woman in all San Francisco that day who acted unconcerned. As the trio sailed past me I hear her say, "O, we'll have a good time as long as our money lasts."

As we stopped on Stockton street to watch a toppling wall I found myself next to an old colored man. As he spoke I recognized in him the negro exhorter. I had sometimes listened when he was holding forth from his open-air platforms. Now he was exclaiming:

"Haven't I prophesied all this? Haven't I told you this wicked town would be consumed with fire and brimstone? But now I'm sorry I spoke."

At the Sequoia Club we rescued Mrs. Solly Walter. Later she and I detached ourselves from the Dunns and walked back to my house. The residence streets looked like circus day in a country village. The women were all sitting on chairs in front yards, secure in the feeling that Van Ness avenue was too wide for fire to cross it. By noon today both sides of the wide boulevard were lined with people and furniture. Sometimes a woman would have saved only one easy chair and was comfortably rocking in it. Again it was a bedroom set that had been snatched from the burning—but always there were phonographs and parrots and dogs and canary birds. Here, as everywhere, the crowd showed no emotion, except when the earth trembled, as it did now and then, slightly. Then everyone would rush for the middle of the street.

This afternoon my old friend Mr. Whitney called for me with a buggy. We made a complete circuit of the fire zone. The people seem to feel that a power too stupendous to combat had taken charge of their destiny, and that the fury of the forces of nature cannot be met by the puny hands of man. We are all learning the lesson of the inevitable.

The open lot near my house is full of people and new comers are constantly arriving. The pillar of fire mounts higher and higher. The heavens south are burning red, while north over Fort Mason smoke hangs low. It frightens me, the smoke, even more than the fire. It is an unreasonable fear I know, and I'm ashamed to tell anyone of it—the fear that the heavens will fall—the sky looks so near. What if we should get caught up in a maelstrom of smoke and only four blocks of unstable earth between us and the bay!

Thursday, April 19.—At Fort Mason. Yesterday's sights and sounds and experiences are forgotten in today's. We rose when the sun looked up over Union street hill—red as wine through the smoke—and dragged our mattresses back to my house with the fire still many blocks away. While we were eating cold food on the balcony, Xavier Martinez, the artist, came up with some friends to see if there was a way of making coffee. There was not, but I offered an acceptable substitute and threw in the house. They accepted. This was certainly lucky because Maynard and Lillian wanted to go home to Sausalito. They urged me to come along, but I refused. I know now why the people who live at the foot of Vesuvius all stay until it is too late to escape the lava. The Dixons departed taking with them a few cherished things on a two-wheeled push-cart.

Vail Bakewell, the lawyer, came over from Oakland on a tug to rescue us and take us over to his home in Oakland. We all refused to go. I, for one, must see the closing act of this monster tragedy, a whole city for a stage, 500,000 actors and everyone playing his part. We were joined by Porter Garnett, the critic, but soon he left us to save his mother from danger.

At four this afternoon a big cloud of smoke came over us—cinders as big as dollars began to fall and a shower of plaster dust. This frightened us. I packed three trunks and the boys carried them into the neighbor's garden. I wrapped a wet blanket around the band-box containing my new spring hat and hid it in a rose bush. We bought a four-wheeled cart from a small boy, made two two-wheeled carts out of it by using the pantry shelves for the body, loaded up one with food and the other with clothes and started out for my friends', the Towarts, sand lots on the other side of the Presidio. Van Ness avenue was full of people and movings—so full it spilled out into every vacant lot and side street. Going was difficult. Our cart broke down. I experienced the most terrible and senseless fear that this great mass of people, animals and things would stampede. After a council we decided to stop here in Fort Mason for the night.

We are in the middle of an immense field—there must be thousands camping here—people of all nations thrown together higglety-pigglety. Our nearest neighbor is an Italian vegetable peddler and he has brought his entire family and household effects. When they went for the second load they left the baby here wailing an obligato to the accompaniment of a German fellow with a fiddle. Behind us sit a newly wed couple beside their trunk. The little bride is quietly weeping while her inexperienced spouse shows plainly that this is too much for one day. In the camps of the Latin races the men are doing all the talking, while among us English speaking people only the women are to be heard. On the top of the hill stood a bearded Italian waving a large chromo* of St. Francis at the ever approaching fire, while he called upon the patron saint to save his city.

11 P.M. Vail Bakewell and Rob Towart have just returned from an adventure. They went over to see if the Towarts' house had burned. It is still standing but it is only a question of a few hours. Fire is coming up all sides of Russian Hill. I started out with Vail on an exploring expedition. The first startling sight was a rose garden, with hundreds of huge roses glowing red in the light of the flames. We had the luck to get inside the fire lines. It was a thrilling experience while it lasted, until we were peremptorily ordered out by the Colonel in command of the troops. We went so close to the fire that I felt my hair curl. We saw some people loot a grocery and bar—the proprietor inviting everyone to help themselves. We went inside. There were no lights, only that ghastly light coming in the windows of the fire across the street. It made me sick.

Outside a puppy sat whining. I took it up in my arms and it was trembling. There were many dogs and cats that had been forgotten or abandoned by their masters. Some we saw ran away from us, back into the burning houses. A cry was raised that we were surrounded by fire, but there was an avenue of escape down the north side where the

* Chromolithograph—a colored lithograph.

hill makes a sheer drop of 50 feet. My nerves still tingle with the excitement of this. Everything has been on such a scale today! Has Fate thus set a measure which will make all other experiences which are to come to me seem puny?

Still later a span of horses broke their tethering straps and came charging into our camp. We scared them away with umbrellas, which we were using for tents. This so upset the tranquillity of our crowd that Vail and I volunteered to go back to my house to fetch some restoratives. We went by way of Van Ness avenue. Everything was burned from there to the ferry up to Vallejo street. It was a most wonderful sight! Many miles—a limitless space of blue flames with the last red glow of big timbers between—of dancing, palpitating, living light. The great dwelling houses on the west side of Van Ness avenue were ablaze. Soldiers were dynamiting them. It was like the booming of artillery fire.

On our way back we saw two men sitting on the front steps of a big house. They asked us in to see how their home had been wrecked by the earthquake, as well as by the fire across the street and the dynamite. We groped around inside, by the fire light. Vail Bakewell tried to play on the pipe organ—but there was no sound. In the street a man came running up to us and presented me with a box of face powder—said he had no use for it and it might come handy!

Friday, April 20.—Fort Mason. 6 A.M. An army surgeon made an inspection of the camp this morning and found a sick child next to us, which he diagnosed as suffering from small-pox. Even this announcement did not create a panic. It seemed all in the day's doings.

1 P.M. We are at the little dock below the Fort waiting for a navy cutter to take us around to the Oakland ferry.

The fire is within two blocks of my house—everyone in my block had been told to leave. Our house has been ordered dynamited. The apathy of the last two days has given way. The firemen are frantic. If they don't stop the fire now the whole Western Addition will go—a policeman with a red face is running up and down in front of the house. A dead Italian lies in the middle of the street opposite my house. Members of his family sit around his body in a circle. I got so scared I couldn't swallow a glass of water. The heat on the balcony was intense—too hot to stay out there. The paint on the woodwork was blistering Everyone was fire mad. My home will surely go.

Jack London and his wife, Charmian, visited San Francisco from their Sonoma Valley ranch, arriving on the last passenger ferry on April 18. All night long they roamed the streets, until Jack's feet blistered and Charmian's ankles became swollen. Years later, Charmian recalled in *The Book of Jack London* that he told her he would never write about what he saw. "What use trying? One could only string big words together and curse the futility of them," he said. He changed his mind, however, when *Collier's* magazine offered him 25 cents a word for his impressions. Deeply in debt, he wrote "The Story of an Eyewitness" which appeared in the May 5, 1906, issue. It is reprinted here as it later appeared in *The Argonaut* under the title "Jack London Tells of the Fire."

Procession of the trunk-pullers

THE EARTHQUAKE SHOOK DOWN IN SAN FRANCISCO hundreds of thousands of dollars' worth of walls and chimneys. But the conflagration that followed burned up hundreds of millions of dollars' worth of property. There is no estimating within hundreds of millions the actual damage wrought. Not in history has a modern imperial city been so completely destroyed. San Francisco is gone. Nothing remains of it but memories and a fringe of dwelling-houses on its outskirts. Its industrial section is wiped out. Its business section is wiped out. Its social and residential section is wiped out. The factories and warehouses, the great stores and newspaper buildings, the hotels and the palaces of the nabobs, are all gone. Remains only the fringe of dwelling houses on the outskirts of what was once San Francisco.

Within an hour after the earthquake shock the smoke of San Francisco's burning was a lurid tower visible a hundred miles away. And for three days and nights this lurid tower swayed in the sky, reddening the sun, darkening the day, and filling the land with smoke.

On Wednesday morning at a quarter past five came the earthquake. A minute later the flames were leaping upward. In a dozen different quarters south of Market Street, in the working-class ghetto, and in the factories, fires started. There was no opposing the flames. There was no organization, no communication. All the cunning adjustments of a twentieth century city had been smashed by the earthquake. The streets were humped into ridges and depressions, and piled with the debris of fallen walls. The steel rails were twisted into perpendicular and horizontal angles. The telephone and telegraph systems were disrupted. And the great water-mains had burst. All the shrewd contrivances and safeguards of man had been thrown out of gear by thirty seconds' twitching of the earth-crust.

By Wednesday afternoon, inside of twelve hours, half the heart of the city was gone. At that time I watched the vast conflagration from out on the bay. It was dead calm. Not a flicker of wind stirred. Yet from every side wind was pouring in upon the city. East, west, north, and south, strong winds were blowing upon the doomed city. The heated air rising made an enormous suck. Thus did the fire of itself build its own colossal chimney through the atmosphere. Day and night this dead calm continued, and yet, near to the flames, the wind was often half a gale, so mighty was the suck.

Wednesday night saw the destruction of the very heart of the city. Dynamite was lavishly used, and many of San Francisco's proudest structures were crumbled by man himself into ruins, but there was no withstanding the onrush of the flames. Time and again successful stands were made by the fire-fighters, but every time the flames flanked around on either side, or came up from the rear, and turned to defeat the hard-won victory.

An enumeration of the buildings destroyed would be a directory of San Francisco. An enumeration of the buildings undestroyed would be a line and several addresses. An enumeration of the deeds of heroism would stock a library and bankrupt the Carnegie medal fund. An enumeration of the dead—will never be made. All vestiges of them were destroyed by the flames. The number of the victims of the earthquake will never be known. South of Market Street, where the loss of life was particularly heavy, was the first to catch fire.

Remarkable as it may seem, Wednesday night while the whole city crashed and roared into ruin, was a quiet night. There were no crowds. There was no shouting and yelling. There was no hysteria, no disorder. I passed Wednesday night in the path of the advancing flames, and in all those terrible hours I saw not one woman who wept, not one man who was excited, not one person who was in the slightest degree panic stricken.

Before the flames, throughout the night, fled tens of thousands of homeless ones. Some were wrapped in blankets. Others carried bundles of bedding and dear household treasures. Sometimes a whole family was harnessed to a carriage or delivery wagon that was weighted down with their possessions. Baby buggies, toy wagons, and go-carts were used as trucks, while every other person was dragging a trunk. Yet everybody was gracious. The most perfect courtesy obtained. Never in all San Francisco's history, were her people so kind and courteous as on this night of terror.

All night these tens of thousands fled before the flames. Many of them, the poor people from the labor ghetto, had fled all day as well. They had left their homes burdened with possessions. Now and again they lightened up, flinging out upon the street clothing and treasures they had dragged for miles.

They held on longest to their trunks, and over these trunks many a strong man broke his heart that night. The hills of San Francisco are steep, and up these hills, mile after mile, were the trunks dragged. Everywhere were trunks, with across them lying their exhausted owners, men and women. Before the march of the flames were flung picket lines of soldiers. And a block at a time, as the flames advanced, these pickets retreated. One of their tasks was to keep the trunk-pullers moving. The exhausted creatures, stirred on by the menace of bayonets, would arise and struggle up the steep pavements, pausing from weakness every five or ten feet.

Often, after surmounting a heart-breaking hill, they would find another wall of flame advancing upon them at right angles and be compelled to change anew the line of their retreat. In the end, completely played out, after toiling for a dozen hours like giants, thousands of them were compelled to abandon their trunks. Here the shopkeepers and soft members of the middle class were at a disadvantage. But the working-men dug holes in vacant lots and backyards and buried their trunks.

At nine o'clock Wednesday evening I walked down through the very heart of the city. I walked through miles and miles of magnificent buildings and towering skyscrapers. Here was no fire. All was in perfect order. The police patrolled the streets. Every building had its watchman at the door. And yet it was doomed, all of it. There was no water. The dynamite was giving out. And at right angles two different conflagrations were sweeping down upon it.

At one o'clock in the morning I walked down through the same section. Everything still stood intact. There was no fire. And yet there was a change. A rain of ashes was falling. The watchmen at the doors were gone. The police had been withdrawn. There were no firemen, no fire-engines, no men fighting with dynamite. The district had been absolutely abandoned. I stood at the corner of Kearny and Market, in the very innermost heart of San Francisco. Kearny Street was deserted. Half a dozen blocks away it was burning on both sides. The street was a wall of flame. And against this wall of flame, silhouetted sharply, were two United States cavalrymen sitting their horses, calming watching. That was all. Not another person was in sight. In the intact heart of the city two troopers sat their horses and watched.

Surrender was complete. There was no water. The sewers had long since been pumped dry. There was no dynamite. Another fire had broken out further uptown, and now from three sides conflagrations were sweeping down. The fourth side had been burned earlier in the day. In that direction stood the tottering walls of the Examiner building, the burned-out Call building, the smoldering ruins of the Grand Hotel, and the gutted, devastated, dynamited Palace Hotel.

The following will illustrate the sweep of the flames and the inability of men to calculate their spread. At eight o'clock Wednesday evening I passed through Union Square. It was packed with refugees. Thousands of them had gone to bed on the grass. Government tents had been set up, supper was being cooked, and the refugees were lining up for free meals.

At half past one in the morning three sides of Union Square were in flames. The fourth side, where stood the great St. Francis Hotel, was still holding out. An hour later, ignited from top and sides, the St. Francis was flaming heavenward. Union Square, heaped high with mountains of trunks, was deserted. Troops, refugees, and all had retreated.

It was at Union Square that I saw a man offering a thousand dollars for a team of horses. He was in charge of a truck piled high with trunks from some hotel. It had been hauled here into what was considered safety, and the horses had been taken out. The flames were on three sides of the Square, and there were no horses.

Also, at this time, standing beside the truck, I urged a man to seek safety in flight. He was all but hemmed in by several conflagrations. He was an old man and he was on crutches. Said he: "Today is my birthday. Last night I was worth thirty-thousand dollars. I bought five bottles of wine, some delicate fish and other things for my birthday dinner. I have had no dinner, and all I own are these crutches."

I convinced him of his danger and started him limping on his way. An hour later, from a distance, I saw the truck-load of trunks burning merrily in the middle of the street.

On Thursday morning, at a quarter past five, just twenty-four hours after the earthquake, I sat on the steps of a small residence on Nob Hill. With me sat Japanese, Italians, Chinese, and negroes—a bit of the cosmopolitan flotsam of the wreck of the city. All about were the palaces of the nabob pioneers of Forty-nine. To the east and south at right angles, were advancing two mighty walls of flame.

I went inside with the owner of the house on the steps of which I sat. He was cool and cheerful and hospitable. "Yesterday morning," he said, "I was worth six hundred thousand dollars. This morning this house is all I have left. It will go in fifteen minutes." He pointed to a large cabinet. "That is my wife's collection of china. This rug upon which we stand is a present. It cost fifteen hundred dollars. Try that piano. Listen to its tone. There are few like it. There are no horses. The flames will be here in fifteen minutes."

Outside the old Mark Hopkins residence a palace was just catching fire. The troops were falling back and driving the refugees before them. From every side came the roaring of flames, the crashing of walls, and the detonations of dynamite.

I passed out of the house. Day was trying to dawn through the smoke-pall. A sickly light was creeping over the face of things. Once only the sun broke through the smoke-pall, blood-red, and showing a quarter its usual size. The smoke-pall itself, viewed from beneath, was a rose color that pulsed and fluttered with lavender shades. Then it turned to mauve and yellow and dun. There was no sun. And so dawned the second day on stricken San Francisco.

An hour later I was creeping past the shattered dome of the City Hall. There was no better exhibit of the destructive force of the earthquake. Most of the stone had been shaken from the great dome, leaving standing the naked framework of steel. Market Street was piled high with the wreckage, and across the wreckage lay the overthrown pillars of the City Hall, shattered into short crosswise sections.

This section of the city with the exception of the Mint and the Post Office, was already a waste of smoking ruins. Here and there through the smoke, creeping warily under the shadows of tottering walls, emerged occasional men and women. It was like the meeting of the handful of survivors after the day of the end of the world.

On Mission Street lay a dozen steers, in a neat row stretching across the street, just as they had been struck down by the flying ruins of the earthquake. The fire had passed through afterward and roasted them. The human dead had been carried away before the fire came. At another place on Mission Street I saw a milk wagon. A steel telegraph pole had smashed down sheer through the driver's seat and crushed the front wheels. The milk cans lay scattered around.

All day Thursday and all Thursday night, all day Friday and Friday night, the flames still raged on.

Friday night saw the flames finally conquered, though not until Russian Hill and Telegraph Hill had been swept and three-quarters of a mile of wharves and docks had been licked up.

The great stand of the fire-fighters was made Thursday night on Van Ness Avenue. Had they failed here, the comparatively few remaining houses of the city would have been swept. Here were the magnificent residences of the second generation of San Francisco nabobs, and these, in a solid zone, were dynamited down across the path of the fire.

Jack London was not happy with his interpretation of what he saw, despite the fact it earned him more money per word than anything else he ever wrote. "It's the best stagger I can make at an impossible thing," he told Charmian. And, in a letter to poet George Sterling on May 31, he wrote, "Hopper's article in *Everybody's* is great. Best story of the Quake I've seen. My congratulations to him."

Streetcar tracks on Union Street, west of Steiner Street.

Eric Temple Bell was to become one of the outstanding mathematicians of his time, a popular historian of mathematics and, as "John Taine," a well-known writer of fantasy and science fiction. In April 1906 he was teaching mathematics at The Lyceum, a prominent preparatory school located in the Phelan Building on Market Street. He had also invested in one of the city's eight telephone companies. After the quake he wrote a long letter to students at his former school in England, the Bedford Modern School, and it was published in the school's magazine, *The Eagle*, in July of that year.

He was not alone in his concern about the outside world seeing the extent of the earthquake damage. The business community felt that visitors and investors would be scared away. A major campaign, spearheaded by the Southern Pacific Company, downplayed the effects of the quake while emphasizing fire damage which could—as it had in the past—devastate any American city.

The consul Bell refers to is the Austrian consul, who had a room adjoining his in a boarding house at 729 California Street.

This photograph was taken in 1903, when he was 20.

ERIC TEMPLE BELL (1883-1960)

"Like wind through a cornfield"

THE STREETS IN THE BUSINESS SECTION were an awful sight. The fire was the best thing that could possibly have happened to San Francisco for its future. If any foreigners or Easterners had seen the City just after the shock, or taken photos of it, its reputation would have been ruined for ever. As it was, the fire ruins have covered it up. Magnificent buildings were twisted like cork-screws, and the side-walks looked like crumpled up paper. In places, goods stored in the wholesale section, in vaults under the pavement, had been forced up 12 to 14 feet into the air. The cracks in the ground could not be exaggerated—though people will now of course cover them up and deny their existence. The street car tracks were twisted high into the air in all imaginable shapes.

The people of San Francisco should erect a monument to the peerless fool who kept the electric current on when the shock came, for it was through him that the city was burned, and therefore really saved. We had to pick our way like cats on hot bricks to avoid the fizzling wires. Within twenty minutes of the shock, K. and I were in the heart of the business section, and by that time, there alone, seven awful fires were raging unchecked. Stone and iron melted and ran, or burned in the terrific heat. But in spite of this the San Francisco fire department could have done their usual work—the best in the world—if there had been water. But all the mains were broken in a thousand places. I'll never forget the look in the firemen's faces, as they tried hydrant after hydrant, only to get a sickening dribble of water. But they didn't wait long. They rushed the hose carts off for dynamite, and in fifteen minutes more San Francisco's most beautiful buildings were sailing into the air. The sight of a fifteen storey structural steel building being dynamited, is very curious. It goes up rather slowly, and on the whole looks like a heap of dirt being given a vigorous kick.

K. and I made a wild dash for the [telephone] Company's offices, and found the fine new fireproof building a wreck. We got some of the books out, but the safe was where the Lord only knows. We began to hunt for it, when suddenly there was a yell in the street, and we made out the word 'dynamite.' The way we got out of that building was nothing slow. Five minutes later it was a heap of bricks and scrap iron. The dynamiting seemed to do absolutely no good. Although there was no wind—it being a beautiful sunny day—the fearful heat just melted things a block away.

Next, we ran back to the house. We dug a common trench in the garden, and buried some valuables into it. The only thing I could not do was to save the Stanford Library books that I had out, and luckily, though two weeks later, we found everything else cooked to a finish, the books were only half baked.

When we were going back for the last time to try and get some of the Consul's papers, the infernal shaking began again. We didn't wait that time, and in my haste to get out of a window on to a roof twelve feet or so below, I made a boss shot, and nearly took the top of my head off on the window-frame. It was so funny, that the others stopped and began to howl with laughter, but they soon made a jump themselves when the roof began to cave in. Altogether, there were seventeen earthquakes that day, four of them severe.

After we had seen that our house was a goner, we separated, for the time being, to look up friends. I went down to our office, on the fifth floor of the Phelan Building, to see the old man,* and managed to help him with some papers and things. The elevator shaft was filled with bricks and timber, and the halls were knee deep in plaster and bricks.

Several watchmen and their wives slept in the building, and on the way down we saw four of them being carried out covered up. The earth beginning to get uneasy again, we made a dash for the tall timber.

* Professor L.H. Grau, head of The Lyceum.

After that, I rejoined the others near the house, and having done all that we could to save anything, we went down town to have a look at things. This was about eight o'clock.

.   .   .

The best thing about the earthquake and fire was the way the people took them. There was no running around the streets, or shrieking, or anything of that sort. Any garbled accounts to the contrary are simply lies. They walked calmly from place to place, and watched the fire with almost indifference, and then with jokes, that were not forced either, but wholly spontaneous. In the whole of those two awful days and nights I did not see a single woman crying, and did not hear a whine or a whimper from anybody. The rich and poor alike just watched and waited, it being useless to try and save anything but a few immediate necessities, and when the intense heat made it necessary to move, they get up with a laugh and say, "Well, I guess we've got to leave the old shack now," and move on a little further to watch the fire.

One of the great trials was the lack of water. We had to drink whisky from time to time, but the children of course could not do that, so they simply had to suffer. Even they did not complain. About ten o'clock we ran into a Stanford friend of mine, who had ridden a wheel* the 35 miles, to come and dig me out, as he thought. ... He looked quite disappointed to see me still alive, and howling. He proposed an expedition into the burning business section, and so off we started. That was a sight. We eluded the soldiers, and walked right through to the water-front. We found a burning store with lots of canned stuff and bread in it, so loaded ourselves and started out of it on a run. The fire swept on a block at a time, but it was quite safe, as there was little danger from the steel buildings, as they seldom fall, but just burn out. We ate as much of our plunder as we could, and gave the rest to the police, who distributed it. That was the last we had for 48 hours, but we didn't feel it in the least.

There was lots of chance to loot jewellery stores, but of course nobody took advantage of it. Nobody thought of profiting by the fire, which says a great deal for the San Francisco people. In nearly all other big fires, &c., there is always more or less of this. As it became

---

* Bicycle.

evident that the whole city was doomed, the unburned stores started giving their food away to the women and children. Towards three o'clock we made another dash through, and got a launch at the water-front to take some telegrams from the Consul across to Oakland.

There was "nothing doing," however, as the soldiers had seized all the wires. The scene from the bay was past all description. San Francisco looked like one roaring furnace, and now we could hear the peculiar sound of the flames, like wind blowing through a field of ripe corn. This was quite loud over in Oakland, eight miles across the bay. Oakland is on the mainland, and was scarcely affected by the shock, and there was no fire. The whole disturbance seems to have been confined to the San Francisco peninsula, which reaches down to San José, and is of very curious formation geologically. The whole shooting match will go under some day.

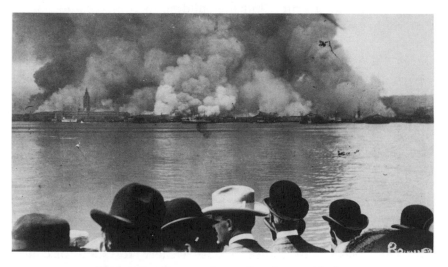

The burning city, seen from a ferry boat on the bay.

Looking down Eddy Street, with the Poodle Dog Restaurant (left) at the corner of Mason Street, the Flood building (center) at Powell Street, and the Emporium across Market Street. These buildings and all others in the neighborhood were completely gutted by fire.

More than 90 years after the quake and fire, eyewitness accounts are still surfacing. As recently as 1997, attorney Jerome M. Garchik purchased the following letter at a flea market in San Francisco, and his wife, newspaper columnist Leah Garchik, included it in her Sunday essay in the San Francisco *Chronicle*. Although the letter says little about the catastrophe that is not told in dozens of similar accounts, it is worth reprinting here because of its overall charm.

According to the 1900 census, Mabel Coxe was the youngest of the three children of Colonel Frank Coxe, U.S. Army Paymaster, and his wife, Ella. In this letter, Mabel is writing to her older brother, Charles, stationed with the U.S. Army in the Philippines.

Family matters

July 3, 1906

MY DEAR CHARLIE

Well, how are the bride and groom? It seems so funny writing to my married brother, he seems so "old and staid" now. When the news came I was sick in bed but I think the surprise knocked all the pains out of me. I know you must be very happy, and you must hurry up and come home with Bessie so we can congratulate you in person. I have been wondering if the quake did it. It seems to have done a lot in that line around here.

Oh, Charlie, it was a dreadful, dreadful time and is pretty bad yet for that matter. Of course shacks are being put up on the ruins and business resumed but it is such a sad sight. At first, that is the first two weeks, there was nothing, absolutely no place where you could get anything. Those who had forethought on the morning of the quake laid in provisions for they knew the worst was yet to come. Some of the grocerymen took advantage of the state of affairs and sold to the highest bidder but the authorities found it out, went in and took such stores. One firm, Goldberg Bowen & Co, are just about killed in this town.

I was out staying all night with Florence when the quake came and everything was dashed around out there. I just hung on to the bed or I would have been pitched out for the shake was so fast and furious. The falling chimney added to the creaking and groaning of the houses, and the falling of plaster, ornaments, furniture etc. was something never to be forgotten.

We were pretty calm, actually waited to throw something around us before we went out to investigate. The first thing we discovered was about a half a block on Union St that had dropped in. Then came the reports that South of Market had been totally destroyed and that there were more buildings wrecked than standing, south of Sutter. Of course I could not get Mama over the phone and I was sure our house had suffered terribly. There was no way to ride in and so I just had to foot it. It was half past seven when I started and I tell you I just flew. I came down Fillmore, and such sights I saw. Every brick building in the town was down and the nearer I got to home the worse it was. Little old frame houses twisted and torn lying half below ground and half above, and when I came to the Pierce Rudolph Storage not a wall was standing on the outside and there was the furniture all exposed.

I drew a sigh of relief when I saw our house still standing. Two houses opposite us had gone entirely to pieces and dropped a whole story in the ground, and they had to chop the places open to get the people out. Everyone was on the streets and poor Mama was a wreck when I got to her. She had the benefit of having your furniture (that book-case and the bamboo arrangement) fall over her head as well as our fine mahogany book-case in the den. Really Charlie that beautiful thing was literally torn to pieces. Glass doors smashed, framework, shelves and even the partitions in splinters. Papa is going to send it to the Crafts and Arts and they say they can repair it.

Mama's beautiful jardiniere is smashed, lots of ornaments, and even the front was dashed out of the piano. The most remarkable thing was the way the big cut-glass vase crashed down over the table and never broke but put some terrible cuts in the table. The kitchen was a wreck, we had to wade through broken dishes, tomato catsup, Worstershire sauce, syrup etc, and I tell you it stayed that way for days. We haven't hardly any of the blue and white china and a few pieces of the white. The dining room suffered the least. Three of Mama's handsomest plates were broken and some smaller things but the cabinet was intact. It is made to tilt a little back so that helped it from going over and I guess it was in a good position for the direction of the shake.

The Whitmans' place was a sight. All the plaster fell from the wall, and Dr. was literally covered up by it in bed. They had to move right out. When Grace Kennedy tried to get out of bed she was thrown down and had all the skin taken off her knee, and she had no sooner gotten up than the chiffonier came tumbling down just where she had fallen. She made for the door but was thrown again before she reached there. Eric Polhemus was shut up in his folding bed but escaped unhurt. The poor old St. Nick!* To think it has gone at last. At the time of the quake the tank on the roof broke and forty thousand gallons of water went right through to the kitchen.

Almost immediately after the quake we heard that South of Market was burning, then fires broke out all over the city and we were encircled. The sight of homeless men and women fleeing through the streets trying to drag all they could save in blankets and sheets or strapped to ladders which were on roller skates, and lawnmowers loaded, and even children's beds;—anything that was on rollers or had wheels; and the sight of the sick and injured, ambulances flying like the wind, automobiles covered with red crosses and even hearses used for carrying people and their belongings, will never fade from my memory.

Of course the excitement, the terrible excitement of the first few days, sort of dazed us and we didn't think much about how things would be days or weeks hence, but when the fire had died and we looked around us we wondered if any of us could ever live in S.F. again. All that Wednesday night of the 18th we walked the streets and watched the flames, but I got so worn out that once in a while I would go into Sharpes** and throw myself down on the floor or the spring which still remained on the bed. It was dreadful during those first two weeks when we couldn't even strike a match, but about a dozen of us had to grope around in the dark at Sharpes and just lie around on the floor. The third night we were told that the only way left for us unless we wanted the flames to encircle us, was for us to walk to Fort Mason and get on a tug. We stuck it out however and the fire stopped three blocks from us one way and four another.

You would have laughed to have seen Ella*** and me standing in line for a loaf of bread. Papa and Snitz hauled the water. We can never again say "Everyone works but Father." One day when we didn't have

*   Hotel St. Nicholas, on Market at Polk Street, where the family lived briefly.
** Apparently the home of friends.
*** Mabel's older sister.

anything to eat I went and stood in line and all I got was some Postum Cereal and a half-size can of condensed milk, and I had to tell a lie to get that as they only gave milk to the babies.

Afterwards when Mama got sick and went to Glenwood I did all the cooking; and on Mamas little curling iron stove. I don't know how I ever did it but somehow it just came, and anything I wanted I just seemed to go ahead and make it. You can bet I learned a lot. I made all kinds of soups, salads, and creamed crab, oysters etc, and cooked meats, vegetables and potatoes and you bet we ate and made up for the starvation period.

When Mama came back from Glenwood she was worse than when she went away, and I walked one whole day all over town trying to get a nurse, and finally succeeded. She made such a lot of work that I got sick too. The day I went down to Glenwood with Mama, the coal man called for us in his wagon and took us down. You would have died laughing but of course everyone did the same. Mama and I sat on the seat with the driver and Papa put one of our kitchen chairs in the back and sat there hanging on to the seat.

The letter goes on to say that the family would be moving on July 14 for two reasons: The rent was being increased to $92.50 a month, and Fillmore Street, where municipal offices and downtown retail stores had relocated, "makes our location regular South of Market. It is awful now."

A search of newspaper files for what might have become of Mabel Coxe in later years turned up several sad and bizarre accounts, all from the year 1915. She first was reported found in a stupor on a San Francisco photographer's doorstep under mysterious circumstances. A few months later she was found unconscious and bruised in a ravine near Auburn, with no clues as to what had happened. The last account, in November, reports her attempted suicide at the home of a County Jail matron in whose custody she was awaiting examination on a charge by her mother that she was an "inebriate." There the newspaper accounts end.

Newspaper Row: The *Call* was in the Spreckels building (right) at Third and Market. The *Examiner* was across Third, and the *Chronicle* (with clock tower) was on the opposite side of Market, at Kearny.

Automobiles were still a novelty in 1906, and most of them were owned and driven—often recklessly—by wealthy young men as a unique form of sport. During the days immediately after the earthquake they gained a new image as a vital and speedy mode of transportation. James Hopper hired "one of the city's gilded youths" to drive him around town in order to cover as much of the city as possible for his newspaper. In this, the final excerpt from his *Everybody's Magazine* article, he gives a vivid picture of what he saw.

Kaleidoscopic vision

I WENT DOWN TO THE *CALL* TO REPORT. The sun was rising behind a smoky pall already floating above the populous district south of Market Street. The *Call* Building, the highest in the city, was unmarred by the earthquake, and so was the building of the *Examiner*, across Third Street from the *Call*, and that of the *Chronicle*, across Market Street from the *Examiner*. The editorial building of the *Call*, however, in the narrow alley back of the main building, was shaky. At the door I met [Fred R.] Bowie, the acting city editor, the first man at his station. "Hopper," he said, "the Brunswick Hotel at Sixth and Folsom is down with hundreds inside of her. You cover that." This order seemed perfectly natural to me. In spite of what we had already seen, our power of realization was behind time as it was to be through the three days' progressive disaster. Going up into the editorial rooms with water to my ankles, I seized a bunch of copy paper and started up Third Street.

At Tehama Street I saw the beginning of the fire which was to sweep all the district south of Market Street. It was swirling up the narrow way with a sound that was almost a scream. Before it the humble population of the district were fleeing, and in its path, as far as I could see, frail shanties went down like card houses. And this marks the true character of the city's agony. Especially in this populous district south of Market Street, but also throughout the city, hundreds were pinned down by the débris, some to a merciful death, other to live hideous minutes. The flames swept over them while the saved looked on impotently. Over the tragedy the fire threw its flaming mantle of hypocrisy, and the full extent of the holocaust will never be known, will remain ever a poignant mystery.

The firemen were there, beginning the tremendous and hopeless fight which, without intermission, they were to continue for three days. Without water (the mains had been burst by the quake) they were attacking the fire with axes, with hooks, with sacks, with their hands, retreating sullenly before it only when its feverish breath burned their clothing and their skins.

I went back to Market Street and stopped an automobile. It was a private machine, chauffeured by one of the city's gilded youths, but he jumped at my offer of $50 for the day's hire, another example of the twisted vision of us all, which refused to acknowledge the true stupendousness of what was happening. I whirred off north into the Latin quarter to see as to the safety of friends I had there. Its destruction was in keeping with the picturesque reputation of the district. The low brick buildings built in the pioneer days had nearly all thrown their fronts into the narrow streets, and their interiors were shown cross-sectioned like the doll houses you see in toy stores. The house of Henry Laffler, the writer, was so, his bookcase, writing-table, and bed showing like furniture on a stage. Beneath the pyramid of bricks that had been the front of the building a dead Chinaman lay, one long yellow hand stretched out of the loose sleeve of his blouse. But a note pinned upon the remnants of the stairs told me that Laffler was safe. I went on to the studio of [Xavier] Martinez, the painter. The old building still stood. The studio was full of bricks, but a neatly stacked pile of paintings in the center told me that the painter was safe. How these two men escaped is beyond my imagination.

Back to the paper we whizzed. We passed firemen fighting the fire, which had jumped Market Street and was beginning to devour the wholesale and financial district. At the paper, I picked up "Scotty" Morrison, our old policeman, and [Glenn] Byers, one of the "cubs." They had walked miles to report. This time we had a nearer appreciation of what was happening and our orders were to cover the progress of the fire and get a list of the dead. As we left, the Grand Opera House, where a few hours before I had been listening to Caruso, was burning with explosive violence together with the back of the editorial rooms. The main *Call* Building was to be our reporting place.

We started first to cover the fire I had seen start on its westward course from Third Street. From that time, I have only a vague kaleidoscopic vision of whirring at whistling speed through a city of the damned. We tried to make the fallen Brunswick Hotel at Sixth and Folsom Streets. We could not make it. The scarlet steeplechaser beat us to it, and when we arrived the crushed structure was only the base of one great flame that rose to heaven with a single twist. By that time we knew that the earthquake had been but a prologue, and that the tragedy was to be written in fire. We went westward to get the western limit of the blaze.

Already we had to make a huge circle to get above it. The whole district south of Market Street was now a pitiful sight. By thousands the multitudes were pattering along the wide streets leading out, heads bowed, eyes dead, silent and stupefied. We stopped in passing at the Southern Pacific Hospital. Carts, trucks, express wagons, vehicles of all kinds laden with wounded, were blocking the gate. Upon the porch stood two internes, and their white aprons were red-spotted as those of butchers. There were 125 wounded inside and eight dead. Among the wounded was Chief Sullivan of the Fire Department. A chimney of the California Hotel had crushed through his house at the first shock of the earthquake, and he and his wife had been taken out of the débris with incredible difficulty. He was to die two days later, spared the bitter, hopeless effort which his men were to know. As we were leaving, two men came to the gate. They were pulling along the street a sheet of corrugated iron upon which lay an old woman with both feet charred. We bore her in and she actually smiled as we laid her upon a cot.

At Thirteenth and Valencia Streets a policeman and a crowd of volunteers were trying to raise the débris of a house where a man and a woman were pinned. One block farther we came to a place where the ground had sunk six feet. A fissure ran along Fourteenth Street for several blocks and the car tracks had been jammed along their length till they rose in angular projections three or four feet high. As we were examining the phenomenon in a narrow way called Treat Avenue a quake occurred. It came upon the fag-end of endurance of the poor folk crowding the alley. Women sank to their knees, drew their shawls about their little ones, and broke out in piercing lamentations, while men ran up and down aimlessly, wringing their hands. An old woman led by a crippled old man came wailing down the steps of a porch, and she was blind. In the center of the street they both fell and all the poor encouragement we could give them could not raise them. They had made up their minds to die. I looked at my watch and was astounded to see that it was only half past eight. On Valencia Street, between Eighteenth and Nineteenth, the Valencia Hotel, a four-story wooden lodging-house was down, its four stories telescoped to the height of one, its upper rooms ripped open with the cross-section effect of a doll-house. A squad of policemen and some fifty volunteers were working with rageful energy at the tangle of walls and rafters. Eleven men were known to have escaped, eight had been taken out dead, and more than one hundred were still in the ruins. The street here was sunk six feet, and again, as I was to see it many times more, I saw that strange angular raise of the tracks as if the ground had been pinched between some gigantic fingers.

We went down toward the fire now. We met it on Eighth Street. From Third it had come along in a swath four blocks wide. From Market to Folsom, from Second to Eighth, it spread its heaving red sea, and with a roar it was rushing on, its advance billow curling like a monstrous comber above a flotsam of fleeing humanity. There were men, women, and children. Men, women, and children—really that is about all I remember of them, except that they were miserable and crushed. Here and there are still little snap-shots in my mind—a woman carrying in a cage a green and red parrot, squawking incessantly, "Hurry, hurry, hurry"; a little smudge-faced girl with long-lashed brown eyes holding in her arms a blind puppy; a man with naked torso carrying upon his head a hideous chromo*; another with a mattress and a cracked mirror. But by this time the cataclysm itself, its manifestation, its ferocious splendor, hypnotized the brain, and humans sank into insignificance as ants caught in the slide of a mountain.

One more scene I remember. On Eighth Street, between Folsom and Howard, was an empty sand lot right in the path of the conflagration. It was full of refugees, and what struck me was their immobility. They sat there upon trunks, upon bundles of clothing. On each side, like the claws of a crab, the fire was closing in upon them. They sat there motionless, as if cast of bronze, as if indeed they were wrought

* Chromolithograph—a colored lithograph.

upon some frieze representing the Misery of Humanity. The fire roared, burning coals showered them, the heat rose, their clothes smoked, and they still sat there, upon their poor little boxes, their bundles of rags, their goods, the pathetic little hoard which they had been able to treasure in their arid lives, a fixed determination in their staring eyes not to leave again, not to move, another step, to die there and then, with the treasures for the saving of which their bodies had no further strength.

We whirled down Harrison Street, along the southern edge of the fire which up to that time was not spreading much toward that side. The streets were choked with trucks, with baby carriages, with cabs, with toy express wagons, and a procession of silent people, stupefied by the incredible and progressive calamity, was marching stolidly out of the city which had proven a trap. Passing Fifth Street, we caught, behind the flaming smother, a glimpse of the Mint, square, squat, like a rock in the flaming sea. Its iron windows were all closed; it brooded there, unmoved, inscrutable as a sphinx. Later we learned that behind those iron doors men had lived through the maelstrom of fire, had lived and fought and had saved the building. West of it, a long white sky-scraper towered, still untouched. It was never touched. I saw it a few days later, rising white, unsullied, above the surrounding desolation. I read its name and the tremendous irony of it staggered me. "The United Undertakers" was written into the granite above the door.

At Third Street we caught the starting-point of the fire. It had worked north as well as west, and the *Call* Building, the tallest sky-scraper in the city, was glowing like a phosphorescent worm. Cataracts of pulverized fire poured out of the thousand windows. The *Examiner* Building, across the way, was burning. The Palace Hotel, treasured perhaps above everything by San Franciscans, was smoking but was still making a magnificent fight. To the east the fire had gone as far as Second Street. There it had leaped Market Street toward the north, and was roaring, a maelstrom of flame, through the wholesale district, before the southeastern breeze. We circled to the north, through the Latin quarter, picturesque in its ruins as it had been in life. I remember passing six dead horses under a pile of bricks on Washington Street. We went up toward the Hayes Valley district, in which heavy volutes of smoke announced another conflagration.

In passing I stopped at The Neptune, where I had been at the time of the earthquake, five hours before. The fire had not yet reached it. I ran up to my room. A key was in the door. "Looters," I said to myself. I pushed open the door. Spick and span in his loose white clothing, Ah Wing, the Chinese chamber-man, was making my bed. The room was swept, the plaster that had fallen gathered in a heap in the hall, my clothes were all hanging in the closet, and he was putting a clean slip about my pillow. Coming out of the whirl of death and devastation, this piece of domestic fidelity absolutely flabbergasted me. I closed the door upon it and left on tip-toe as in the presence of some sacred rite. I'd like to see Ah Wing again. When, the next morning, it struck me at last that it was time to take my things out, I wasn't able to get within fifteen blocks of The Neptune. Now, all that remains is the arch of the door, and a nameless chaos of pulverized and half volatilized things in the cellar, among them the results of Ah Wing's industry. I devoutly hope he is alive, with a little hoard of gold in his wide sleeves, enough to buy him a ticket on the P.M.* to old Canton.

We went up to Hayes Valley to examine the fire there. We passed the City Hall, the building upon which the city had spent six millions. It had crumbled at the assault of the quake and was now a ruin, noble with a beauty that it had lacked when entire. Here and there a massive column rose with its architrave, giving an effect of Babylonian splendor. Above, the dome, divorced of stone, showed its naked skeleton, twisted as from some monstrous torture. The Central Emergency Hospital was blocked with an avalanche of huge stones.

The fire, we found, already covered four square blocks and was sweeping toward the east. We went before it and stopped at the Mechanic's Pavilion, the Madison Square Garden of San Francisco. All the morning it had been used as a great hospital, but now, before the menace of the fire, the last patients were being transferred to the Military Hospital at the Presidio. We waited till the fire came. The immense wooden structure caught with almost explosive violence, and when we left the ruins of the City Hall were catching. We circled the fire south of Market Street again and found that it had reached Twelfth Street. At one o'clock we tried to report to the *Chronicle*

* Pacific Mail Steamship Company.

Building. The Examiner, the Palace Hotel, and the Grand were burning fiercely by that time and we could not reach it. We started on another tour of the fires.

It was just about that time that the wind, which had been slight and from the east, turned to a spanking breeze from the northwest. This sealed the doom of the city. By the time we had arrived at the fire south of Market Street, it had spread from Fourteenth Street down to the bay; and this immense frontage, driven by the wind, was moving south and east, the blocks literally melting before its advance. We circled far to the south. We stopped at St. Mary's Hospital, on Rincon Hill, at the southeast corner of the city. The whole city below, from Fourteenth Street to the ferries, was one great flame, which smacked in the wind like the stupendous silken flag of some cosmic anarchy. Below the silken, whirring sound of it, there was a muttered roar as if thousands of tumbrils were rolling over an endless bridge, and the dynamite, used now in a last effort to confine the conflagration, pulsed in dull reverberations. The patients of the hospital were being removed to steamers lying in the bay below.

We circled along the water-front, everything to the west of us a flaming chaos. Up Market Street the great buildings writhed like so many live beings in the agony of fire. The entire wholesale district from the bay to Sansome and north to Washington was burning. As they burned, the buildings crashed down upon what the earthquake had thrown, and the streets were as those of a barricaded city in the throes of its last assault. The United States Twenty-second Infantry was garrisoned at the Appraiser's Building, and all along Washington Street the troopers, aided by volunteers, were noosing ropes about the wooden shacks, relics of the sixties, and pulling them down in gigantic tugs-of-war, one hundred men to a rope. At the Hall of Justice, in the midst of the Latin quarter, the Mayor, the Chief of Police, and their staffs together with the Citizens' Committee appointed immediately after the earthquake, were gathered in the basement. In the half-darkness, beneath the low-vaulted ceiling, they sat at long tables, their faces yellow in the light of the sputtering candles, and conferred in whispers. Near them was stretched a long line of stiff forms beneath white sheets.

Out in Portsmouth Square, in front, the prisoners of the jail sat huddled in handcuffed groups. While we were there they began to move the dead from the hall, for the fire was very near now, and soon a line of sheeted figures lay in the green grass before the [Robert Louis] Stevenson monument. By five o'clock the Hall of Justice was burning, the headquarters had been removed to the big Fairmont Hotel on the tip-top of Nob Hill, the prisoners to Alcatraz, and the dead lay underground, the Stephenson bark, its bronze sails swollen with the eagerness of departure, their monument.

Almost at the same time the fire which had swept the wholesale district below Sansome, jumped Kearny Street and with a rattle of eagerness fastened upon Chinatown, with its carved balconies, its multi-colored signs, its painted and gilded flimsiness. At the same time, doubling back, it came down Montgomery, San Francisco's Wall Street, and Kearny, fairly whistling down the deep, narrow corridors. By eight o'clock the Kohl and Mills Building and the Merchants' Exchange flamed like torches and the destruction of the business blocks of the city was complete.

At seven o'clock the staffs of the *Call* and the *Chronicle* met for a conference in the editorial rooms of the *Evening Bulletin*. The pink glow of the fire, near-by on three sides now, was the only light. The orders given to the *Chronicle* men was: "The men of the *Chronicle* will meet at the *Chronicle* Building to-morrow at one o'clock, if there is any *Chronicle*." That given to the *Call* was: "The men of the *Call* will meet at the Fairmont to-morrow at one o'clock, if there is any to-morrow." There was a to-morrow, but long before one o'clock the *Chronicle* was a gutted ruin and the magnificent Fairmont, like a great Greek temple upon its hill, was blazing like a funeral pyre.

At eight o'clock I was standing on the corner of Market and Montgomery. The whole south side of Market Street was on fire from end to end. There was a lull in the wind, and before me the Palace and Grand Hotels were burning with a sort of quiet mournfulness. Suddenly the great Crocker Building, on the north side of the street, began to burn, slowly, one window-shade here, one window-shade there, with a sort of flippant deliberation. Half an hour after it began to purr softly, then, with a roar, the flames poured out of all the openings. This was the beginning of what might be called the fourth main fire. It went north, caught the *Chronicle*, and then steeple-chased up Geary, Post, and Sutter Streets, melting before it the rich retail section and then the private hotel district. At ten o'clock the huge new St.

Francis Hotel on Union Square was burning. The fire spread as it went west. It united with that of Chinatown, then with that of Hayes Valley, and the three, hand in hand in formidable alliance, marched, keeping step, toward the west with a frontage of nearly two miles.

All night the city burned with a copper glow, and all night the dynamite of the fire fighters boomed at slow intervals, the pulse of the great city in its agony. When the sun rose, a red wafer behind clouds of smoke that were as crape, the tidal wave of flame had swept three-quarters of it. Nob Hill, the Fairmont, the homes of the pioneer millionaires, Mark Hopkins's, with its art treasures were aglow, a ruby tiara upon the city. Before the irresistible advance, the people were fleeing toward the sea. For the third time the headquarters of the Government had been changed, this time to the North End Police Station. By eleven o'clock that was in danger, and another exodus was made to Franklin Hall, on Fillmore Street, once suburb, now center.

I walked down Market Street late in the afternoon of the second day. It was as if I walked through a dead city, not a city recently dead, but one overcome by some cataclysm ages past, and dug out of its lava. Fragments of wall rose on all sides, columns twisted but solid in their warp, as if petrified in the midst of their writhing from the fiery ordeal. Across them a yellow smoke passed slowly. Above all, a heavy, brooding silence lay. And really there was nothing else. Contortion of stone, smoke of destruction, and a great silence—that was all.

Although he does not say so here, Hopper lost a great many manuscripts and printed copies of his earlier writings when his home at the Neptune burned. In later years he became a popular short story writer and novelist. During World War I he was sent to France as war correspondent for *Collier's* magazine. He was one of the founding members of the bohemian colony that gathered at Carmel, attracting such literary luminaries as George Sterling, Upton Sinclair, Jack London, Mary Austin, and Sinclair Lewis.

His affection for Carmel was tempered only by his love for his native Paris, where he returned to live for a while. He died in Carmel just one month after his 80th birthday.

Another newspaperman rushing around San Francisco that first morning was Harry Coleman, staff photographer for the *Examiner*. He recorded these impressions in his autobiography, *Give Us a Little Smile, Baby* (1943).

Picturing the city

W HEN [THE QUAKE] WAS OVER I was weak, trembling and gasping for breath. Like a soldier on a battlefield without his gun, I was stranded far from my camera in the midst of the biggest picture story of my career. Yanking on my clothes, I started on a dead run down Pine Street toward the center of the city. Streets were clogged in the middle with stupefied people, massed in terror as far as possible from falling missiles. Some were crying, some laughed hysterically, others applied emergency treatment to bleeding heads and torn bodies, and still others worked desperately over lifeless bodies.

I ran on, splashing down avenues flooded by broken water mains, under overhanging entanglements of high-powered electric wires which were spitting fire as they twisted menacingly from tottering poles. Often I had to climb across wide fissures and over barricades of fallen débris where entire building fronts were spread across the street. I paused for breath in front of the Olympic Club. There a deluge of water from its shattered swimming pool was pouring through the entrance. I hurried on to Kearny Street, past Lotta's Fountain, to my newspaper building. The exterior looked all right, but the interior was a mass of ruins. Marble steps were piled high with fallen tile and plaster, but I had to gain the seventh floor where my picture equipment was in a locker. Somehow I got up to the art room, the last lap across a narrow, loosened foot-bridge which connected our studio with the main building. The room was knee-deep in wreckage. Our lop-sided metal lockers were intact, however, and my camera appeared to be in working order.

To make my first picture, a general view, I climbed to the roof of the Hearst building and counted sixteen ribbons of smoke stretching skyward. Each marked a separate fire in that crushed city, where more than twenty-eight thousand buildings were in ruins. Pointed in any direction that morning, my camera was bound to be focused on a good news picture.

I saw miles of flames raging as smoke-blackened firemen stood helplessly by dry hydrants, watching their useless hoses curl up in the fire. With my cheeks almost blistered and my hair singed with the terrific heat, I shot pictures down Market Street past the Palace and Grand Hotels, through smoking canyons of red-hot twisted girders, down to the wrecked ferry building, into Front Street and along the twisted rails of the Belt Line railroad, where the fire tugs *Active* and *Leslie* were pumping feeble streams of bay water on the roofs of wooden wharves, while excited seamen and stevedores trampled out sparks as they fell from the sky.

Threading my way over hot, cobbled streets, through swarms of stampeding rats, I continued my photographing up Mission Street into the lodging-house district, where great tongues of fire and clouds of smoke were everywhere, and the injured were trying to bandage each other's wounds with handkerchiefs and shreds of cloth. I pictured the frenzied crowds, standing aquiver, afraid to re-enter their houses to gather up what remained of their belongings. Frantic men separated from their families, pitiful mothers dragging frightened children, and sailors pulling sea-chests formed a human tide of refugees which flooded past my lens as they struggled toward the waterfront.

I went on west, past the wreck of the Opera House, where only a few hours ago Edith Walker had sung in the "Queen of Sheba" before such jeweled first-nighters as Mrs. Herman Oelrichs, Mrs. James Flood and Mrs. Frederick Kohl. I pointed my camera toward the wrecked footlight pit and remembered that I had an overnight assignment to meet [theater critic] Ashton Stevens that morning on this very spot to photograph Caruso, Fremstadt and Alfred Hertz, the impresario, in their rehearsal for Wednesday night's production of "Lohengrin."

Trampling on through "Carmen" posters which lay torn and scorched in the street, I passed the shell of St. Patrick's Church and, a few blocks farther on, pictured the United States Mint, where Super-intendent Frank Leach and his small crew lined the roof to stamp out embers blowing from nearby buildings. They prevented it from igniting and saved more than three hundred million dollars in the vaults. On the Mission Street side of the white marble post-office building, I stood erect in the sunken street and rested my elbows on the sidewalk. On Valencia Street, I photographed the wreck of Woodward's Pavilion and the flaming ruins of a four-story hotel. Then I journeyed back through the grime and heat toward Market Street, past the tumbled ruins of the Eleventh Street Episcopal Church and the magnificent new City Hall, now completely razed.

Through the smoke, I photographed sparks falling on the roof of St. Mary's Cathedral at Van Ness Avenue and O'Farrell Street, while bucket brigades of heroic priests fought against disheartening odds to save the big church, miraculously, from destruction. My next subject was the Emporium, greatest department store in the West, which was now a series of gaping canyons interspersed with walls.

My camera felt as though it weighed a ton as I lugged it into Powell Street, through Union Square Park, where scantily clothed guests from downtown hotels had taken refuge. There I found the awful-eyed Caruso, his million-dollar throat wrapped in a soiled bath towel, clinging to a framed portrait of Theodore Roosevelt. With him were [Marcella] Sembrich, [Josephine] Jacoby, [Antonio] Scotti, [Archangelo] Rossi, and other lesser lights of the Metropolitan Opera Company.

A few squares down Geary Street, the "Call" and "Chronicle" buildings, skyscrapers of the day, were burning with their cornices piled in the street. I went back to the "Examiner" building for a new supply of films, but it was too late. Flames from the nearby Winchester Hotel had reached our studio. I made one more exposure of that scene on my last photographic film as the clouds of smoke poured along both sides of Third Street. My day's picturing was ended. Standing on the broken sidewalk in front of the plant, utterly fatigued, I looked down toward the wrecked presses, buried beneath tons of débris, and it occurred to me then for the first time that newspapers could not be issued. Where were my editors? What could be done with my pictures if it were possible for me to finish them?

At the time, the *Examiner* and *Call* were on opposite corners of Third Street on the south side of Market Street. The *Chronicle* was across Market, at Kearny. All were morning papers. The *Bulletin*, an evening paper, was at Kearny and Bush streets. The *Call* building was on fire by mid-morning, and the *Examiner* by noon. The *Chronicle* building, although severely damaged by the quake, did not succumb to the flames until that night. The *Bulletin* building was then relatively free of damage, but later burned.

Michael de Young, owner of the *Chronicle*, offered to share his facilities with the *Call* and *Examiner*, and throughout the day combined crews of the three papers wrote their stories, set type, and prepared to bring out an extra edition. But all of this came to naught when their water supply was cut off and they were unable to turn over their presses. Efforts to produce the *Bulletin* met with similar failure.

Later in the day the three papers sent a deputation to the Oakland *Tribune*, an afternoon paper. The proprietor, W. Dargie, immediately placed his plant, paper, and staff at their disposal, enabling them to produce a four-page paper that bore the masthead *The Call=Chronicle=Examiner*. It had no advertisements or photographs, but provided the first detailed story of that dreadful day and was circulated free to news-hungry San Franciscans, who had heard all sorts of rumors about a universal cataclysm destroying New York and Chicago.

The appearance of this paper on the morning of April 19 ensured that the *Call*, *Chronicle*, and *Examiner* could uphold a prime goal of any newspaper: not to miss a day's issue.

The Call=Chronicle=Examiner

SAN FRANCISCO, THURSDAY, APRIL 19, 1906.

EARTHQUAKE AND FIRE: SAN FRANCISCO IN RUINS

DEATH AND DESTRUCTION HAVE BEEN THE FATE OF SAN FRANCISCO. SHAKEN BY A TEMBLOR AT 5:13 O'CLOCK YESTERDAY MORNING, THE SHOCK LASTING 48 SECONDS, AND SCOURGED BY FLAMES THAT RAGED DIAMETRICALLY IN ALL DIRECTIONS, THE CITY IS A MASS OF SMOULDERING RUINS. AT SIX O'CLOCK LAST EVENING THE FLAMES SEEMINGLY PLAYING WITH INCREASED VIGOR, THREATENED TO DESTROY SUCH SECTIONS AS THEIR FURY HAD SPARED DURING THE EARLIER PORTION OF THE DAY. BUILDING THEIR PATH IN A TRIANGULAR CIRCUIT FROM THE START IN THE EARLY MORNING, THEY JOCKEYED AS THE DAY WANED, LEFT THE BUSINESS SECTION, WHICH THEY HAD ENTIRELY DEVASTATED, AND SKIPPED IN A DOZEN DIRECTIONS TO THE RESIDENCE PORTIONS. AS NIGHT FELL THEY HAD MADE THEIR WAY OVER INTO THE NORTH BEACH SECTION AND SPRINGING ANEW TO THE SOUTH THEY REACHED OUT ALONG THE SHIPPING SECTION DOWN THE BAY SHORE, OVER THE HILLS AND ACROSS TOWARD THIRD AND TOWNSEND STREETS. WAREHOUSES, WHOLESALE HOUSES AND MANUFACTURING CONCERNS FELL IN THEIR PATH. THIS COMPLETED THE DESTRUCTION OF THE ENTIRE DISTRICT KNOWN AS THE "SOUTH OF MARKET STREET." HOW FAR THEY ARE REACHING TO THE SOUTH ACROSS THE CHANNEL CANNOT BE TOLD AS THIS PART OF THE CITY IS SHUT OFF FROM SAN FRANCISCO PAPERS.

AFTER DARKNESS, THOUSANDS OF THE HOMELESS WERE MAKING THEIR WAY WITH THEIR BLANKETS AND SCANT PROVISIONS TO GOLDEN GATE PARK AND THE BEACH TO FIND SHELTER. THOSE IN THE HOMES ON THE HILLS JUST NORTH OF THE HAYES VALLEY WRECKED SECTION PILED THEIR BELONGINGS IN THE STREETS AND EXPRESS WAGONS AND AUTOMOBILES WERE HAULING THE THINGS AWAY TO THE SPARSELY SETTLED REGIONS. EVERYBODY IN SAN FRANCISCO IS PREPARED TO LEAVE THE CITY, FOR THE BELIEF IS FIRM THAT SAN FRANCISCO WILL BE TOTALLY DESTROYED.

DOWNTOWN EVERYTHING IS RUIN. NOT A BUSINESS HOUSE STANDS. THEATRES ARE CRUMBLED INTO HEAPS. FACTORIES AND COMMISSION HOUSES LIE SMOULDERING ON THEIR FORMER SITES. ALL OF THE NEWSPAPER PLANTS HAVE BEEN RENDERED USELESS, THE "CALL" AND THE "EXAMINER" BUILDINGS, EXCLUDING THE "CALL'S" EDITORIAL ROOMS ON STEVENSON STREET BEING ENTIRELY DESTROYED.

IT IS ESTIMATED THAT THE LOSS IN SAN FRANCISCO WILL REACH FROM $150,000,000 TO $200,000,000. THESE FIGURES ARE IN THE ROUGH AND NOTHING CAN BE TOLD UNTIL PARTIAL ACCOUNTING IS TAKEN.

ON EVERY SIDE THERE WAS DEATH AND SUFFERING YESTERDAY. HUNDREDS WERE INJURED, EITHER BURNED, CRUSHED OR STRUCK BY FALLING PIECES FROM THE BUILDINGS, AND ONE OF TEN DIED WHILE ON THE OPERATING TABLE AT MECHANICS' PAVILION, IMPROVISED AS A HOSPITAL FOR THE COMFORT AND CARE OF THE INJURED. THE NUMBER OF DEAD IS NOT KNOWN BUT IT IS ESTIMATED THAT AT LEAST 500 MET THEIR DEATH IN THE HORROR.

AT NINE O'CLOCK, UNDER A SPECIAL MESSAGE FROM PRESIDENT ROOSEVELT, THE CITY WAS PLACED UNDER MARTIAL LAW. HUNDREDS OF TROOPS PATROLLED THE STREETS AND DROVE THE CROWDS BACK, WHILE HUNDREDS MORE WERE SET AT WORK ASSISTING THE FIRE AND POLICE DEPARTMENTS. THE STRICTEST ORDERS WERE ISSUED, AND IN TRUE MILITARY SPIRIT THE SOLDIERS OBEYED. DURING THE AFTERNOON THREE THIEVES MET THEIR DEATH BY RIFLE BULLETS WHILE AT WORK IN THE RUINS. THE CURIOUS WERE DRIVEN BACK AT THE BREASTS OF THE HORSES THAT THE CAVALRYMEN RODE AND ALL THE CROWDS WERE FORCED FROM THE LEVEL DISTRICT TO THE HILLY SECTION BEYOND TO THE NORTH.

THE WATER SUPPLY WAS ENTIRELY CUT OFF, AND MAY BE IT WAS JUST AS WELL, FOR THE LINES OF FIRE DEPARTMENT WOULD HAVE BEEN ABSOLUTELY USELESS AT ANY STAGE. ASSISTANT CHIEF DOUGHERTY SUPERVISED THE WORK OF HIS MEN AND EARLY IN THE MORNING IT WAS SEEN THAT THE ONLY POSSIBLE CHANCE TO SAVE THE CITY LAY IN EFFORT TO CHECK THE FLAMES BY THE USE OF DYNAMITE. DURING THE DAY A BLAST COULD BE HEARD IN ANY SECTION AT INTERVALS OF ONLY A FEW MINUTES, AND BUILDINGS NOT DESTROYED BY FIRE WERE BLOWN TO ATOMS. BUT THROUGH THE GAPS MADE THE FLAMES JUMPED AND ALTHOUGH THE FAILURES OF THE HEROIC EFFORTS OF THE POLICE FIREMEN AND SOLDIERS WERE AT TIMES SICKENING, THE WORK WAS CONTINUED WITH A DESPERATION THAT WILL LIVE AS ONE OF THE FEATURES OF THE TERRIBLE DISASTER. MEN WORKED LIKE FIENDS TO COMBAT THE LAUGHING, ROARING, ONRUSHING FIRE DEMON.

NO HOPE LEFT FOR SAFETY OF ANY BUILDINGS

San Francisco seems doomed to entire destruction. With the raging of the flames just before dark, the hope was that with the use of the tons of dynamite, the course of the fire might be checked and confined to the triangular sections it had cut out for its path. But on the Barbary Coast the fire broke out anew and as night closed in the flames were eating their way into parts untouched in their ravages during the day. To the south and the north they spread; down to the docks and out into the resident section. In and to the north of Hayes Valley. By six o'clock practically all of St. Ignatius' great buildings were no more. They had been leveled to the fiery heap that marked what was once the metropolis of the West.

The first of the big structures to go to ruin was the Call Building, the famous skyscraper. At eleven o'clock the big 18-story building was a furnace. Flames leaped from every window and shot skyward from the dome. In less than two hours nothing remained but the tall skeleton.

By five o'clock the Palace Hotel was in ruins. The old hostelry, famous the world over, withstood the seige until the last and although dynamite was used in frequent blasts to drive

Continued on Page Two.

BLOW BUILDINGS UP TO CHECK FLAMES

The dynamiting of buildings in the track of the fire, to stay the progress of the flames, was in charge of John Bermingham, Jr., superintendent of the California Powder Works. Several experienced men from the powder works, assisted by policemen and members of the fire department, did the hazardous work of blowing up the buildings. They were razed to sets of threes, but the open spaces where the shattered buildings fell were quickly turned into holocausts of flame. The work was most effective in the business blocks east of Kearny street.

WHOLE CITY IS ABLAZE

At 10 o'clock last night the Occidental Hotel was destroyed by the flames which swept unchecked across Montgomery street and attacked the block bounded by Montgomery, Sutter, Bush and Kearny. The one Merchants' Exchange building was a mass of flames from basement to tower.

The Union Trust building and other buildings in that block were threatened by the flames.

Shortly after 10 o'clock the fire had eaten its way southward from Portsmouth Square to Kearny and California streets. The entire section from Bush to Kearny to Montgomery side of Kearny street also fired.

All the building adjoining the Hall of Justice were ablaze and the firemen were striving to save the structure by using dynamite. It almost a certainty that every building contained in the section bounded by Clay, Kearny, Market and East streets will be consumed.

The flames had eaten their way eastward to the residence section as far as Gough street. There, by dynamiting blocks after blocks, the firemen succeeded in checking the devouring element.

CHURCH OF SAINT IGNATIUS IS DESTROYED

The magnificent church and College of St. Ignatius, on the northwest corner of Van Ness avenue and Hayes street represents in its destruction a material loss of over $1,000,000. The actual cost of the great building was over $500,000, but during the years which have elapsed since its erection the church has been enriched by paintings and frescoes, which were priceless. Some of them were works of art which can never be replaced, however willing those interested in the church might be to meet any expense in the effort.

MAYOR CONFERS WITH MILITARY AND CITIZENS

At 1 o'clock yesterday afternoon 50 representative citizens of San Francisco met the Mayor, the Chief of Police and the United States Military authorities in the police office in the basement of the Hall of Justice. They had been summoned thither by Mayor Schmitz early in the forenoon, the fearful possibilities of the situation having forced themselves upon him immediately after the shock of earthquake in the morning, and the news which at once reached him of the completeness of the disaster. His first move in making out a list of citizens from whom to seek advice and assistance, and in summoning them to the conference. It was called at the Hall of Justice, as virtually the first news which reached the Mayor regarding the extent of the disaster was that of the ruin of the City Hall. He did not realize that even while the conference was to be going on corridors would be crashing down and windows falling in fragments in the Hall of Justice also, and that before sterner stones desperate efforts would be made to blow the structure up in the vain endeavor by this means to check the advance of the flames in the northern section of the downtown district.

All, or nearly all of the citizens summoned to the conference

Continued on Page Two.

No longer able to take photos, Harry Coleman volunteered his services as an emergency policeman and was assigned star number 871. His first duty was to gather beds and bedding from buildings close to the fire and take them to the hospital being established at the Mechanics' Pavilion. He then went on a similar errand gathering medications and surgical supplies from drug stores. When the Pavilion caught fire, he helped evacuate the patients to the hastily prepared hospital at the Presidio.

He continues his and the *Examiner's* story in this droll excerpt from his autobiography.

Newshounds raid mayor's cellar

THERE WAS A SLOW, CONTINUOUS return to order by Thursday night. Although the fires were still out of control, military fire fighters were dynamiting homes along wide Van Ness Avenue in an attempt to save the section known as the Western Addition. Our newspapers printed limited editions on the presses at Oakland and local staffs generally drifted together. The "Examiner" group rendez-voused at Harbor View Baths, a spot on the waterfront where news and pictures could be assembled and dispatched across the bay. The convenient location served us well, but there was little shelter and no space for living quarters; even camping room was scarce.

These obstacles were overcome with the arrival of our first "Examiner" launch from the Oakland side. Samuel M. Shortridge, later a United States Senator from California, was a stowaway in the cabin and his landing solved all the domestic problems of our staff. The baldish, elongated barrister, who had been refused an official permit to enter San Francisco, showed his appreciation for our help in his illegal entry by offering the use of his spacious residence nearby as working headquarters for our staff. He went home and his adopted news family trailed along with him.

With the gang comfortably bivouacked in the Pierce Street mansion, we pooled our reserves and lines of contact were soon established. Shortridge's cook stove and culinary goods were transplanted into the street, where a field kitchen was set up. This transfer was necessary because of a proclamation which forbade the lighting of fires indoors. Sing, Sam's Oriental houseboy, appeared to enjoy the novelty of preparing meals in the gutter. We designated a task force to keep the larder stocked, an easy assignment by that time because food was arriving in the city by relief trainloads and every news launch brought us more provisions from Oakland. Another crew carried over our duffel, typewriters and general office equipment from Harbor View, which soon buried the last trace of domestic order in the Shortridge ménage. Every room was a paper-cluttered workshop. Handsomely carpeted halls were in a hell of a mess, topsy-turvy with extraneous cots, blankets and disordered garments.

The interior of Sam's mansion at that stage reminded me of a movie set depicting an old plantation, or the country squire's home, commandeered by hostile invading troops and occupied as field headquarters. The sombre, intermittent rumble of dynamite blasts and the blowing palls of soot and smoke added to the illusion.

From the Shortridge portals, couriers raced to and from press boats on the waterfront and kept news bulletins moving in a constant flow. Telegraph and telephone lines were out, no one was allowed to leave or enter the city, and so the only means of sending out news and pictures from the staff, marooned in the city, was by means of our chartered newspaper launches, which made the contact with our editors and the printing plants in Oakland.

A rigid blackout was maintained in the city. The lighting system was in ruins, and as a military precaution against starting new fires, lights were doused and none were permitted in any house. After sundown, we drew the shades tightly in our Pierce Street news headquarters. Reporters ground out copy in the unsteady glow of flickering kerosene lanterns or candles stuffed into empty bottles. But a semi-orderly routine had been restored in our emergency news camp. We had a brief chance for rest and relaxation, the first period of letdown. In that sudden period of fatigue and edgy nerves, the need was sharp for alcohol, but in all that grand residence there was not a single snifter. The authorities had executed the Mayor's order prohibiting the sale of intoxicants. Saloon doors were nailed shut; Army, Navy and police officers had destroyed or confiscated the total civilian supply. The $64 dollar question was, to put it in the vernacular of the moment— where could a guy rustle up a belt?

We were contemplating this question gloomily when word arrived that they were actually fighting the fire with wine on North

Beach. That was the last straw. We gathered in the rumpus room to elect a board of strategy and formulate a campaign. Gazing around the table, we could see a chain of dull, circular press badges upon the lapels of those present—a chain broken only by my shining police officer star Number 871. It was, at the moment, a star of hope. Douglas Erskine, the sports staff sparkplug, got an idea from it and unfolded his plan to us.

"The Mayor has proclaimed that all intoxicating liquors be confiscated. Is that correct?" Doug asked.

The ayes were unanimous.

"Hasn't he placed the responsibility of finding those forbidden beverages and the authority to do away with them upon the gallant members of his police force?"

Another affirmative roar.

"Well, Police Officer Harry Coleman is delinquent in his sworn duty and I recommend that he get to hell out on his beat and start on a fluid drive at once."

I tried to boo him down, but it did no good and I knew that I was the goat. In accepting the empty honor, however, I remembered the exact location of a wine cellar in the immediate neighborhood and announced to the gang that I was about to make a confiscation. I also indicated that a few well-selected press representatives would be allowed to accompany me on this enterprise. Homer Norton and Frank Hamilton, top reporters, were so assigned and left in the wake of Officer 871.

Only a few blocks away I halted, with my fingers crossed, in front of the home of Mayor Schmitz. I led the way up the steps past an Army sentry and the police guard. The affable chief executive responded in person to my ring at his front door.

"Hello, boys, you must have some news for me," he exclaimed, waiting anxiously for me to speak.

"You're damn right and important news," I told him, with an air of uncompromising authority, and offering no apologies for our untimely visit.

"Well, Harry, what kind of a pose do you want?"

"This is not Harry speaking, Your Honor. This is Police Officer 871, duly sworn guardian of the law in the City of San Francisco. I am here in line with that duty during a great emergency to enforce, with violence if necessary, your own special order with reference to the search and seizure of all intoxicants."

The weary Mayor, never above enjoying a good joke, reddened and appeared puzzled. For a moment he didn't get it, but then he tumbled. An amused chortle came from him. He replied apologetically, only half-suppressing an old-fashioned belly laugh: "Very well, officer, you certainly beat me to the punch this time. I surrender. But a forced entry will not be necessary. I'll get the key to the situation and divvy up if you high-binders will take care of the carrying charges and promise not to divulge the location of your raid to the press."

In a fine, mellow mood, we reconnoitered through the Mayor's abundant cellar. By the time we wound up our pillaging and stumbled up the stairs, we were a trifle stiff. We carried all we could and every available pocket was loaded with booty. But the payoff came when our party turned a downhill corner under full sail and the tension on Norton's linen duster became too great. A button popped and a full flagon of our precious cargo shattered on the pavement, almost in front of an astonished naval lieutenant and a regular police sergeant. The crash scared hell out of them. They both sniffed and looked questioningly at the wrecked contraband, and then they noted the slick new police star on my poncho.

"We're confiscating it and I'll have the gang half-shot at sunrise," I told them.

"Okay, officer," they replied, with knowing winks.

These two wide-angle shots taken by U.S. Navy photographers emphasize the devastation of downtown San Francisco.

Before being appointed superintendent of the San Francisco Mint in 1897, Frank Leach had had a lengthy career as a newspaper editor and publisher. When he arrived at the Ferry Building from Oakland the morning of the quake he had to walk a long, circuitous route to reach the Mint. He went along the waterfront to Pacific Street, then along Kearny, Sutter and Post streets to Union Square. At Market and Powell he was stopped by soldiers who refused to let him through, despite his pleading that he was a government official. Eventually a policeman recognized him and escorted him across the street to the Mint at Fifth and Mission.

What happened when he got inside the building is recounted in this excerpt from Leach's autobiography, *Recollections of a Newspaper Man*, published in 1917.

The classic Greek Revival-style building opened in 1874 during the Comstock Lode silver boom. It served as a mint until 1937, when it was replaced by the more modern structure that now overlooks the Upper Market Street part of town from atop Mint Hill. At present the Old Mint is closed to the public, and its future is uncertain.

Saving the Mint — from the inside!

INSIDE THE MINT BUILDING I was greatly pleased to find
fifty of our employees, whose sense of loyalty to duty had not been
modified by fear of earthquake or the horror of being penned up in a
big building surrounded by fire. They were there to do their best to
help save the property of the government, and they went about the
work in a simple, every-day manner, but nevertheless with earnest,
willing, and active spirit. I felt proud to be Superintendent of that
band of faithful and brave men. The captain of the watch, T.W.
Hawes, had directed the work with excellent judgment until I arrived.
They had fought the fire away from getting a foothold in the building
from the east and south sides, but we all knew the worst was to come
when the flames reached the big buildings to the west and north of us.

I made a trip over the inside of the building and had things made
snug and had all inflammable material removed from proximity to
the openings in the walls on the north and west sides. A survey from
the roof about 1 o'clock in the afternoon made our position look
rather perilous. It did not seem probable that the structure could
withstand that terrific mass of flames that was sweeping down upon
us from Market Street. The fire that had cut across Mission Street to
the west of us had swept out northwesterly to Market Street, then east
as if to join hands with the other branch of the fire then raging in and
on both sides of the big Emporium Building; it had thus marshaled
the elements of destruction and was now marching them down on the
mint building. The battle would soon be on. Lieutenant Armstrong of
the United States army was thoughtful enough to bring a squad of ten

soldiers from Fort Miley to help in any way the men could be of service to us. These with our own men made a fighting crew of sixty, which was divided up into squads for work on each floor, from the basement to the roof.

Fortunately for us, we had a good supply of water. In fact, it is a matter of interest to know that, some months previous, the suggestion came to me that we should have the building piped and fire hydrants and hose at suitable places installed on each floor to protect the building from any fire originating on the inside. It was only about ten days before the great disaster came upon us that the last hydrants of the system were put in place on the roof. Our water supply was independent of outside sources being derived from an artesian well in the court. With a strong pump in the boiler room we were able to force a good stream to any part of the roof. Then the two large tanks located on the roof, filled with water, gave us a strong head for two hose streams at the basement floor. Without this protection the building would, without question, have been gutted by the flames. But even these alone would not have been sufficient to keep the fire from gaining a foothold. On the second and third floors the men worked almost wholly with buckets.

Every man stuck to the post where he had been placed. There was not a whimper, though some knew their homes were in the path of the fire, and all felt there was possibly something else besides the safety of the building depending upon the issue of the contest with the great mass of fire that was soon to sweep against us. I know I had decided that, if we should be unable to stand the heat of the flames being against and over the building, or should be driven out by the flames taking possession of the structure, what I should try to do to preserve the lives of the brave men defending the property. I formed a plan of retreat, if the worst came, but said nothing of it to the men. If the mint building had burned it would have been warm work for us, in more than one sense, in getting outside of the fire zone, but I think we would have succeeded, for the buildings to the south of us had been burned away, so we could have gone to the streets, where we would only have had to endure the heat of the ruins until an opening was made in the fire circle surrounding us. We possibly would have had to remain inside the fire zone, like cattle in a huge corral until the fire burned out at some point to enable us to make an exit.

However, we did not have much time for speculation, or long to wait for the contest to begin. We had scarcely finished placing the men, when, inside, the building was made almost dark as night by a mass of black smoke that swept in upon us just ahead of the advancing flames; then, following, came a tremendous shower of red hot cinders, big and small, which fell on our building as thick as hail in a storm, and piled up on the roof in drifts nearly two feet deep at one place against a fire wall for a distance of twenty feet. The court in the center of the building was open to the sky, and in it were much wood and timber. Here the sparks and cinders fell as thick as elsewhere, a dozen little fires were starting at various places in the court, and the men with the hose streams at each end of the court had all they could do to keep those fires down and new ones from starting.

In the height of this feature of the fight I went out into the court to show a soldier who was handling one line of hose how to get the most efficiency from the stream of water. Before I could get back my clothes and hat were scorched by the falling cinders. The difficulty of keeping the fire from getting a foothold here greatly increased my fear that the mint was doomed to destruction. Finally the shower of living coals abated somewhat, making the fight in the court easier, so I passed to the upper floor, where I felt that the hardest struggle against the flames would soon take place.

The buildings across the alley from the mint were on fire, and soon great masses of flames shot against the side of our building as if directed against us by a huge blow-pipe. The glass in our windows, exposed to this great heat, did not crack and break, but melted down like butter; the sandstone and granite, of which the building was constructed, began to flake off with explosive noises like the firing of artillery. The heat was now intense. It did not seem possible for the structure to withstand this terrific onslaught. The roar of the conflagration and crashing of falling buildings, together with the noises given off from the exploding stones of our building, were enough to strike terror in our hearts, if we had had time to think about it.

At times the concussions from the explosions were heavy enough to make the floor quiver. Once I thought a portion of the northern wall and roof had fallen in, so loud and heavy was the crashing noise. Great tongues of flame flashed into open windows where the glass had been melted out, and threatened to seize upon the woodwork of the interior of the tier of rooms around that side of the building. Now came the climax. Would we succeed in keeping the fire out, or should we have to retreat and leave the fire fiend to finish the destruction of the mint unhindered? Every man was alive to the situation, and with hose and buckets of water they managed to be on hand at every place when most needed—first in this room and then in that. The men in relays dashed into the rooms to play water on the flames; they met a fierce heat; though scorched was their flesh, each relay would remain in these places, which were veritable furnaces, as long as they could hold their breaths, then come out to be relieved by another crew of willing fighters.

How long this particular feature of the contest went on I have little idea, but just when we thought we were getting the best of the fight another cloud of dense, black, choking smoke suddenly joined the flames and drove us back to the other end of the building, and some of the men, more sensitive to the stifling smoke, were compelled to go to the floors below. I thought the building was now doomed, beyond question, but to our surprise the smoke soon cleared up and the men, with a cheer, went dashing into the fight again. Every advantage gained by them was told by their yells of exultation. We were gaining in the fight when word came to me that the roof was now on fire and the flames were getting beyond the control of the men there, who only had buckets to fight with. The roof men wanted a hose stream, but I sent word back that the hose was needed on the third floor for a while longer and that as soon as we were out of danger at this point we would attack the roof fire from underneath in the attic. I knew the roof would burn slowly, as it was covered with copper roofing plates.

The explosions of the stones in our walls grew fainter, and finally we heard no more of them. The flames ceased their efforts to find entrance to our stronghold through the windows, but the heat reflected from the mass of red hot ruins to the north of us was almost unbearable; we could not see what the situation was outside, or tell just what other or further experience was in store for us. However, we began to feel that the fight was nearly won and that, after all, we were going to save the building. We were now able to keep the interiors of the rooms which were most threatened wet down by the bucket men, so I sent the men with the hose to extinguish the roof fire, which was quickly done. In a half hour or so our defensive work was over. I now had time to take some observations, and made a trip over the building for that purpose. I found that the building had not been seriously injured, and that with careful watching and preventing the lodgment of cinders, there would be no further danger of the mint being destroyed.

The fight was won. The mint was saved.

The end of the battle came about 5 o'clock in the evening, having begun in the early morning. When he finally walked out of the building, Leach was shocked by what he saw.

"Turn which way you would, the view presented was one of utter ruin, desolation, and loneliness," he wrote. "The buildings ... were piles of smoking and blazing ruins. The street was encumbered with fallen trolley poles and tangled wires and other indestructible debris from the burned buildings. Not a human being was to be seen. It seemed as if all the people and buildings of the city but the mint and its defenders had been destroyed. It was a most depressing scene of desolation."

With most of the banks in ruins, the Mint became the financial center and savior of the city's financial situation. Leach set up a transfer system whereby funds deposited in sub-treasuries throughout the country could be transferred to businesses and individuals in San Francisco by way of the telegraph. In this way, over 40 million dollars was transferred during the first two weeks.

The story of the fight to save the Palace Hotel is told by James Byrne in this third excerpt from his book *Recollections of the Fire*. The time was about 1 o'clock on Wednesday afternoon.

Fighting for the Palace

T HE FIRE FROM THE SOUTH AND WEST had then crossed Third Street and was burning along the north side of Jessie Street towards the hotel. The hotel fire brigade of bellboys and other help was out on the fire escapes along Annie and Jessie streets and were playing the hose upon the walls and wooden bay-windows of the hotel to prevent these latter from catching fire. They had plenty of water in the hose and were doing splendid work.

At that time the Palace Hotel had its own water supply and pumping plant on Jessie Street. This kept the roof tanks filled and supplied a continuous head of water to the amateur fire fighters. Some months previously, on Election night, November, 1905, a fire had broken out in the *Chronicle* building a block west of the hotel on the opposite side of Market Street at Kearny. This fire was extinguished chiefly by water from the Palace Hotel's hydrant near the corner of Market and New Montgomery streets.

When, as happened some months before the earthquake, Fire Chief Sullivan came to inspect fire protection conditions at the Palace, Colonel [John C.] Kirkpatrick, the manager, had chaffed the Chief, reminding him that it was largely the Palace Hotel's water supply rather than the city's, that had saved the *Chronicle* building on that occasion.

I went and talked to some of the bellboys who were working on the hose, and complimented them on their work, promising I would tell Colonel Kirkpatrick what I had seen them do as soon as he returned.

The heat on the fire escapes was at times terrific, and the boys were often compelled to hold an arm up to protect their faces while trying to manage the hose with only one hand. Nevertheless they stuck to their job manfully, and they fought off the fire on the west and south sides of the hotel so successfully that it seemed to me at this time,—I suppose it was somewhere about 9:30 o'clock,—that no menace to the Palace any longer existed unless the fire came up from the east side and through the Grand Hotel on the east side of New Montgomery Street. My view was that, if the hotel staff were able to hold off the fire that menaced the buildings from across the narrow thoroughfares of Annie Street on the west and Jessie Street on the south until the fires in these sections had burnt themselves out, then, if fire did not threaten from the Grand Hotel, across the wider space of New Montgomery Street, the entire staff and water supply would be available in helping to save the front of the hotel.

.   .   .

While I was standing on the corner of New Montgomery and Market streets I saw a Fire Department hose cart come up Market Street from the eastward. It stopped at one or two hydrants on the way, and came on again. Then it stopped at the Palace Hotel hydrant, screwed on a hose and went off with the hose into Sansome Street.

I knew it was the hotel's water supply and that as soon as the pressure was reduced at the hydrant there would be no pressure left to supply the workers on the hotel fire escapes.

Therefore I went back into the hotel, and told the head clerk about it. He did not seem to believe that the street hydrant was supplied by the hotel, and therefore did not attempt to interfere with the Fire Department men. Probably it would have done no good if he had tried to interfere with "the constituted authorities" at such a moment.

But what I knew must happen did happen. The supply to the workers on the fire escapes ceased as soon as the pressure was lowered by opening the street hydrant; and a few minutes later when I again climbed upstairs I found the head bell-boy weeping bitterly because he and his colleagues now found themselves powerless, and he knew that all their work of the morning had been wasted effort.

Shortly after this all the guests were notified to leave the Palace, and it was then understood that the last hope of saving the place had been abandoned.

The Palace Hotel survived the earthquake with minimal damage but was later gutted by fire, despite heroic efforts by the staff to save it.

When it became obvious that the Palace Hotel would burn, James Byrne, who was staying at the hotel with his mother (Mrs. Margaret Irvine) prior to their sailing for Europe, took their luggage to the Pacific Union Club and arranged for it to be stored in the cellar there, under the sidewalk. In the trunks was his mother's most valuable jewelry. When the club building (at the corner of Post and Stockton) was totally destroyed by the fire, he was not too concerned, believing the trunks to be safe. But he was in for a surprise, as he explained in this final excerpt from *Reflections of the Fire*.

Mrs. Irvine's jewels

It was about two weeks after the earthquake when there seemed to be the first chance of burrowing into the ruins of the [Pacific Union] Club which were even then red hot when one dug down a foot or so into the ashes. The entire structure of the building itself was reduced practically to ruins and some shapeless remnants of twisted steel beams and columns.

But the sidewalk over the cellar on the Post Street side, where I had directed the trunks to be stored, seemed cool and safe enough. There was a manhole leading from the sidewalk down to this cellar. This manhole was far too small for me to creep through; but I had one of the boys of the Club retained for that purpose, and the first day the place seemed cool enough and safe enough, we had the iron top lifted off the manhole and I lowered the boy through the opening into the basement.

There was an old newspaper lying in the cellar nearly under the manhole. It was unscorched; but no trunks were visible. It was the same on the Stockton Street side of the basement where the laundry was. Everything was safe and practically unspoilt, the ironing tables, the linen, and all the rest remained uninjured.

But there were no trunks there. The boys had not followed my instructions and the trunks had been destroyed.

Fortunately, I knew every inch of that building and every twist and turn in it. As chairman of the building committee, I had taken great interest in its erection, and, so to speak, had watched every brick as it was laid. Therefore I knew that, as the trunks were not under either sidewalk, they must be in one of two passages leading from the stairway, down which I had seen them taken by the Club boys when I brought them in. I also knew that every part of the building, except the places under the sidewalk, was practically in ashes.

I had a friend in Shreve's, the jewelers, and I went and asked him was there any chance that the jewels in the trunk might have survived the fire. He assured me that they very probably had done so; but that I should be very careful about trying to retrieve them, and that if I located the trunk I should go slowly so as not to allow the jewels to get chilled too quickly. If that happened, they would be likely to crack and split into bits; but if they were allowed to cool off very gradually they would probably be preserved intact.

That was at any rate reassuring. My next task was to locate the trunks. To accomplish that I had to get men to do the digging, and the ashes were still red hot below the surface.

I went down to see Mr. W.G. Stafford who owned a coal yard on East Street [now the Embarcadero] between Howard and Folsom streets, and asked him if he could let me have a gang of his stevedores to do the digging.

.   .   .

Stafford quickly got me the stevedores to do the digging in quest of the buried jewels, and they set to work cheerily on the job. Most of them regarded it as a great joke. They were not told what we were really looking for, but were given to understand that they were expected to recover some valuable papers from the ruins. This they regarded as a nonsensical endeavor; nevertheless they worked carefully and well.

When they got down to the concrete flooring of the cellar we had to lay planks for them to stand on because the concrete was still as hot as a stove-lid.

After about seven days' work we came to the trunks. When eventually we found a couple of trunk handles and realized we had located the lost treasure, we became very, very careful. The handles and hinges had survived the heat; but the trunk itself and most that it contained were calcined into ashes.

We scooped up these ashes, and all the ashes thereabouts, in buckets and boxes, and took them out to the Golf Club where Mrs.

Guthrie, who was then manager of the Club, sifted them carefully and recovered practically every one of my mother's jewels.

Some of them turned up while the men were scooping out the ashes, and I remember being greatly amused by the expression of amazement used by the Swedish foreman of the stevedores when the first one came to light:

"Golly!" said he, "dot vas a diamont as big as a moon! Ven you tells me you vas looking here for papers, I thinks you vas a damn fool!"

A few days later Byrne and his mother finally left on their trip to Europe.

Byrne was a charter member of the Golf Club which at the time of the earthquake and fire was located in the Presidio. He served as the club's president in 1909-1910.

If, as some say, God spanked the town
   For being over frisky,
Why did He burn the churches down
   And save Hotaling's whisky?

As we learn from the following account by Edward M. Lind, divine intervention took human form in saving the whisky. Lind was cashier and manager of A.P. Hotaling & Company, the wholesale liquor merchants located in the block bounded by Jackson, Sansome, Washington, and Montgomery streets. Separating their offices and warehouse was Jones Alley, which has since been renamed Hotaling Street. On the first day of the cataclysm, the block appeared to be in no danger from fire. Lind retrieved all the money from the safe—approximately $2,000—and left it in the care of his parents in Oakland. By noon on the second day, Thursday, he learned that the army was planning to dynamite the Hotaling buildings.

Lind's lengthy yet compelling account of the fight to save the whisky was published in *The Argonaut* on July 17 and 24, 1926. It is excerpted here, with *whisky* spelled as it appears in the *Argonaut* story and in contemporary Hotaling advertisements.

The ditty as quoted above has become part of the folklore of San Francisco but as with much folklore is not completely true to its origin. Charles Kellogg Field wrote the original in response to the claim of a local cleric that God had punished the city for its sinful ways. Almost immediately, it was commercialized by Hotaling, who changed the last line to suit the company's promotional needs. Field's wording, as printed in his autobiography, *The Story of Cheerio by Himself*, is:

If, as one says, God spanked the town
   For being overfrisky,
Why did He burn the churches down
   And save The Old Kirk Whisky?

How they saved Hotaling's Whisky

M R. THOMAS KIRKPATRICK, our general manager, had consulted with the representatives of the Hotaling Estate and had agreed with them that if the buildings were likely to be destroyed by the fire, or dynamited by the soldiery, every effort should be made to save at least a part of the stock. When he arrived on the scene some time about noon on Thursday, the military were already in control of that entire district. It was understood that orders had been issued to save the Federal buildings at all hazards. It was also understood that Captain Orrin R. Wolfe, of the Twenty-second United States Infantry, who commanded the troops in our district, had planned to dynamite our buildings as soon as the fire threatened that section.

Like many others whose property was menaced by dynamiting, or had already been dynamited, we were exercised over devising other means of saving the place. Mr. Kirkpatrick tried to get in touch with Captain Wolfe, but was unable to do so. Presently, however, Captain O.C. Hamlet of the Revenue Cutter Service chanced along and we appealed to him to intercede with Captain Wolfe on our behalf. This he did, and as a result of his kindly offices Mr. [John] Christensen [business manager] and myself were able to secure an interview with Captain Wolfe in the Plaza, where he then had his headquarters.

We explained that whereas Hotaling & Company were ready and even anxious to do all the authorities might want, nevertheless we felt it our duty to point out what the result of dynamiting our premises would be: On account of the large stock of whisky in the warehouse, the consequences of a dynamite explosion would be the immediate combustion of all this vast amount of highly inflammable spirit, which would flow all over the place in a liquid wave of flame, and be virtually certain to destroy instead of save the adjacent Appraisers Building.

On the other hand, if we were permitted to remove the stocks of whisky in the warehouses, amounting to some five thousand barrels, we could take them into the devastated area east of Battery Street, where no further risk of fire existed, and thus preserve our property and materially reduce the peril of a greater catastrophe if it became necessary to dynamite our premises.

After some considerable deliberation Captain Wolfe eventually gave his consent to our plan, and it was then up to Mr. Christensen and myself to put it into execution.

Off we hurried to the waterfront, and there we started scouring the docks and wharves for men who would serve our purpose. Our lure was pay at the rate of a dollar an hour to every man that would lay hands on a barrel of Old Kirk whisky and roll it down, from our warehouse at Jackson Street at Jones Alley, two blocks and a half to Battery Street.

We were able to get eighty men for the job, and they were a mixed lot. Some of them were good stout stevedores and sailor men; others were the scourings of the waterfront, thieves and all the rest of it.

One of these latter I found particularly useful. He was an expert safe-breaker who could open any lock by listening to the fall of the tumblers as he worked the combination. The earthquake had so upset one of our safes that I could not open it. But when I promised this man an extra dollar or so, and also promised not to reveal his abilities to the soldiers or the police, he contrived to get the thing open for me in a few minutes. I don't know how he did it, because part of the bargain was that he should be left entirely alone while he was on the job.

Another gentleman who volunteered was a rather miserable looking little scamp who frankly acknowledged that he worked for a house of ill repute higher up on Jackson Street toward Chinatown, where he said that he cooked and played the piano as occasion required. He proved an excellent cook, and after we had saved the whisky he remained on our force while we had to guard the warehouse and live in it, doing our cooking on the street in a stove we commandeered from the establishment of Bertin & Lepori at 520

Washington Street, close to Jones Alley, who were wholesale grocers and sold stoves and other hardware as well as spices and mineral waters.

At all times, I should explain, we were authorized by the military to help ourselves to whatever supplies we needed and could find in any of the abandoned stores in our vicinity.

Well, this regiment of eighty men started rolling the barrels out of the warehouse and down Jackson Street to the corner of Battery Street, where we stored them in the street itself and in the vacant lot on the southwest corner. By nightfall they had twelve hundred barrels on the corner, and there was no money to pay them.

I had foreseen this difficulty and had gone across the bay to scare up the money. My parents were not at home, and I had to go to Bill Kent, a customer of Hotaling & Company, who had a saloon at Twelfth Street and Broadway in Oakland, and borrow fifteen hundred dollars in cash on my personal i.o.u.

By the time I got this money I found that my troubles had only begun, because an embargo had been placed against anybody entering San Francisco from the east bay cities, and I had to find Governor Pardee, and fight for an interview with him before I could secure the necessary passes to enable me to return.

Meanwhile I had left Alfred McKinnon, our publicity man, who is now [1926] in the movie business in Hollywood, in charge of our regiment. I knew the sort of men they were. Some of them were armed with pistols that the military had issued to us for the protection of the whisky, which nobody was allowed to touch. I knew that they might spare McKinnon for a while; but if they found me, and I was not able to pay them, I would assuredly be shot. And all the time the wages account was mounting at the rate of eighty dollars an hour. But eventually I did get back with the cash, just in time to prevent a riot.

The whisky was then parked at Jackson and Battery streets. A number of soldiers had been ordered to patrol it, and see that we had armed guards always on watch. Failing in these conditions, the head of every barrel was to be stove in and the contents run into the sewer. It was some task to secure, much less to select, men who seemed to be reliable enough for this sort of a job; but eventually we picked a few who agreed to stay up all night and help us with the guard duty. These would only agree to this on payment of twenty-five dollars for the night.

These men were all armed, and were instructed by the military officer in charge of the locality to fire upon any person, soldier or civilian, that laid hands on any barrel of whisky. The whisky was not to be used as a beverage at any hazard; and it would have cost his life to any man that attempted to broach one of those barrels that night.

By the time we had our guards established the fire was beginning to sweep down in our direction from Chinatown to the westward. Shortly after midnight the fire had leaped across Washington Street at Kearny, from the Hall of Justice to the New Western Hotel. North and west of that area, the fire was blazing in the district above Montgomery Avenue and Dupont Street.*

A number of marines under Naval Lieutenant Frederick N. Freeman were working heroically on some buildings on Montgomery Avenue, above Broadway, and were using dynamite to make a fire-break. The dynamite had been brought to that locality by Mr. Abe Ruef, the political boss of that period, who had, and still has, important property interests in that part of the city.

Ruef had asked the firemen and others to do all they could to save that end of town, and had also asked the marines to do all they could to help the work. But there was no water, and practically all these men could use for fighting the fire thereabouts was dynamite. This dynamite acted on Montgomery Avenue just as it had acted down the hill at Washington and Sansome streets the previous day. The debris took fire and burned furiously immediately after each explosion.

The Commercial Hotel, on the northeast corner of Kearny Street and Montgomery Avenue, was owned by Mr. Ruef, and particular efforts were made to stop the flames before they reached it.

If these efforts had proved successful, our chances in the block lower down the hill would have been greatly improved. But they were not successful. Presently the flames got their grip on the structure and it went the way of the rest. The district west of Montgomery Avenue as far up as Stockton Street was by this time completely burnt, and the fire had started in the gore** of Montgomery Avenue and Montgomery Street, now occupied by the Fugazi Bank Building at Montgomery and Columbus Avenue. This was where the old Maguire's Opera House had been before the building had to be partly demolished

* Now Columbus Avenue and Grant Avenue.
** gore = a triangular piece of land.

to make way for Montgomery Avenue, which was cut through during the early seventies.

The windowless east wall of this old theater building along the west side of Montgomery protected part of our block—the gore bounded by Montgomery, Jackson, Sansome and Washington streets. Facing it on the east side of Montgomery Street was an old hotel on the northeast corner of Washington Street, the office building owned by H. & W. Pierce of the Crown Paper Mills and the Willamette Pulp and Paper Company, some other intervening small buildings, then a lodging house of sorts on the southeast corner of Jackson Street, and across the way from this, on the northwest corner, was the old Eiffel Tower restaurant.

Some hours after midnight Thursday, the fire had worked its way down into this gore. The area south and west of the avenue was by this time completely burnt in this section; but the area north of Jackson and Montgomery streets was still intact.

By this time also the fire hose that had been used with such good effect on Wednesday afternoon was again connected with a U.S. navy tug, the Leslie, that pumped water through it from the bay over Telegraph Hill and down Broadway to Montgomery Street. A small stream was available through this hose, and this stream saved our block. The hose was too weak and leaky to deliver any high pressure at the nozzle. Even a good hose would have lost through porosity when carrying a stream, as this hose had to do, over a distance of nearly a mile.

About this time Lieutenant [Sidney W.] Brewster of the U.S. Marines came along with a detachment of marines on their way back to Fort Mason, and they turned in to help with that lone fire hose. It was carried to the roof of the building on the southeast corner of Jackson and Montgomery streets and played upon the fire by Lieutenant Brewster himself.

Occasionally the stream would weaken when the hose sprang a new leak somewhere along its mile of splicings. Then he would close the nozzle until the power picked up again, and then he would renew the combat.

The stream from this hose was not directed upon the fire itself, upon which it would only be wasted; but upon the dead wall on the west side of Montgomery Street fronting us.

The experience of the previous twenty-four hours had taught us that if the wall fell outward the fire would instantly spread to the adjoining buildings, whereas if we could cause it to fall inward it would serve to quench the flames upon which it fell. Therefore the water was played upon the outside of the wall so as to make it fall inward if possible.

Meanwhile all of us, including men that the marines had impressed for the purpose, were working like frantic bees, doing all we could to help. We dragged the hose hither and yon as ordered, helped to direct the nozzle, and scoured through the building itself, carrying out the lamps and tossing the bedding and furniture and everything else that was inflammable through the windows into the street for others to carry away from the point of danger.

Fortunately the water supply held good at the critical period, and after what seemed an interminable time the wall fell inward, westward, with a crash, and the progress of the fire was thus stopped.

That was on the night and early morning of Thursday and Friday. Toward dawn on Friday the wind shifted. Where earlier in the night there had been but little breeze save from the draught caused by the conflagration, a stiff westerly wind now blew up. The fire also shifted. It curled along the foot of Telegraph Hill, and thence headed back, south, in our direction.

This was a bad fire. The shacks went like tinder, and a whole block would be destroyed in thirty minutes.

Shortly after daylight we gathered all the men we could find for the purpose; and as the consent of the military was still ours, we started our new regiment rescuing more whisky from the warehouse at Jackson Street and Jones Alley, and rolling the barrels down to where we had the other twelve hundred, at Jackson and Battery streets.

Sleepless though we were after our strenuous night, everybody worked with a will. Our own employees directed and helped in getting the barrels down from their tiers and out into the street. Others of these were stationed along the way from Jones Alley to Battery Street to egg on and spur into greater activity those who lagged in their barrel rolling.

The elevators customarily used for lifting the barrels from the tiers were out of commission, so ropes had to be used to lower the casks down the stairways. It was ticklish work, especially considering the haste and excitement attending it. Nevertheless out of all we rescued we lost only two barrels of whisky. These slipped from the ropes and rolled down the stairs and were smashed against the wall opposite.

There was no time for meals while this hurried salvage was going on. But bottles of the best imported ale and stout were distributed among the workers for their sustenance; and in this way our force was maintained intact and enthusiastic.

Before noon we had added another thousand barrels to our dump at Battery Street; but the fire was then sweeping down the hill and was menacing us from close at hand. It had already passed Broadway and was devastating the Pacific Street section of the Barbary Coast, a block to the north of Jackson Street.

Our barrel rollers were already becoming nervous and wanted to quit. Many of them were afraid to enter the buildings, fearing an explosion and a holocaust, and would not handle a barrel until it had been rolled out on the street.

Meanwhile the Barbary Coast had become an inferno. The flames had eaten through the block from Pacific Street, and the buildings on the north side of Jackson Street were beginning to burn toward us from the rear. It was only by all sorts of threats and cajoleries that we could keep any of the men on the job at this period, while the sparks and smoke were playing all around us.

Eventually it became impossible to risk further salvage in the open, so we closed all the iron shutters, tore down the wooden signs of A.P. Hotaling & Company, and abandoned the property for the time being to what seemed its certain and fiery fate.

Then we went down the street and joined the military guards at the Appraisers Building. Here everything was in confusion. Hope had been abandoned. The air was filling with live sparks and choking smoke, while numbers of government clerks and officials were removing important records to places of temporary safety.

Then the wind veered and began to blow from the southeast; that is to say in the face of the conflagration that was driving down from the north and west of us. This inspired everybody with a new hope, and instead of despairing, we all began to think of possible methods of salvage.

We hurried off and got a wine pump from the warehouse of A Finke's Widow, at 809 Montgomery Street, just north of Jackson, and another from George Dondero, of the Swiss American Wine Company at 530 Washington Street, near Jones Alley, back to back of Hotaling's.

We dropped the end of one of these through the manhole of a sewer at Battery and Jackson streets, and the other into the saltwater seepage in the excavations for the present Custom House at the old Post Office site diagonally across the street from where the barrels were stored. Then we got some empty puncheons, stove in their heads and pumped into them a *compote* of the sewage and seepage.

This we did so that we could have something wherewith to dampen the thousands of barrels of whisky we now had stored in the open at Battery and Jackson streets, and thus prevent their bursting in the heat of the adjacent conflagration.

This gave us a still greater idea: When the wind shifted and began blowing the flames away from our side of the street, it seemed possible that we might save the entire block. We told our plan to the soldiers and they at once joined us.

A number of buckets and tin pails were commandeered from a deserted grocery store on our block, and a bucket brigade was formed to carry pails of our mixture from Battery Street up Jackson to Montgomery Street.

It was at the corner of Montgomery and Jackson streets that the menace was at its worst. The old Eiffel Tower restaurant building on the northeast corner, which was higher than any other structure thereabouts, was in full blaze, and the sparks from this fire threatened at any moment to start another blaze in the old lodging house across the street on the southeast corner, which was part of our block. If that happened we knew we were done for.

The hose we had been using so successfully all through the night had been taken away, or burnt by the fire on Telegraph Hill, and we had only our buckets to depend on. These had to be passed in through the lodging house door and up the winding stairway to the attic, and then up a rickety ladder through a small manhole to the roof, and scattered over the exposed woodwork or on live sparks as they fell.

It was the toughest job up to that hour. On the preceding night, some silly fool had taken away the ladder while Lieutenant Brewster and a couple more of us were on the roof with the hose. If we had then been compelled to flee from the roof, we would probably have broken our legs jumping down from the manhole in the darkness. This time nobody took away the ladder; but while I was passing up a bucket of the mixed sewage and seepage, the man I was handing it to stubbed his toe on something, and the contents of the bucket fell plump on my head and all over me. It was horrible. But there was no time for washing up or any of that sort of business just then.

One side of Jackson Street was a roaring fury of flame, with walls toppling and smoke choking people. Along the other side we had to keep the buckets going no matter how we blistered or smarted. On the roof of the lodging house it felt like a barbecue. The buckets could not come quick enough, and the evil-smelling stuff made a steam that was suffocating as it evaporated on the roasting woodwork.

Finally the Eiffel Tower house collapsed. Our side of the street was still unscathed, and danger from that source was ended. Nearly all the low buildings on the north side of Jackson Street from Montgomery Avenue to Battery Street were wiped out during that stage of the conflagration. The Sub-Post Office near Battery Street was saved by the soldiers who had aided us at the corner of Montgomery Street, and whom we then assisted at the Post Office with our bucket brigade.

After that, we waited only half an hour or so to see that the area was really safe. Then, having posted the required guards over the whisky on Battery Street, we went back to the warehouse and so to sleep.

That night the fire was stopped; but early on Saturday morning we were again on the job seeking men to roll the whisky back into the warehouse. This took the greater part of the day, and even then our task was not ended. We had still to guard our whisky. We dared not leave it under lock and key, for we knew that all the other stocks of whisky in the city had been destroyed by the authorities to prevent use of the liquor during the period of fire and desolation. Even the liquor that might have been saved was thus destroyed. They feared the results that might ensue upon its distribution. The embargo was still in force, and what was practically martial law was still the law in the burnt districts.

Therefore we had to keep a responsible watch upon our whisky. Accordingly eight of us were locked up in our building every night;

and there we had to remain until the next morning, because anybody seen about the streets in these districts was shot.

I had friends that used to come and spend the night with us and thus help to relieve the tedium of our imprisonment.

Young Volkman, of C.M. Volkman & Co., the seeds merchants of Sansome Street, who were then at 408 Front Street near Clay, was one of these. He got it into his head one night that he would like to go out for a breath of fresh air. He tried to do so. There was a rifle shot almost as soon as he got out of the door, and he popped back in again. The bullet mark is still on the wall where it hit when it missed him.

Considering the conditions, however, we had a pretty fair time. We had a good stove, and we had the cook from the disreputable house that we had enlisted as a barrel roller. We got pretty good meat while it lasted from Patek's, the wholesale butcher, at the corner of Washington and Sansome streets, and we had all the groceries we needed from the various deserted grocery stores. The only thing we lacked was baker's bread.

Isidore Zellerbach of the Zellerbach Paper Company on Sansome Street was another visitor that would pass an occasional night with us; Frederick G. Wright, of the Willamette Pulp and Paper Company, whose offices were on Montgomery Street between Washington and Jackson streets, was another. The clock in their office stopped at 5:15 the morning of the earthquake and is still in the old building, with its hands still set at 5:15.

He was very helpful. On the Saturday after the fire when I needed more money to pay the barrel rollers and others I went over to the Hotaling's bank at San Rafael to cash a check for the purpose. The manager refused to cash a check on the firm for me on the grounds that I had no authority to draw one. Explanations could not be substantiated; so I had to come back empty handed. I would have been in a tight place over money matters for the second time that week, on the firm's account each time, if it had not been for Wright, who dug up the necessary funds. Thereafter I got proper check books and authorizations and could get all the cash that was needed.

Our guard at the warehouse was kept up for six days. Four of us would sleep until midnight while the other four made hourly inspections of the premises to see that no smouldering spark had survived the fire. At midnight we changed about and the early watchers turned in.

On Sunday night, the porch in the rear of the Columbia Coffee &
Spice Co., two doors to the east of us, at 423 Jackson Street, broke out in
flames from a spark that had been smouldering in it since the preceding
Friday. If it had not been for the careful watch we were keeping, the fire
might have gained headway enough to start a real fire; and then, after all
our trouble, Hotaling's and the whisky would have gone up in smoke.

This advertisement appeared in the *San Francisco Call* three weeks later. Two points
worth noting: Sales were to be *cash only* since checks and exchanges were useless; and
the whisky was being shipped "to all points *outside* of San Francisco" (the ban on
liquor sales within the city remained in effect for 10 weeks).

In this next piece, Louise Herrick Wall draws for us a poignant picture of the city as it appeared a week after the main fires had been extinguished. It is part of her article "Heroic San Francisco," which appeared in the August 1906 issue of *The Century Magazine*.

LOUISE HERRICK WALL (b. 1866)

The dignity of ruins

In a lull of work, on the morning of April 28, just ten days after the beginning of the fire, a valiant relief-worker took me in her automobile for a three-days' trip through the ruins of San Francisco. As we entered the intensely congested street from the Oakland ferry, most of the fires were mere feebly smoking ash-heaps, and certain streets had been partly cleared of overhanging poles and wires. The eyes, unveiled of smoke, could now range across the wasted city from one notable ruin of house or church or hotel, with a growing sense of the majesty and the dignity of the ruins set in space. Strange and terrible as is the destruction, San Francisco was never so nearly beautiful. There is no blackening of the ruins; the heat seems to have been so intense that it consumed all its own smoke and charcoal, leaving faintly colored surfaces of crumbled iron, marble, and brick. The ruins stretch out in the softest pastel shades of pink and fawn and mauve, making the wasted districts look like a beautiful city a thousand years dead—an elder Troy or Babylon.

The streets so recently thronged with violently active refugees seeking for any place of safety were lined with tents and shanties. The ingenuity of the home-building instinct is astonishing. There are hundreds of decent shelters made of fire-warped corrugated iron, of window-shutters, of wooden doors torn from wrecked buildings. One especially complete little nook was built between the ends of two adjacent Pacific Avenue cars and fitted with stove and seats. Tents were made of coats and bed-comfortables. Down near the old fish-market were some piratical-looking tents made by the fisher-folk, of old sail-cloths and spars, with a rakish list to leeward, as though ready to ship a crew and set sail in any of the elements.

On this tenth day from the fire the park showed hundreds of acres of lawn covered with well-arranged tents set among the blooming roses and flowering shrubs of the park's conventional flower beds. The shadow of leaves plays on clean canvas, and rescued canaries hang at the tent-peaks chirping contentment. Here and there a hurrying load of furniture or a laden foot-passenger recalls the exodus of a few days before, but these grow hourly more unusual.

The most foreign element in the park is the great crowd that collects about the Relief Camps, where thousands stand in the bread-line three times each day to be fed. The Los Angeles Relief Camp is especially complete in its equipment. In front of its great cooking tents tables are spread with shining rows of tins. They chose a sheltered cove of green sward, an acre or so in extent, surrounded by trees, and nothing could be more orderly or pleasant to look upon than the arrangement of their work.

New buildings of redwood, depots to receive a part of the 27,000 tons of food supplies sent in by neighboring cities and States, have been run up and completed in a week. Here food is handled and distributed to the homeless refugees by the military. The generosity and good-will of every State in the Union has reached out and touched and given its healing virtue to California. San Francisco has been borne up in safety on the goodness of the world, as a sea-gull, at sea, sleeps safely on the wing.

A young doctor who was hurrying through Utah to offer his services in San Francisco says that he could not buy bread to eat in Ogden. The bakers had cut down the local supply: Ogden had to wait, they were baking bread by the car-load for San Francisco. All the schools in Ogden were closed on that day that the children might collect food supplies to carry to the waiting relief cars.

Go where you will in San Francisco to-day, you find yourself inevitably drawn back to the great battle-field of Van Ness Avenue. Here the last desperate fight was made by the half-dead firemen, the professional and amateur dynamiters, the blackened engineers, and military and civil chiefs of the city. It was here that the automobiles loaded with dynamite rushed in their perilous loads. Van Ness Avenue, with the anguished Western Addition behind it, was the last stand of hope. The history of the struggle is written in the ashes and complete ruin of the eastern and southern sides of the avenue and in the partly burned lines of houses, with their shattered windows and the dynamited gaps between houses, of the western side. Here and there the fire leaped the avenue and dynamite snatched from the flames the twice-doomed houses of those rich merchants and financiers who had built to themselves a "house upon the sand." Books, pictures, rare Japanese art collections, and the treasures of two generations of wealthy San Franciscans, were sacrificed that night by dynamite to save what was left of the city.

On the west side of Van Ness stands the Catholic cathedral of St. Mary's. The big brick building was too shaken by the earthquake to be safe for worship, but three times on Sunday, the 29th, mass was celebrated by hundreds of worshipers, who knelt with bared heads on the steps of the cathedral. At their back stretched for miles the wasted city, raising broken shafts of delicately tinted ruin against the even grayness of the morning sky, while in front the people bowed before the unseen altar of their unseen God.

No quarter of the whole town is more strangely altered than what was once the congested picturesqueness of Chinatown. Where the wooden buildings have melted into ash a stout property-line of heavy wire, reinforced by an armed guard, has been stretched across to prevent any further looting of the heathen by the Christian hordes.

To one who has loved this Chinese quarter, which exercised upon some minds a fascination undimmed by familiarity, the destruction of Chinatown is the most poignant loss of the San Francisco fire. The faults of dirty, smelly, delightful old Chinatown will prevent its ever being what it has been.

As I sat on a little embankment, where a bazaar had stood, amid the hot ashes of Chinatown, a tingling in the throat from the acrid smoke that curled up from the burrowing little fires about me, I could think of no more joyful consolation than that Robert Louis Stevenson had not lived to feel the pang of this desolation. Just below me the shaken house where he had lived and the little golden galleon of his monument outlived the ruin of the quarter that he had loved.

Against the property-line, looking in on the ruins, several Chinese merchants stood and talked in low voices. I went up to one tall Cantonese with an impulse to say something of the sorrow I felt in the blow to his honest, loyal people in the loss of their homes and trade.

"Bye and bye," he said slowly and without swagger, "we build all new."

Yes, they might build it new, but the old haunt of opium dreams was gone.

The contrast between old Chinatown, or even what remains of it now, and the new Chinese encampment at Fort Point is absolute. The tent city of the Chinese, after one or two removals, has finally been concentrated in an open, rolling stretch of country near the bay, with the purple Marin hills beyond. Just now the green fields are washed with the yellow, white, violet, and orange of mustard, lupine, and poppy flowers. A sweet, breezy empty, salubrious place, it must seem most strangely unhomelike to its new dwellers. I heard the meadow-larks calling across the swales above the sound of "tent-peg that answered to hammer-nose." Under close military inspection, soldiers in khaki and Chinamen in black broadcloth were raising scores of clean, new tents, in ordered rows, over the bruised meadow flowers of yesterday. The whole equipment here was noticeably good; from tents and ropes to stoves and shining refuse-cans, the material was new and sound, the best I had seen issued by the government to refugees.

Behind the newly rising city of khaki tents was the big white tent of the medical department, with its red cross insignia winding and unwinding itself on the staff. Cows were browsing in the meadows and the earth lay innocently blooming, as if there had been no harm intended by those few seconds when the hide of our great mastodon-earth twinkled away the fly-like vexation of man and his little works.

The Catholic cathedral of St. Mary's at Van Ness Avenue and O'Farrell Street survived the earthquake and its aftermath, but was destroyed by fire in 1962. Today, the site is occupied by KRON Television.

The view from Telegraph Hill, looking south toward Market Street.

For many people, the earthquake and fire brought about a time for reflection—a re-evaluation of life's priorities. Such sentiments can be found in a number of the surviving letters and journals. But few people were able to express their feelings more eloquently than Charles B. Sedgwick in this excerpt from "The fall of San Francisco: Some personal observations," an article he wrote for the May-June 1906 issue of *The British-Californian,* a periodical published in San Francisco.

Sublime spectacle

THAT NIGHT I CLIMBED TO THE SUMMIT OF Russian Hill to view the conflagration, and never shall I forget the sight. It was weirdly beautiful. A thousand banners of flame were streaming in the cloudless sky from spires and domes and lofty roofs, the under-scene being a sea of glowing gold, angry and tumultuous, but brilliant beyond anything I had ever seen or conceived of; and magnificent in irresistible power, its great flaming waves leaping upon or dashing against the strongest creations of man and obliterating them. Noise as of a hundred battles in progress, with myriad giant guns in play, told of the fierce, relentless destruction as towering buildings, eaten loose, toppled and fell, or were lifted skyward by thundering dynamite, to then scatter and drop, throwing up huge fiery splashes from the burning sea.

Soul-stirring, sublime, the spectacle was, notwithstanding its seeming Devilishness, and it would have been worth all that it cost could we only have afforded it. It fascinated, thrilled, took one out of oneself and made him part of another life: another life in which might is mightier, time quicker and things altogether on a more stupendous and potent scale than here on this little, slow, imperfect earth. In face of that tremendous force, pulling down in an hour that which it had taken communities of men years to rear, we seemed puny and futile indeed; laughably, if not so pitiably, weak. Mere worms, or, having the patience and industry, ants—our habitations, cities and great life-works subject to as easy destruction as are the wonderful creations of ants at the hands of humans when in the mood. That man cannot see himself, in relation to the great scheme of things, as a mere ant is the sadness in the thought, for could he so see, he would cease this toilsome building for a day and add his effort, little though it be, to that which is omnipotent and everlasting.

The bay, as I passed down the hill, appealed to me as having never looked more serene and peaceful, lit up as it was by a bright moon and with reflected lights from the shipping gleaming prettily on its calm waters. A strong contrast, indeed, to the turbulent scenes being enacted on the other side of the eminence!

A view from Russian Hill, by portrait photographer J.B. Monaco. The men facing the camera are Monaco's brother-in-law and nephew.

The streets were full of people, recumbent, and some in sound sleep. They seemed to find a greater sense of security close to mother earth. In my wanderings I passed through Washington Square, and there I witnessed a strange sight, the living and the dead lying peacefully side by side on the green sward. All through the night the police wagons brought their dead to the public squares, and the down-town undertakers did the same thing, not knowing where else to take them, I suppose. The living would roll over closer, to make room for their silent brothers. I could not help thinking how wonderfully adaptable is human nature. Had anybody told these living refugees, the day before, that their bed-fellows of the morrow night would be corpses, they would doubtless have had their shivers. As it was, they did not mind in the least.

When the sun rose once again all was bustle and animation, for it was felt that the homes would surely go that day. The exodus began in earnest, the farsighted ones making for the big Golden Gate Park and distant open spaces, others moving on but a few blocks at a time. Every street leading away from the doomed city was thronged with people, who, while not perhaps gay, could not be said to be sad or despondent. Folks were dressed in their best, presenting an uncommonly smart appearance—for refugees. Each carried that which he or she most prized: mothers, their babies; old maids, their dogs and parrots; young ladies, their "other hat" and a bountiful supply of candy; children, their toys and bags of peanuts and popcorn; and the men, sensible fellows, bundles of bedding and grub.

A spirit of good nature and helpfulness prevailed, and cheerfulness was common. The gentler sex was radiant; women love moving. The children thought they were on a picnic. The men did a little quiet groaning under their loads, and were seen to be talking energetically to themselves at times—but I am sure they were not swearing.

There was much kindliness. The old and feeble, the blind, the lame, were tenderly aided. The strong helped the weak with their burdens, and when pause was made for refreshment, food was voluntarily divided; the milk was given to the children, and any little delicacies that could be found were pressed upon the aged and the ailing.

This goodness and self-sacrifice came natural to some, but even the selfish, the sordid and the greedy became transformed that day— and, indeed, throughout that trying period—and true humanity reigned. It was beautiful to behold, and gave one a glimpse of human kind in a new and a glorious light.

Would that it could always be so! No one richer, none poorer, than his fellow; no coveting the other's goods; no envy; no greedy grasping for more than one's fair share of that given for all. True it is, I reflected, that money is the root of all evil, the curse of our civilization, seeing that it is the instrument which frail mortals use to take unjust advantages. What a difference those few days when there was no money, or when money had no value!

Charles Sedgwick also recalled some lighter moments for his
British-Californian article. The vignettes reprinted here begin
with a scene on Market Street as the fire reached Fourth Street.
Firemen, unable to do anything, were standing idly; soldiers
were on guard at the banks; and the police were admonishing
people to "pick up their duds and git."

The funny side

Wʜɪʟᴇ ᴅʀᴀᴍᴀᴛɪᴄ ᴇɴᴏᴜɢʜ, the scene was in no wise pathetic. There was much laughter and joking, but no tears. One cheerful idiot went by in a wagon drumming on a piano "There'll be a hot time in the old town tonight," which struck many as being exquisitely appropriate, for applause was generous. Another chap, who no doubt fondly imagined himself a second edition of the Nero who fiddled while Rome was burning, dashed along in an automobile, the while energetically scraping on a violin. At first I thought it was Mayor Schmitz practicing up for his old trade, but when I considered that the tune was not Irish, I realized my mistake.

There were many attempts at gaiety, and I do not think they were all feigned. That half of San Francisco which was ever gay and careless was true to itself to the last; it never could take life seriously, and it did not take its own destruction seriously.

Some incidents were legitimately funny, ludicrous enough to bring a smile to the gravest face. I was passing the Occidental Hotel in the course of the morning and heard a lady, who was standing on the curb, hail a passing trooper.

"Ho, Mr. Soldier," she cried, "please take me out of this dreadful place. I cannot stand it a minute longer."

"You are safe enough where you are, madam—for a time," answered the man on horseback. "And I have no conveyance."

"But I must get away immediately. I never did like this town, and I'll never come back. I can do without a carriage; I will ride with you," responded the lady.

"Where do you wish to go, madam?"

"To Canada."

Looking at the poor, skinny animal whose back was all but breaking under its already ample load, and then at the portly proportions of the good dame in distress one could not repress a smile.

"I will call for you later," said the two-hundred-pound "boy in blue," as he gallantly rode away, intending, of course, to do no such thing.

.   .   .

Ever since the day of the great exodus, and indeed on that day too, I had noticed that the people seemed different, particularly the women. The latter had lost that graceful contour for which California ladies are famous. They had become squatty; in fact, as broad as long, just as one is made to appear by those grotesque mirrors at the Chutes. The phenomenon troubled me, for there was no accounting for it. Not a fairy-like form had I beheld anywhere, and in a community where formerly they had been common. I began to wonder if anything was the matter with my brain, or if my optics had ceased to see right.

Finally, one day, I remarked on the strange affair to an acquaintance. He smiled.

"Oh," said he, "I suppose it is with them all as with my wife. You see, she has on four skirts, five waists, three shirts and—"

"Enough!" I cried. "The mystery is explained."

And it also explained to me another circumstance which at the time I had considered odd. That of extra clothing, the women folks appeared to be taking along only hats. I shall not be so ready to condemn women as unpractical, in future.

.   .   .

On my way down town in the early morning I had noticed a group of people up Ellis Street and went to see what was the matter. A lodging house had collapsed, and it was said several people had been taken away, dead, and many more rescued who were badly injured. Men were still digging and scraping among the debris to find someone who at intervals called for help. An individual who appeared to be directing things kept calling out, "Where's your head? Where's your head?" Only a grunt came in reply at long intervals, but after a time a man's leg was uncovered and a few minutes later they had the poor fellow on his feet. They did not greet him, did not say "Glad to find you alive;" nor did he thank his deliverers. He cleared his throat, shook the plaster-dust from his nightgown, and looking slowly around with a faint smile said: "Somebody was asking where my head was. If you look closely you will see that it is on my shoulders."

The crowd grinned. The perspiring chief-rescuer was hot. "This is no time to spring your chestnuts, you chump," said he, walking away in manifest disgust.

Probably the most endearing image that many San Franciscans have of the 1906 tragedy is of the Italian tenor Enrico
Caruso running frantically around the Palace Hotel twirling
his moustache and muttering "'ell of a place! I never come
back!"—as he never did. If the eyewitness accounts of the numerous *sightings* of him during those few days are accurate, it
would seem that he did put on a comic offstage performance.
Credit for the "never come back" remark appears to rest with
photographer Arnold Genthe, who said he saw Caruso outside the St. Francis Hotel, dressed in a fur coat over pajamas.
Other writers tell of seeing him in similar attire in different
parts of town. On Thursday the 19th he was seen on Sloat
Boulevard looking for the nearest railroad station.

The tenor told his own version in *The Sketch* of London,
and it was reprinted in the July 1, 1906, issue of *The Theater*
magazine with the title, "Caruso on the Earthquake."

This portrait of Caruso as Don José appeared in the *San
Francisco Chronicle* on the morning of April 18, 1906, accom-
panying a review of the previous evening's performance of
Carmen.

Caruso talks back

Y OU ASK ME TO SAY WHAT I SAW and what I did during
the terrible days which witnessed the destruction of San Francisco?
Well, there have been many accounts of my so-called adventures published in the American papers, and most of them have not been quite
correct. Some of the papers said that I was terribly frightened, that I
went half crazy with fear, that I dragged my valise out of the hotel into
the square and sat upon it and wept; but all this is untrue. I was
frightened, as many others were, but I did not lose my head. I was
stopping at the [Palace] Hotel, where many of my fellow-artists were
staying, and very comfortable I was. I had a room on the fifth floor,
and on Tuesday evening, the night before the great catastrophe, I
went to bed feeling very contented. I had sung in "Carmen" that
night, and the opera had gone with fine *éclat*. We were all pleased,
and, as I said before, I went to bed that night feeling happy and contented.

But what an awakening! You must know that I am not a very
heavy sleeper—I always wake early, and when I feel restless I get up
and go for a walk. So on the Wednesday morning early I wake up
about 5 o'clock, feeling my bed rocking as though I am in a ship on
the ocean, and for a moment I think I am dreaming that I am crossing
the water on my way to my beautiful country. And so I take no notice
for the moment, and then, as the rocking continues, I get up and go
to the window, raise the shade and look out. And what I see makes me
tremble with fear. I see the buildings toppling over, big pieces of
masonry falling, and from the street below I hear the cries and
screams of men and women and children.

I remain speechless, thinking I am in some dreadful nightmare, and for something like forty seconds I stand there, while the buildings fall and my room still rocks like a boat on the sea. And during that forty seconds I think of forty thousand different things. All that I have ever done in my life passes before me, and I remember trivial things and important things. I think of my first appearance in grand opera, and I feel nervous as to my reception, and again I think I am going through last night's "Carmen."

And then I gather my faculties together and call for my valet. He comes rushing in quite cool, and, without any tremor in his voice, says: "It is nothing." But all the same he advises me to dress quickly and go into the open, lest the hotel fall and crush us to powder. By this time the plaster on the ceiling has fallen in a great shower, covering the bed and the carpet and the furniture, and I, too, begin to think it is time to "get busy." My valet gives me some clothes; I know not what the garments are but I get into a pair of trousers and into a coat and draw some socks on and my shoes, and every now and again the room trembles, so that I jump and feel very nervous. I do not deny that I feel nervous, for I still think the building will fall to the ground and crush us. And all the time we hear the sound of crashing masonry and the cries of frightened people.

Then we run down the stairs and into the street, and my valet, brave fellow that he is, goes back and bundles all my things into trunks and drags them down six flights of stairs and out into the open one by one. While he is gone back for another and another, I watch those that have already arrived, and presently someone comes and tries to take my trunks, saying they are his. I say, "No, they are mine"; but he does not go away. Then a soldier comes up to me; I tell him that this man wants to take my trunks, and that I am Caruso, the artist who sang in "Carmen" the night before. He remembers me and makes the man who takes an interest in my baggage "skiddoo," as Americans say.

Then I make my way to Union Square, where I see some of my friends, and one of them tells me that he has lost everything except his voice, but he is thankful that he has still got that. And they tell me to come to a house that is still standing; but I say houses are not safe, nothing is safe but the open square, and I prefer to remain in a place where there is no fear of being buried by falling buildings. So I lie down in the square for a little rest, while my valet goes and looks after the luggage, and soon I begin to see the flames and all the city seems to be on fire. All the day I wander about, and I tell my valet we must try and get away, but the soldiers will not let us pass. We can find no vehicle to take our luggage, and this night we are forced to sleep on the hard ground in the open. My limbs ache yet from so rough a bed.

Then my valet succeeds in getting a man with a cart, who says that he will take us to the Oakland Ferry for a certain sum, and we agree to his terms. We pile the luggage in the cart and climb in after it, and the man whips up his horse and we start. We pass terrible scenes on the way: buildings in ruins, and everywhere there seems to be smoke and dust. The driver seems in no hurry, which makes me impatient at times, for I am longing to return to New York, where I know I shall find a ship to take me to my beautiful Italy and my wife and my little boys.

When we arrive at Oakland we find a train there which is just about to start, and the officials are very polite, take charge of my luggage, and tell me go get on board, which I am very glad to do. The trip to New York seems very long and tedious, and I sleep very little, for I can still feel the terrible rocking which made me sick. Even now I can only sleep an hour at a time, for the experience was a terrible one.

It had taken eight 60-foot rail cars to ship all of the opera company's magnificent costumes and sets to San Francisco, yet all that was saved could have been carried back in a shopping basket, according to a report in *Sunset Magazine*.

Caruso arrived in New York on April 24 and, wrote a *New York Times* reporter, "denied with some bitterness that he had displayed his embonpoint in pajamas." Caruso said that by the time he reached Union Square he was wearing trousers and a waistcoat. But the legend lives on!

"Annie Laurie" was the nom de plume of journalist Winifred Black Bonfils. She wrote this piece, published April 22 under the headline "Annie Laurie Tells of the Spectral City," while on the staff of the San Francisco *Examiner*. The Happy Hooligan she refers to was a popular cartoon character that appeared regularly in Hearst's Sunday newspapers from 1900 to 1932. In place of a hat he wore a tin can.

ANNIE LAURIE (1865-1936)

"The real
San Francisco"

I HAVE BEEN IN SAN FRANCISCO, the city of the core of my heart, just six hours to-day. In those six hours I, a stranger, was three times offered food and twice offered water. A smooth-faced chunk of a boy saw that I looked tired and asked me to ride with him in his two-wheeled cart perched on the mattress he was taking to some homeless friends. A young fellow with the old letters U.S.A. on his collar went out of his way to offer to find people for me, and a woman with eyes soft with gentle pity asked me if I had any place to sleep. If I had not she said that she would take me home with her.

And then I knew that the dreadful story of death and hopeless misery the blackened ruins were trying to tell me was false. San Francisco, the best loved of the world, is not dead, and can never die while one man or woman with the true spirit that made the old San Francisco what it was still lives.

The beautiful streets, the smiling parks, the friendly houses of friends, the gay restaurants—these things were only a little bit of the outside dress of San Francisco. The real San Francisco is just as much alive to-day as it was some seven sweet years ago when the whole city was gay with flags to welcome our boys home from the Philippines.

San Francisco in ruins!

Why, you couldn't kill San Francisco with a dozen earthquakes and a hundred fires. That isn't the kind of stuff San Francisco is made of, and it's taken just exactly these last four days of hideous horror to let even us, who thought we knew the temper of our own people, to get in under the silly varnish of the surface and really know them at all.

I met a woman out in Jefferson square to-day who ought to sit for a picture of the Incarnation of the Spirit of San Francisco. She was standing in a funny little square tent made partly of boards and partly of ragged bits of cloth. She wore a dress that had been through the fire with her, but her bright hair was brushed neatly back from her rosy face. She was washing dishes, petting a dog, talking baby talk to a baby and bossing some half-dozen of boys, all at the same time.

"Run down to the edge of the pavement with these beans," she said to one boy, "and see if you can't find somebody's fire to warm 'em a little by. Hike over to the commissary wagon; they're giving out eggs there. The baby can't eat these beans. Where are those blankets? Didn't I tell you rascals to put them out to air? Oh, yes; I've got thirteen boarders. Yes; we all sleep in this tent. No; they don't pay me a cent. Burnt out? Who isn't?

"What's the use of being blue about it, though? Didn't yer see our totem at the door? Allow me to present you. This is our friend, Happy Hooligan."

And there on the ridgepole of the tent was perched a little wooden Happy Hooligan on top of a crudely painted sign which said: "Cheer up."

Happy Hooligan isn't the handsomest creature in the world, nor even the most refined; but the rabbits brought him to that baby on Easter and that baby's blessed mother had the good sense and the good heart to bring him along with the little handful of things she was able to save. I've never been very fond of Happy myself. I don't fancy his taste in hats; but after this I'll never see his ugly face in the cheapest kind of picture again without thinking of that woman out there at Jefferson square, homeless, without a dollar, cold and not overly well fed—but a California woman, for all that.

When I came down over the mountains this morning out of the hateful gray desert into the green glory of California and saw the yellow poppies dancing in the only sunshine that ever really shines I kept saying over and over to myself what we've all heard General Barnes say so many times:

"California is God's country, and God smiled when he made it."

God did smile when he made California, and he's smiling yet at all our foolish little perplexities and anxieties and want of faith and courage. Let's look back at him up through the smoke and cinders, and smile, too—just to see what will happen.

Happy Hooligan, as he appeared on a Valentine card.

Winifred Bonfils later gained fame not only as a journalist— her "Annie Laurie" and "Winifred Black" columns appeared regularly in Hearst newspapers—but also for her involvement with national and international battles against drug abuse. In addition, she helped found several charities. Her investigative reporting of San Francisco's public hospitals resulted in a number of reforms. So profound was her impact on the city that when she died in 1936 her body was laid in state in City Hall.

Officer Henry C. Schmitt was patroling the Harbor District when the earthquake hit, and he narrowly missed being killed by a collapsing wall. His duties kept him downtown until early afternoon, when he was finally able to go home to his family at 505 Dolores Street, in the Mission district.

The Schmitts slept at home on the first night, but at about 8 o'clock on Thursday evening the fire was getting closer and they were forced to leave. With the help of neighbors, Schmitt saved his brand new kitchen stove from the third floor flat. The following is from *The Argonaut*, May 8, 1926.

HENRY C. SCHMITT (b. 1861)

Street life,
with stove and piano

T HE MILITARY HAD THEN DRAWN a guard around the place, but when I showed my police badge, they allowed us to pass, and up we went, two flights of stairs to our flat, where I unlimbered the stove from its boiler and other connections. Then we carried it out and across the street to the northwest corner of Dolores and Eighteenth streets, and set it up outside the wall of the Mission High School.

We were so pleased with this bit of work that we went back for the piano. That was a real job, because of the stairs and the fire which was then burning the place. But eventually we got a piece of rope and hitched it on the newel post of the banisters, and thus lowered the whole piano down into the street, safe and sound except for a knob or two that got rubbed off as it banged down the stairs. We rolled it on its own castors across to the corner where we had the stove and our bedding, and only lost one castor on the journey. In that way our new corner was elegantly furnished.

Before we were able to get out the piano the roof of the house was on fire. But in spite of this one of the soldiers went up to our flat after we reached the street, and threw some more furniture out of the window. He threw out a nice couch we had. I was looking at him as he threw it out and was looking at the couch on the ground when and after it fell.

You talk about people doing strange things during that fire. There is no doubt that nearly everybody became half queer over it: I stood across the street watching my own couch drop to the ground. A

[223]

man I did not know from Adam quietly walked over, picked up that couch—my couch—hoisted it on his shoulder and walked away with it. Did I call out to him, or try to stop him, or run after him—I, a policeman, looking at a fellow walk off with one of my best pieces of furniture? Not a bit of it. I just kept looking at him. It did not occur to me that there was anything unusual, anything for me to worry about, in the man making off with my couch. But very often afterward I wondered what had come over me, and was sorry for losing that couch when it was too late. It would have been useful at our new corner.

But we had the stove and the piano, and these made the focus and rallying center of the most curious gathering of homeless refugees out of all that were then compelled to camp abroad in San Francisco.

The old Hebrew Cemetery in the block bounded by Eighteenth, Dolores, Nineteenth and Church streets was then being turned into a park; and, as a preparatory measure, it had been covered thickly with manure. To that open space flocked hundreds of poor people of the working classes, from the cheaper residence quarters further south, who had been rendered homeless by the fire. It was a pitiable thing to see those poor things, when the fire drew nearer and was sending showers of sparks and live cinders over them, trying to protect their clothes and quilts and things by piling the damp manure over them. Others were mere babies. Others were sick and ailing, and unable to help themselves.

Well, when I brought out the stove, which we still have in the house we are now [1926] living in, I brought out the flue as well and we rigged up the finest out-door kitchen in that part of San Francisco. We had also salvaged a big washboiler, and some of the boys around the neighborhood dug up another big one so we were well equipped. Mrs. Schmitt and the two girls soon set to work cooking in them, and making tea and stew for all that could not help themselves.

The girls would go out moseying around the graveyard, and come back and tell of some poor old woman with nobody to look after her, or some poor old sick man, or some children with the mother helpless. And they would fill up a can with coffee or tea, and milk; and another can with meat stew, and off they would go with them. Empty fruit and vegetable cans were our soup tureens, cups, saucers, plates and side dishes. They were very handy.

The grocer on the corner put out all his supplies the first day; so we had plenty of tea and coffee and sugar and butter and everything; as well as canned goods, while they lasted, and then the Red Cross people began supplying things.

The wholesale butchers used to send out meat for the refugee camps from the Potrero; and when a wagon was passing our place the man would dump out a few fine slabs of meat on the corner, and that kept the stew-boiler going. It was the same with the dairyman from down the Peninsula. They always dumped down one or two big ten-gallon cans of milk at our corner as they drove by. So all that Mrs. Schmitt and the girls had to do was keep awake and keep the boilers full and the fire going.

There was a sort of amusement artist that used to sing and play at entertainments around our end of the city. His name was Billy Delaney. He was very helpful and good tempered; so he was appointed chief commissariat officer to the stove and its establishment. He would sally out, with a soldier as escort, and collect wood from the ruins, and coal from the coal yards, or anywhere else, and draw water for the boilers, and help to feed the crowd that was always hungry.

A child would come slinking up to the kitchen, with a tomato can half full of cold water, and ask leave to heat it on the stove so as to make her mother a cup of coffee. Then Billy Delaney would find two cans, and get Mrs. Schmitt to fill them up with good real coffee, and nice stew for the child. And that is the way it kept going all the time.

Then when the dynamite explosions were making the night noisy, and keeping everybody awake and anxious, the girls or some of the refugees would play the piano, and Billy Delaney and other folks would start singing; so that the place became homey and sociable, considering it was on the sidewalk, outside the high school, and the town all around it was on fire.

The soldiers were quartered in the high school yard, but the lavatories there were reserved for the women and children from our corner of the cemetery.

All through the days of the trouble, I think, our corner was the best looked after, and certainly our stove was the best in that part of the Mission. The fire only went two blocks beyond us, and was stopped on Friday, April 20, at Twentieth and Dolores streets.

William F. Burke was secretary to the San Francisco postmaster at the time of the earthquake and assistant postmaster from 1909 until he retired in 1941. The compelling account that follows is part of his story in the *Argonaut* series.

The Beaux Arts classical style Post Office building at Seventh and Mission streets had been open only since August 1905 and was one of the few buildings downtown to survive the holocaust. When the quake struck, there were 46 men on duty in the building. Others came in after the temblor, but soldiers ordered everyone out when fires threatened the building. Ten men on the third floor refused to leave, and it is through their efforts that the building was saved. The fire roared all around them as it moved uptown. Windows were shattered by the heat, and flames poured in, but these men beat them with mail sacks soaked in water from the freight elevator tank.

For two days after the fire, crews righted equipment and re-sorted mail that had been tossed to the floor by the quake. On April 20 the Post Office re-opened for business, true to its claim: *Neither snow nor rain nor heat nor gloom of night stays these carriers from the swift completion of their appointed rounds.*

Neither snow, nor rain, nor earthquake...

O N THE MORNING OF FRIDAY, THE 20TH OF APRIL, the officials of the Post Office, the Railway Mail Service and the Inspection Division gathered to make plans for the rehabilitation of the Mail Service. The theory of the postmaster was that the first need of stricken citizens of the city was to get word to their friends on the outside that, while they were still alive, they were in great need. The telegraph lines were all down, and the best proof of the inadequacy of the telegraph service was the fact that thousands of telegrams were being mailed under two-cent stamps in the Post Office, the telegraph companies trusting to the postal service to deliver them. So the first care was the outgoing mail. Wagons and automobiles were impressed and sent out to the different stations to gather in what the carriers had already collected from the boxes. These collections during the day were hurried to the main post office, where the clerks, after setting their cases upright and re-arranging the disorganized furniture, undertook the distribution of the mail. In the meantime other wagons were impressed at the Ferry Station, where the mail was piling high, and these hauled the incoming sacks to the main office, where it was distributed in readiness for dispatch to the stations.

It was also decided to cover the camps with an outgoing service as quickly as possible, and automobiles were impressed for that purpose. I took one of them to cover the Presidio and Golden Gate Park and any intermediate gathering I could find, the plan being to inform the people that collections would be made from their camps in the afternoon and that those who desired to communicate with their friends should be ready with their mail.

The service between the main office and stations was at that time handled by the street cars. Cars carrying mail bore the United States Mail signs, and I stopped at the old Sacramento Street car barn, on Sacramento Street beyond Presidio Avenue, secured one of these signs and hung it on the top of the front of our auto. The effect was electrical. As the people saw the machine bearing the mail sign coming, they cheered and shouted in a state bordering on hysteria. We told them where the collections would be made in the afternoon and asked that they spread the news. As we went on into the Presidio there was almost a riot, and the people crowded around the machine and blocked its progress. It was evidently taken as the first sign of rehabilitation and, as it proceeded, the mail automobile left hope in its wake. It was the same in the park.

The news spread rapidly, and also the fact that the Post Office would handle everything, stamped or unstamped, as long as it had an address to which it could be sent. When I went back in the afternoon, over the rounds of the morning, to collect the mail from the camps, the wonderful mass of communications that poured into the automobile was a study in the sudden misery that had overtaken the city. Bits of cardboard, cuffs, pieces of wrapping paper, bits of newspapers with an address on the margin, pages of books and sticks of wood all served as a means to let somebody in the outside world know that friends were alive and in need among the ruins.

Altogether we gathered a wagon load of as curious mail as was ever handled; and as it was brought to the machine we threw it into mail pouches. When we had covered the last of the camps in the Presidio, the Richmond District and the park, we made our way to the main office where this curious mail could be distributed in the best way possible to get it to its destination. It came to our knowledge later that not one piece of this mail that was properly addressed failed of delivery.

It was never denied that in handling mail without stamps, the Postmaster was in direct violation of the regulations and personally liable for the amount of the stamps on every letter so handled, but stamps could not be gotten on sale and so the risk was taken. At the close of the day between wagons and automobiles and carriers, 95

The Post Office at Seventh and Mission streets was saved by 10 postal workers who refused orders to leave the building and fought the fire from inside.

pouches of letters carrying mail composed of rags and tatters and odds and ends—and burdened with a weight of woe bigger than had ever left the city in a mail sack—were made up for dispatch. In impressed wagons they found their way through the ruins over piles of brick that blocked the streets and under walls that tottered and dropped bricks as they passed, to the Ferry Station where they were sent out of the city. With them were sent 287 sacks of papers.

In the meantime, further anxieties began to develop within the service. Transportation had of course been paralyzed and, save for an occasional lift on a wagon or automobile, the employees of the office had to make their way to and from work on foot. This meant that none of the employees could go home to lunch and there were no restaurants where they could eat. Besides, the problem of securing food through the bread lines was one of slow and uncertain solution. Also it was found that many of the Post Office employees were kidnapped by the soldiers and put to work on the brick pile. Passes from the Postmaster cured much of this trouble, and the carriers' uniforms always gave them free way, but the clerks were being continually stopped until the simple expedient of snapping a mail lock into a button hole on their coats solved the difficulty definitely and completely. A man who wore one of Uncle Sam's mail pouch locks could go anywhere, and we had no more trouble.

The question of feeding the men at the main office, where had been gathered all of the work from the downtown burned district, was a serious question until the navy came to their relief. Tremendous quantities of naval stores were being landed at the Folsom Street dock, and, upon the order of the Postmaster, wagon loads of these were sent to the main office where messes were arranged and where the men were given not only their own meals, but were allowed to take home provisions for their families. In that way, they were able to remain at work to rehabilitate the mail service and at the same time meet the necessities of providing for their families at home.

Because of this the permanent force of the main office grew rapidly and within a few days every man was in his place.

Before Monday, the 23, regular communication was established between all the stations left standing and the main office, and between the main office and the Ferry and the Third and Townsend Street

Depot; and with the return to activity came problems numerous and complicated.

Oakland, filled with refugees, finding its mail swelling to far greater bulk than it was able to handle, sent over to the stricken city for assistance. Calls of the same kind came from Berkeley and Alameda, and from Los Angeles authorities a similar request was made that from the San Francisco Post Office force of clerks and carriers assistance be allowed them to handle the mail that was rapidly running far beyond their control. By order of the Department, forty-two clerks and twenty-five carriers were sent to Oakland, and four clerks to Berkeley, and then the Postmaster declared that he could spare no more of his force. While the clerks and carriers were ordered away under the belief that the postal activity of San Francisco had been reduced nearly one-half, it was found that the actual work of the office had increased to an insurmountable extent.

And not only had the work increased to an insurmountable extent, but it had become immensely more complicated as well. In a way the furnishing of assistance from the San Francisco Post Office force to cities not so stricken was like taking the life preserver from a drowning man and telling him to swim for it. If ever a post office needed every man it had, and if ever a forlorn and shattered organization needed to be let alone instead of being harried and curtailed, it was the force of the San Francisco Post Office. Mr. [Arthur G.] Fisk, the postmaster, stormed and protested; the men wailed and objected, the hours of work lengthened and the mail piled higher and higher; but the disorganized and shortened force plugged along loyally at its work and brought order out of chaos. Seventy-three men out of the force of the San Francisco office in 1906 meant more than three hundred would today [1926]; moreover, the men drafted for service elsewhere included some of the best we had. It was some months before these men were returned, and in the meantime the complete rehabilitation of the service was seriously delayed.

It was then, and has been the theory of the public since, that with one-half of the city burned and one-half of its people away, the full force of clerks and carriers left in the San Francisco Post Office could handle what remained with ease and dispatch, but it took no more than a day to make it apparent that the reverse was the case. Before a week had passed, 75,000 forwarding orders and changes of address had been turned into the office, and these increased in number until by the first of June nearly 200,000 had been received and recorded, and mail was working subject to their direction. These forwarding orders were sent first to the carrier who delivered at the old address, and then to the carrier who delivered at the new address for record. Letters addressed to locations in the burnt district went direct to the carrier who had always delivered them; he, having a forwarding order on his book, endorsed them with the new address, remailed them, and in due time they were delivered.

Frequently, however, three or four or even half a dozen members of the same firm, or its employees, would send in forwarding orders, each of them directing the mail to a different location, and business mail was sent, under their orders, all over the State. It frequently happened that carriers who delivered in the burnt district worked never so hard in their districts prior to April 18 as they did at their desks after that day, keeping track of mail that poured in upon them and directing it to any one of the half dozen addresses which perhaps they had on file to control it.

I remember a typical instance of the way mail had to be handled. It was in the case of a firm that had been burnt out in the downtown district and had immediately relocated its office in the home of one of its employees in the Richmond District. The proprietor's residence had been destroyed as well as his place of business. Within a short time he found a home for himself and his family in the Mission and took with him his office as well. Then he found a location on Fillmore Street and started again in business at that address. All this happened within a very few weeks. So it came about that his mail, still coming addressed to his original place of business in the burned district, was first marked up to his temporary address in the Richmond District, then was marked up to his address in the Mission, and then was sent over to his Fillmore Street address.

A constant stream of mail was going the rounds of his various addresses, finally arriving at its true destination with a delay of perhaps thirty-six or forty-eight hours. This situation was multiplied by thousands and meant that every piece of mail for the burned district received anywhere from two to four rehandlings before it finally reached home. A system of short cuts was subsequently devised whereby a great deal of this reforwarding was obviated, but that was not until some weeks later.

It might naturally be asked why was this not done at once. Because it was impossible, and because it was inadvisable and dangerous in the conditions in which the service was just after the catastrophe. It was impossible because no one had ever met such a situation before; and, it may be said, as soon as we got used to the problem we found a solution for it. It was inadvisable and dangerous because our only hope of maintaining service lay in handling the situation in the way in which we were accustomed to handle the mail, inadequate for the time being though it might be. Our only safety lay in creeping along by known methods until we had grasped the full significance of the complicated task before us, and could risk experimenting with it. Until the service could be restored to what might be called normal in such a state of affairs, any new plan that might break down,—and any innovation was certain to break down,—would have led to hopeless confusion, and discredit.

It was a frequent and sometimes a bitter inquiry to the Postmaster from people who thought their mail was not coming rapidly enough: "Why don't you take carriers from the burnt district and put them out where the houses are still standing?" It was always evident to everybody working in the San Francisco Post Office in the days succeeding the fire why this was not done.

It soon became necessary to divide delivery districts and change boundaries, and otherwise alter the postal map of the City, and each change meant new latitude for error on the part of the clerks, and increased labor and study to maintain the distribution.

In the Registry Division the problems of delivering registered mail under the system of receipts prescribed by the Department became almost insurmountable, and the increase in the registers caused by persons sending letters to lost friends in the hope of thereby finding them grew so fast that the clerks could not keep up with it.

Day by day there poured in upon the Postmaster frantic letters of inquiry. First these were from nearby towns, and then from farther away, until within a week they were coming, it seemed, from all over the world. Some of them were from mothers and fathers in search of children; some were from children in search of parents; from relatives; from friends; from mere acquaintances; some evidently from mere curiosity seekers; but all attested the utter lack of any avenue of information outside of the postal service. These inquiries were handled by clerks detailed especially for the purpose. Where the tone of the letter was sincere, and it was possible to give the information without interfering with the already over-wrought Departments of the office, this was done despite regulations that declare no information shall be given by the Post Office regarding addresses. Inquiries as to the burning of certain houses, or numbers on streets, or hotels, could easily be answered; inquiries for prominent firms and prominent people were also easily answered, but more asking for obscure parties or for the safety of unknown people, and some even for people named only by their first names, presented an impossible amount of work at that time, and so a great many of these were turned over to the relief bureaus in the hope that through the relief registers some of the people sought might be found.

Then began to follow letters from the newspapers and magazines offering to submit galley lists to be corrected; asking if certain subscribers were still receiving mail at their old addresses and submitting typewritten sheets with names, and inquiries as to how soon second class matter would start moving again.

For the time being second class matter was put aside to wait. For the few days first succeeding April 18 letter mail, stamped or unstamped, was given the right of way. It was assumed that letters and not papers were what the people wanted, and all efforts were bent toward dispatching and delivering the letters that came and went. When finally there was time to turn attention to the mass of second, third and fourth class matter that waited handling, the amount that had accumulated was appalling. At one time the number of sacks awaiting distribution went well into the thousands. When this was finally attacked, it was first picked over for the sacks of third and fourth class matter so that catalogues, blank forms, stationery and hundred other things that were being sent into the city, for the use of the business men in their efforts to re-establish themselves, might be gotten together, sent out to the stations and delivered.

Before this was all done, it was necessary for the Postmaster to issue an order putting every clerk in the service on a twelve-hour day, taking Sundays away from carriers, working them overtime in violation of the law, which says they shall not work more than eight hours.

Everybody worked at fullest tension and without any unwillingness. The work was well done, and congestion was relieved sooner than it sometimes takes to dispose of the accumulations attendant on the Christmas rush of business.

Stamps were placed on sale at the different stations on April 20, as soon as communication with the main office was established; but, for many days after, the unstamped letters continued to pour in. There was no guarantee as to how these letters would fare in the hands of other post offices, nor was there any warrant or law for handling them in San Francisco, so notices were placed at all mail drops warning the people that letters unstamped would not be handled as paid mail but would be treated as "dead" and sent to the department in Washington. Spiteful and denunciatory letters poured in upon the Postmaster in reply to these notices, all from writers who did not know that not for weeks after the notices were displayed was a single unstamped letter delayed in its course. No man without money and without stamps who trusted to the postal service of San Francisco and dropped his unstamped letter in the mails found he had trusted in vain. Thousands of these unstamped letters, typewritten and bearing well-known return cards, were caught and returned to the firms that sent them, but no unstamped letter that bore evidence of coming from a man who could not afford stamps was delayed in transit.

The Seventh Street Post Office building, which from its beginning also housed federal courts and other government agencies, was severely damaged during the 1989 Loma Prieta earthquake. It was closed for complete renovation and seismic retrofitting and re-opened in January 1997 as the United States Court of Appeals for the Ninth Circuit, handling federal appeals for nine western states. The Postal Service did not return as tenant.

At the time of the earthquake, photographer Arnold Genthe, who had gone to San Francisco in 1895 from his native Germany, was already well-known for his soft-focus portraiture and street scenes. Sadly, all of his work—except for negatives of pre-1906 Chinatown which he had fortuitously stored in a friend's safe—was lost in the fire. Undaunted, he carried his camera around the stricken city and captured images that gained him even greater fame, and assured him a place in American photographic history. In his 1936 autobiography, *As I Remember*, he tells the stories behind some of those pictures.

God poses, photographer exposes

IN THE FRANK COWDERYS' HOME ON MAPLE STREET and later on in the Octavia Street home of Dr. Millicent Cosgrave (whose friendship throughout these years has meant so much to me) I had found a haven of rest. For several weeks I did not concern myself with any thought of the future. I blithely continued to take photographs. Of the pictures I had made during the fire, there are several, I believe, that will be of lasting interest. There is particularly the one scene that I recorded the morning of the first day of the fire (on Sacramento Street, looking toward the Bay) which shows, in a pictorially effective composition, the results of the earthquake, the beginning of the fire and the attitude of the people. On the right is a house, the front of which had collapsed into the street. The occupants are sitting on chairs calmly watching the approach of the fire. Groups of people are standing in the street, motionless, gazing at the clouds of smoke. When the fire crept up close, they would just move up a block. It is hard to believe that such a scene actually occurred in the way the photograph represents it.

Several people upon seeing it have exclaimed, "Oh, is that a still from a Cecil De Mille picture?" To which the answer has been, "No the director of this scene was the Lord himself." A few months ago an interview about my work—I had told the story of that fire picture—appeared in a New York paper with the headline, "His pictures posed by the Lord, says photographer."

The ruins of Nob Hill became a rich field for my camera. All that remained standing of the Towne residence on California Street was the marble columned entrance. The picture I made of it by moonlight brought out its classic beauty. Charles K. Field found the title for it, "Portals of the Past," by which the portico is known today. It has been removed to Golden Gate Park where in a setting of cypresses it remains a noble monument to a noble past. Charles Rollo Peters made a large painting of it, using my photograph, for the Bohemian Club, and for once the photographer was given credit by a painter. Over his signature on the canvas he inscribed, "With thanks to Arnold Genthe."

On the other side of California Street, in front of the Huntington home, were two marble lions, the traditional commonplace guardians of a home of wealth. The terrific heat of the flames had broken off parts of the stone here and there, simplifying and ennobling their form, as a great sculptor might have done. Of another house all that remained were some chimneys and a foreground of steps. Beyond them was devastation with only the lights of the Mission District visible in the distance. It was another scene that had to be taken by moonlight so as to bring out its full significance. I called the picture "Steps That Lead to Nowhere."

Genthe's most famous photograph, taken from Sacramento Street
looking toward the bay.

These columns are all that remained of the Nob Hill residence of Albion N. Towne. Poet Charles K. Field gave them the name "Portals of the Past." This photograph was shot by Arnold Genthe and printed by Ansel Adams.

In this final account from his memoirs, Harry Coleman proves that some photographers will go to any length to get *the* picture. He knew that the most dramatic shots would be from the highest point in the city and, with all downtown skyscrapers reduced to shells, the badly damaged dome of City Hall was the best possibility. In spite of obvious dangers, he and a reporter set about to get the shot. Later, aerial photographs were taken by the Army Signal Corps using cameras attached to balloons and exposed by means of an electric cable held by a photographer on the ground. But Coleman's image gains greater fascination when we realize how he made it.

At the feet of a goddess

Photographic supplies and other strategic materials were coming to me from across the bay and my camera was in full-time service again. I walked through the desolate streets, gouged by dynamite and seared by flames. On the once swanky uplands of Nob Hill, I found Dr. Arnold Genthe, whose photographic skill has become legendary. His camera was focused through the "Portals of the Past," marble pillars which towered alone overlooking the unforgettable picture of the lowland wastes. Only here and there a small wooden structure remained untouched and unscarred in the center of destruction. Iron wheels hung on twisted rails on California Street hills, where the cars had been halted by snapping cables.

I photographed funerals winding through long bread lines, and cinder-smeared congregations singing hallelujahs and seeking solace as they knelt before ashcan pulpits where ministers held street services in the shadows of crumbled altars. Two hundred and fifty thousand refugees, hungry but not depressed, were sleeping in parks and public squares.

With Jack London, I made snaps of the broker, the baker and the candlestick maker, tossing bricks at the point of the same bayonet. All able-bodied men were made to do their bit in clearing the streets. When they finished the section allotted to them, each man was given a card which permitted him to pass through the lines. I made pictures of the exodus at the ferry building, where thousands of evacuees were going away on trains which asked no fares.

The most desirable news picture obtainable was an overhead view of the great expanse of five hundred and fourteen blocks of smoldering wastes. The highest point in the interior of those districts devastated by the fire was the dismantled tower of City Hall. Looking up through a dizzy mass of twisted steel, the climb to the top seemed impossible. Nevertheless, an *Examiner* reporter named Bill Levings and I undertook the job.

The remembrance of that climb still chills me. Chief of Police Dinan had refused flatly to give me a permit to climb to the top of the building because he said it would be like granting me permission to commit suicide and thus he would be an accessory. Only when I had signed a paper releasing both him and the city from all responsibility would he grant my permit, grudgingly.

The most accessible point of entrance to the wreck was at the southwest corner of Larkin and Grove Streets. From there we climbed over piles of crumbled masonry, through a broken window in the main rotunda of the first floor, and after sliding precariously over several tumbled walls, we found parts of a stairway which led to the second floor. Then we scrambled up the iron grating of an elevator shaft. Reaching the third floor, we were somewhat confused to find that the earthquake's twistings had separated the main building from the tower by more than fifty feet. Several crooked girders led across the chasm and we crawled over one of them. Halfway across, I stepped on a loose stone and came perilously close to falling, but the twenty pounds of camera I carried saved me. When I gained the wall on the opposite side, I was so weak that I had to lie flat on top of the two-foot wall and wait until I got over the shakes.

Still pale, and only slightly less giddy, I walked along the broken section of wall in an effort to find the way to the tower, only to discover that there was no connection except by the roof and no way to get there except by crawling back over the same twisted girder again. Nevertheless, Levings and I did it, and from the third floor we broke through the ventilator to the roof. From that point, we smashed the glass and climbed the interlaced iron work of the inner dome to the apex. There a small, spiral stairway leading to the top of the dome had been broken in many places and was scarcely secure enough to hold us, but we kept on going until we reached a small platform, 300 feet above the earth, upon which rested a tottering ball surmounting the dome. We could go no higher. Cooped deep in the ball and crouched at the very feet of the Goddess of Liberty, I held my camera and photographed the ruined city.

The trip down was dangerous, but the experiences we had on the way up helped us and we found it easier. Looking like a pair of chimney sweeps, we reached the ground exactly four hours from the time we started.

Harry Coleman went on to become photographic director of the San Francisco *Examiner* and supervisor of photography, art, and engraving for all Hearst newspapers. He also served as picture editor for International News Photos.

This is the photograph Harry Coleman took from his perch inside the "tottering ball surmounting the dome" of the devastated City Hall (insert). It was published as a supplement to the *Examiner* on June 10, 1906. On the right, Market Street runs toward the bay. The large white building to the right of Market Street is the Post Office at Seventh and Mission streets. The Hall of Records building, lower center, sat beside the City Hall on City Hall Avenue, which can be seen running parallel with Market Street.

A principal cause of rancor between San Franciscans and the troops assigned to the city was the brutal manner in which people were forced from their own buildings, even when there was no immediate danger. Ostensibly, the troops were following orders intended to save the civilians from harm, but the archives contain a number of complaints of incidents in which this was carried to extremes, and with little or no tact. Frank Hittell was an attorney living on Turk Street. His account in *The Argonaut* of March 19 and 26, 1927, accused troops of preventing people from answering calls for help from exhausted and overworked firefighters.

Holding back
the volunteers

LATE ON WEDNESDAY, the first day of the fire, I was at the corner of Gough Street and Golden Gate Avenue when a fireman approached a crowd of men who were being kept back by the military, and asked for volunteers. So thoroughly cowed were the citizens by the soldiers that no one responded, although I knew that every man of them was willing to help. I went forward and was stopped by a soldier who ordered me back. I refused to go back, informed him that I was responding to the call of a fireman for volunteers, and finally, after prolonged argument, was permitted to pass.

The firemen inquired why more men did not come, and I told them that they were willing enough, but were afraid of the soldiers. They urged me to try to get volunteers through the lines. I went back, and was told by a soldier that I could not again pass the lines. I replied that I should not only again pass the lines, but that I should bring twenty men with me as volunteers. The soldier said that he would not permit them to pass. I got the volunteers without difficulty, and returned to the line established by the military when we were stopped.

After a long parley, the firemen coming back and imploring the soldiers to permit these volunteers to pass, we were finally permitted to do so. At this time, an inconsiderable number of firemen were fighting this fire.

They had, they told me, been at work since one o'clock in the morning, having been called out on the "cannery fire" in the vicinity of Telegraph Hill, which preceded the earthquake. Without the assistance of these volunteers which, as time passed, augmented in numbers, despite the resistance of the military, these exhausted firemen could never have stopped the westward advance of the flames from Gough and Golden Gate, and the Western Addition would have been destroyed by fire. As it was, the citizens turned the fire back to the east. The fire was effectually stopped. Only by resistance to the military authorities was this result achieved.

On Thursday afternoon persons to me unknown set fire to the east side of Van Ness Avenue for the purpose of preventing the fire from crossing the avenue to the west. At this time all south of Turk Street had been burned and the wind was from the northwest. Instead of setting fire to the buildings on the east side of Van Ness near Turk, and permitting the fire to work slowly to the north against the wind, some incompetent person set fire to the building far to the north, and the flames came roaring down gaining in volume as they progressed, till soon the structures on the west side of Van Ness began to catch fire. At this time, I was in Lafayette Square. A man came rushing up with a call for volunteers, and I dropped my work and followed him.

As I approached Van Ness Avenue, a soldier rushed up and struck me with the side of his gun barrel, and ordered me back. I was angry at the blow, and refused to go. At this moment, Captain Helms, head of a private detective agency, a man with an air of authority, came up and was ordered back. In vivid language he told the soldier that he would not be stopped, gun or no gun, displayed his own weapon, and a badge he wore, and the soldier, overawed, allowed us to proceed. Other volunteers behind us got through somehow, and so we began to work efficiently on the fire. The military cordon relaxed sufficiently to permit several hundred citizens to act as volunteer firemen. There were at this time two lines of hose on Van Ness Avenue, and two engines, one of which was manned by a donkey-engine engineer. I believe that there were only two or three firemen: before the fire was extinguished, there were several hundred citizens at work.

As soon as the fire would catch at any point, the men in great numbers took up the hose bodily and carried it along the block, put out the flames, and then rushed with it to some new danger point. When the [Richard R.] Wallace house, at 799 Van Ness Avenue, later occupied by Tait's Restaurant, caught fire, steam was not up in one of the engines, and the pressure was great enough to throw water only a few feet from the nozzle of the hose. With incredible labor of many men the hose was taken to the top of the house, and hung over the sides. Toward five o'clock Thursday afternoon, the flames on the west side of Van Ness had again been extinguished by the efforts of citizens, despite the hindrances put in their way by the soldiers. No dynamite was used, only a few firemen were present, the military did much to hinder, and yet the fire was put out.

Ten blocks farther north on Van Ness Avenue, the fire raged on through that Thursday night. The narrator here is James Stetson, a 73-year-old widower living at number 1801, on the northwest corner of Clay Street. He was forced at bayonet point from his home, but sneaked back and saved a neighbor's house—and, consequently, the entire block—from burning.

Stetson arrived in San Francisco in 1852 and later became prominently involved with the city's railroad companies. His memoirs, *San Francisco During the Eventful Days of April, 1906: Personal Recollections*, were published privately in 1906 and subsequently re-published in two slightly amended versions. This is an excerpt from the first edition.

The defiant Mr. Stetson

At 3 o'clock [Thursday] the soldiers drove the people north on Van Ness and west up Franklin Street, saying that they were going to dynamite the east side of Van Ness. From my window I watched the movements of the fire-fighters and dynamiters. They first set fire to every house on the east side of Van Ness Avenue between Washington and Bush streets, and by 3:30 nearly every one was on fire. Their method was this: A soldier would, with a vessel like a fruit-dish in his hand, containing some inflammable stuff, enter the house, climb to the second floor, go to the front window, open it, pull down the shade and curtain, and set fire to the contents of his dish. In a short time the shades and curtain would be in a blaze. When the fire started slowly, to give it a draught they would throw bricks and stones up to the windows to break the glass.

From 4 to 4:30 St. Luke's and the Presbyterian churches and all the houses from Bush to Washington were on fire. At about this time they began dynamiting. This was called back-firing, and, as the line of fire was at Polk Street, the idea was to meet the flames and not allow them to cross Van Ness Avenue. The explosions of dynamite were felt fearfully in my house; those within two blocks would jar and shake the house violently, breaking the windows, and at the same time setting off the burglar alarm. As the windows would break it tore the shades and curtains, covered the floor with glass, and cracked the walls. After it was over I found that it had demolished in my house twelve plates and fifty-four sheets of glass, each measuring about thirty by fifty inches.

At 4:45 I was ordered out of my house by the soldiers,—not in a quiet manner, but with an order that there was no mistaking its terms and meaning,—about like this: "Get out of this house!" I replied: "But this is my house and I have a right to stay here if I choose." "Get out d—n quick, and make no talk about it, either!" So a soldier with a bayonet on his gun marched me up Clay Street to Gough amid flames, smoke, and explosions. I stayed at Gough Street for a while, looking down upon my house, expecting every minute to see the flames coming out of it. I watched from Gough Street with much anxiety, and made up my mind that I would see if I could not get back into my house. The heat was so intense that it had driven the guards away from Van Ness Avenue; so, seeing no one near, I quietly slipped down the north side of Washington Street to Franklin.

As no one was around there, I continued to Washington and Van Ness and, putting up my coat-collar and protecting the side of my face with my hat, I ran along Van Ness to my front door and quickly got into the house again at 5:40, being kept out fifty-five minutes. As I had reluctantly ascended Clay Street in charge of the soldier, I held back long enough to see the steeple of the Presbyterian Church fall. When I returned, Mr. Merrill's house had been dynamited, and the two churches, the Bradbury houses, and the Gunn house had shared the same fate.

On getting into my house again, I found the Neustadter house, at the corner of Sacramento and Van Ness, was half-consumed, but it had not set on fire the Spreckels residence, and as at this time Mr. Merrill's house, which had been dynamited the second time, was so demolished, I felt that I could consider that my house had passed the critical time, for I hoped that Mr. Merrill's house in burning would not endanger the west side of Van Ness.

But now a new danger threatened. The range of blocks from the north side of Washington Street to the south side of Jackson were on fire from Hyde Street, and the flames coming toward Van Ness Avenue, with the possibility of crossing. The Spreckels stable on Sacramento and also the houses back of the Neustadter residence were now on fire. This would set fire to the three Gorovan cottages, two other two-story houses, and the dynamited house of Mr. Gunn, all fronting on Clay Street. So I watched from my front window to see Washington and Jackson, and then going to my back window to see the threatened danger from Clay Street. The Wenban residence, at the corner of Jackson and Van Ness, was well on fire at 6:15; at 6:55 it fell in. The Clay Street danger began at about 7:30 P.M. At 8:15 the whole front as here described was blazing and at its full height. My windows were so hot that I could not bear my hand on them. I opened one and felt the woodwork, which was equally hot. I had buckets of water in the front and rear rooms, with an improvised swab, ready to put out any small fire which would be within my reach. I watched the situation for an hour, and as the flames died down a little I had hope, and at 10 P.M. I felt satisfied that it would not cross Van Ness Avenue, and neither would it cross Clay Street.

At this time I ventured out and saw a small flame, about as large as my two hands, just starting on the tower of Mrs. Schwabacher's house, which is next to mine on Clay Street. A very few people were around. I saw James Walton of the Twenty-eighth Coast Artillery, C.C. Jones, of 2176 Fulton Street, and David Miller Ferguson, of Oakland. I said I would give any man ten dollars who would go up and put out that fire. They went into the house with a can of water, climbed the stairs and opened a window, and in a few minutes put it out. Two of the men would accept nothing; the soldier, the next day, accepted ten dollars. Had Mrs. Schwabacher's house gone, all in the block would have gone; the fire would have crossed to the north, up Pacific, Broadway, and Vallejo, and probably over to Fillmore, when very little would have been left of the residence portion of the city.

Now again another danger came. Another tier of blocks, from Leavenworth to Van Ness, between Jackson and Pacific, had taken fire. This was about 10:15 P.M. At 11:15 it had got to Van Ness, and Bothin's house was fully on fire, but although it was entirely consumed, the fire did not cross to the west side of Van Ness. The wind during all the day and evening was steady from the northwest,—not a very strong wind, but it helped protect the west side of Van Ness. At 12 o'clock on the beginning of the 20th I saw smoke coming out of the chimney of the Spreckels mansion. I went out and spoke to a fireman, and he said he had been into the house and that it was full of smoke and on fire. At 1 o'clock the house was on fire in the upper rooms, at 1:30 it was blazing out of the upper windows, and in a short time afterwards was wholly on fire. The fire caught the house from the rear by the blaze from the Gorovan cottages. I felt quite sure that if any one had been on guard inside with a bucket of water the fire could have been put out.

When the Spreckels house was well on fire I knew, from its having an iron frame, hollow tile partitions, and stone outside walls, there would be no danger to my house. As I was quite tired, I told the man Ferguson that I would go into my house and take a nap. He asked me what room I would sleep in, and he promised if they were about to dynamite my house, or any other danger threatened, he would knock on my window to give me warning to get out. I went in and lay down on a lounge in the library and slept until 5 A.M. When I awoke and looked out the flames were pouring from every window of the Spreckels mansion. At 10 A.M. the house was thoroughly burned out.

In the morning I went over to the California Street [Railway Company's] engine-house, and found it in ruins. Beams, pipes, iron columns, tie-rods, car-trucks, bricks, mortar, ashes, and debris of every description filled the place. The engine-room was hot, but I looked into it. It was a sad sight to me, for I had something to do with it from its earliest existence. The form of everything was there, but rods, cranks, beams, and pipes were bent and burned, whether beyond hope of restoration I could not tell. No one was there or on the street, and I came away with uncertain feelings. I had hope, but whether the loss would be total or partial I could not say. A further examination showed much damage—one shaft thirteen inches in diameter was bent out of line one inch; one eight inches in diameter, seven eighths of an inch; some of the large sheaves badly twisted. A new cable coiled on a reel was so badly burned in the portion exposed as to render the whole useless. Brass oilers and fillers on the engine-frames were comparatively uninjured. The tank contained 6,000 gallons of fuel oil, and with its contents was uninjured. The granite blocks on which the engines and drivers rested were badly cracked by the heat, and in some places entirely destroyed. The portions of the cables in use that were in the engine-room were ruined, and on the street were burned off in five different places. The prospect of ever repairing and getting this machinery and appliances in operation again seemed impossible.

Thanks to James Stetson's efforts as president of the California Street Railway Company, the cars were running again within five months. He died in 1909 in the house he fought to save.

[254]

James Stetson lived in this mansion at 1801 Van Ness Avenue, at the
northwest corner of Clay Street.

This excerpt from a letter written by Elmer Enewold gives us a glimpse into what it was like being part of the National Guard patrolling the city's streets—and a rare confession to having shot at a civilian. Interestingly, it also indicates that even he, a guardsman, believed that martial law was in effect. Enewold wrote the letter to his father, Lawrence Enewold, in Omaha, and dated it "Frisco May 3 1906." The original is in the California Historical Society archives.

A letter from a National Guardsman

I REPORTED AT THE ARMORY to see what was doing. They kept us down there until about 4 P.M. that afternoon when 60 of us were ordered out to the Broadway Street jail to guard that. We marched down Geary to Market to Montgomery and up Montgomery. Just as we turned off Market to Montgomery the Palace and Grand Hotel took fire and in a few minutes both big structures were ablaze, and it was an awe inspiring thing to behold. After proceeding up Montgomery to Clay Street fire broke out on both sides of Montgomery for two solid blocks. We were ordered into the middle of the street and went at the double quick through that blazing hell of flying glass and bricks lickety-cut. I tell you it was the nearest hell I ever hope to be.

In a short time we reached the jail, which I suppose you know is in the Tenderloin District and about the worst part of town. They kept us busy breaking into saloons and putting the liquors into the streets, and keeping the Italians in order. The fire was gaining steadily now as the water mains had broken and no water was obtainable. The brave firemen were retreating step by step, block by block, doing their best to beat back the demon that was eating up our beautiful and dearly beloved Frisco, but to no use.

· · ·

The fire had now come up and taken hold of the Hall of Justice. In a few minutes it was a blazing pile, the flames reaching high in the air. We were beginning to get anxious now as there remained only a few blocks between us and the fire. My thoughts were of the folks at home. I had not seen them since early that morning. I wondered if the fire had reached them or how they were and if they were also fleeing before the fire. I picked up a piece of paper lying in the gutter and scribbled a few lines to the folks letting them know I was OK and still alive and kicking. This was done by the glare of the fire. I got a man to deliver it on his way out there to his folks. I found out later that Mother had received it OK and it relieved her mind a great deal.

It was about 3 A.M. (the 19th) when the fire had come up within a block of the jail. The officials were getting anxious now and were going to turn all the prisoners loose, but our Captain volunteered to take them out and deliver them to the Military Authorities at Fort Mason. There were about 300 of them against us 60 boys. All the murderers and hard cases were hand-cuffed to a long chain so they were safe from escape. The others were lined up between us fellows. We were 30 on each side. The order was given to load, fix bayonets and to shoot to kill in case anyone of the prisoners attempted to break the line. Then our long march began along the northern part of the city to Fort Mason which was reached about 7 A.M. Here we turned the prisoners over to the Military Officers and not waiting for breakfast started back to town.

Passing Jackson and Van Ness I fell out of line and ran down to the house to see the folks. Grandpa Kaiser, Jergenson and Warming were there. They told me that Ma and the girls had gone to Troiels. This relieved me a great deal. Knowing that they at least were safe, I again joined my company and we started down town.

[The guardsmen were then assigned to Jefferson Park to help with the distribution of food and coffee supplies to about 3,000 refugees gathered there.]

During that terrible night no one slept—it was impossible [with] the heat and terror. About 4 A.M. half of our Battalion were ordered on out to Golden Gate Park to take care of the people lying out there in tents made of sheets, blankets or carpet, in fact anything that would shelter them from the cold and fog that you know comes over the city in the evening. As we swung into line down the streets cheer after cheer greeted us from the people lined up on both sides of the streets showing that our work had at least been appreciated, and it made us boys feel pretty good because the National Guard never had a very good name before. It was rather an inspiring sight with marching troops and the glare of the fast approaching fire. But then again it reminded one of the retreat from a ruined city.

After a long and tiresome march we at last reached the Park. Being too tired to pitch our little tents that we carry with us, we laid down on the grass and were all soon asleep. The next day we were kept busy going into grocery stores and taking on the goods we could lay our hands on, these being given to the people that were quartered in the Park. And by the way you should see our beautiful Park now, the road beds all cut up by heavy teams and the lawns tramped down by hundreds of feet.

The next night, I think it was Saturday evening, it started to rain like the dickens and you don't know how sorry I felt for the poor people laying, some with only a bed sheet over them. But when morning came the sun broke out bright and clear and things were soon dried out.

You said in your last letter to the folks that you hoped I had not shot anyone. Well in this line I have had only one experience. One evening during guard duty over the ruins at the end of 3rd Street, I saw a man about a quarter of a block away from me bending over something on the ground. I yelled at him to get out, but he paid no attention to me, so I up and fired at him. I missed of course, but the shot must of scared him, for he started to run. I was just getting ready to shoot again, when a shot was fired from across the street and the fellow toppled over. This was fired by a *regular* who had seen him run after my shot was fired. When the two of us reached the fallen man we found he had been shot through the neck and was stone dead. It proved to be a negro. An officer came along and ordered us to throw the body into the still burning ruins, so in it went. We went back to see what he was after and found a body of a man half buried under a heap of bricks. This we dug out and laid over the some 20 or more that had been killed in the collapse of a lodging house. This was my only experience in the way of shooting. But I have had several others that will never be forgotten in my life time.

One morning while on guard in the pan-handle of the Park I saw a crowd of people standing around a bakery wagon. On going down to see if I could not get a pie or something myself I found that the driver was asking 50¢ for a loaf of bread. Of course this was outrageous and the poor people could never afford a price like this, although one or two had bought being they wanted it so bad. But I knew that the majority would have to go without so I leveled my gun at the driver and told the people to line up and get a loaf apiece. Well Pa we cleaned that wagon out in a couple of minutes and the crowd thought I was just OK.

When all the bread was gone I told the fellow to get up on his wagon and get out of the Park as soon as he could otherwise I would make things pretty hard for him. He was awful mad as you can imagine but he took my bluff and got out. This was the first time I had ever turned highwayman and I really had no authority to do what I did. But the people were in want and the man was trying to rob them, so I had to think quickly before he got away and being that *Martial Law* controlled the city I took the chance of bluffing the baker and won out. The people got all he had for nothing just because he tried to rob them first, and in my heart I think I did right.

Of course we are having little occurrences every day but they don't amount to much. I only did my best for the sufferers around me, hoping all the time that somebody was taking as good care of my own dear ones who I had not seen since early morning the first day of the earthquake. A whole week had gone by now and I had not even heard from them.

The letter goes on to say that after a week Enewold finally had a day off, and he found his folks staying with another family. Friends had helped them salvage some furniture before their house burned down. He used his authority as a National Guardsman to commandeer first an express wagon and then an automobile to help his mother move into a house that had been deserted. However, the owner of the house returned, and the family had to move again, this time into one room at a friend's house.

From Guard Sam.

San Francisco under Martial Law, April 18, 1906.
Copyrighted, 1906, by the Rieder-Cardinell Co., Los Angeles and Oakland

It so happened that on the morning of April 18 the cadet corps of the University of California, Berkeley, was having its annual inspection and display of maneuvers and competitive drill. Rumors spread that the cadets might be called to active duty in San Francisco, and regimental ranks swelled beyond full quota as former cadets showed up, eager to participate. The decision to go was finally made, and cadets—aware that they would have to be self-sufficient—rushed local stores for cheese, crackers, and canned foods, and dashed home to get their own blankets. Plans to transport 600 officers, cadets and other personnel across the bay took a few hours, and it was not until late that night that they finally left Berkeley.

Corporal Irvine Pressley Aten (class of 1908) was one of those cadets. His account appeared in *The Argonaut* on March 26, 1927, and is excerpted here. He and his fellow cadets landed at the San Francisco Ferry Building at 11 o'clock on Wednesday night and were marched to the corner of Golden Gate Avenue and Divisadero Street. The cadets remained in San Francisco for two nights and two days performing regular guard duty. In those days, many grocery stores had a bar in the rear. These were referred to as "grocery saloons."

This photograph appeared in *Blue and Gold*, the university year book for 1908.

The shooting of Cadet Aten

AFTER STATIONING THE SENTRIES we corporals rolled up in our blankets to catch some sleep; but owing to the cold, the hard ground, and the frequent calls of the guard we got none. As our company (D Company, Captain Elliott) was short of privates I walked a post from 4 o'clock to 8 o'clock a.m., during which time nothing unusual happened. At daybreak, however, screaming autos came rushing by, and I had to slow them down at the crossing. In the gutter on Divisadero Street I found two dollars in nickels and dimes. These I gave to an old woman who told me that bread had gone up to $1 a loaf.

At 8 o'clock I was relieved and our detachment went off duty until noon. I tried to sleep for an hour, and then proposed to Robinson, my college room-mate, who also belonged to D Company, that we walk down Golden Gate Avenue to the fire which was then raging about twelve or fifteen blocks below us to the eastward.

Presently we arrived at the corner of Eddy and Polk streets, where we met two Berkeley men, Hillman and Volmer, who were the first two college men other than Cadets that we had encountered thus far.

The fire was then burning fiercely at the lower end of the block on Eddy Street, and a regular soldier stationed about the middle of the block was having a hard time of it trying to hold back citizens that wanted to get into their homes to remove their valuables. He was cursing and threatening them and even pointing his gun at some of them so as to frighten them away.

When he saw us he beckoned and hailed us, asked who we were, and then requested us to enter and clear out the grocery saloon on the

[263]

corner of Polk and Eddy streets, because the soldiers on the other side of the block had already started dynamiting the buildings.

Robinson and I were without our rifles and were hesitant about going in with only our belts and bayonets. Just then, however, two more of our fellows came along. Frank Kleaberger, of Class 1908, and Austin Burton, of Class 1909. They were in uniform and carried their revolvers. The regular then again asked us to clear out the saloon, and being thus reinforced by Kleaberger and Burton, the four of us pushed our way into the place.

It would be hard to describe the howling, drunken, fighting mob we encountered there, and we had literally to push our way through them. Kleaberger jumped behind the bar, pulled out his gun, and prevented any more men from getting liquor, while Robinson, Burton and myself began hustling out the men that were drinking, but not paying much attention to the women and children that were scrambling for and carrying out the groceries.

We had just got the crowd nicely moving when I heard a rifle shot outside and pushed my way through the crush to learn the cause. As I reached the doorway, ongling* my way through the crowd, I caught a glimpse of a soldier standing on the sidewalk on the Eddy Street side of the entrance. At the same instant another soldier on the Polk Street side fired and I was hit.

Several more shots were fired, but went over the heads of the crowd into the ceiling while the place rapidly cleared. There was no excuse whatever for this shooting. We Cadets were clearing the store without having to resort to strong measures. No material resistance was being offered, and a random shot into such a crowd of men, women and children could not be justified. It may be that the soldier that did the shooting was drunk. It may be that he was simply too excited, too inexperienced. Anyhow I was shot, and people said that a civilian was also hit. But of that I know nothing definite.

Kleaberger said he saw the soldier afterward standing near the doorway of the saloon, carrying his gun, muzzle down, and shaking like a leaf. Remarks I subsequently overheard in the hospital incline me to the belief that the man was drunk.

* Clawing.

When hit, I did not at first realize what had happened. My left foot felt numb and my left leg contracted spasmodically as if a bomb had exploded near my foot. My weight must have been on my right leg because I did not go down, but hopped out into the street where the boys found me and helped me to a cot on the other side. My thigh bone had been shattered just below the hip joint.

One of the soldiers that had come down the street with this shooting party helped to carry me up to Jefferson Square, whence later I was taken to the Presidio Hospital. But none of us thought of noting his regimental or other insignia, so nobody seems ever to have found out who did the shooting.

The relief doctor at Jefferson Square found that the bullet had broken the thigh bone just below the joint. He pulled a picket off the fence and made a splint. Meanwhile the boys had impressed the services of an express wagon and I was taken to the Lane Hospital. There they found that the water supply had just given out; so they took me to the Presidio Hospital where we arrived about 12:30 midday.

Here the doctor gave me some of the most excruciating moments I ever endured, after which I knew definitely where my leg had been broken. I was taken to the surgical ward, which was already filled to overflowing. It held only forty-four beds, and I was patient No. 54.

But a kind-hearted soldier who was convalescing surrendered his bed to me. It was in the center of the ward, and I occupied that bed all the time I was in the hospital.

Several deaths occurred during the first forty-eight hours, by which time the ward was adjusted to its proper capacity. Fire Chief Sullivan was among those who died while I was there. The patients that died were nearly all persons that had been hurt in the earthquake.

Three patients suffering from gunshot wounds inflicted by soldiers were received in the ward while I was there. One of these was a Chinaman who had been a prisoner and tried to escape. He was shot through the head and subsequently died from the wound. Another was a Japanese that ran away when a soldier challenged him, and was shot through the hand, the head and the shoulder. He recovered. The third was myself. There were seven hundred patients in the place, and as far as I could learn, we three were the only ones shot by the military. There was a report that a patient in the women's surgical ward had been hit by a stray bullet. But this I did not verify. Two cases of accidental shooting were brought in; but these had absolutely nothing to do with the policing of the city by the soldiers.

Naturally enough, the hospital was overstrained by the pressure of the first few days, the congestion of patients and lack of nurses, food and water. I went in at noon on Thursday, and did not get a bath until the following Monday morning. During that period my only nourishment was liquor and raw eggs. As a matter of fact I did not want any food, but there were others that did want it. By Monday, however, everything was ship-shape again, and the hospital was running on lines of military precision.

Saving my leg was a serious question for some days. On Saturday Dr. Reinhardt was at the hospital. I was given chloroform and my leg was fixed with a brick extension. This was made of three bricks, a rope and a pulley, and was so arranged that the weight would stretch my leg and keep it at its proper length. At the end of the week Dr. Huntington assured me that I would get through in good shape. He took an x-ray that showed the bone badly shattered for a length of three inches, with several particles shot into the muscles. The bullet had broken into three pieces. These had lodged on different sides of the bone. They were not removed, and remain as my souvenirs of the San Francisco fire.

For nearly two weeks following the earthquake no visitors were allowed at the hospital. On Thursday and Friday night we could hear the blasting of dynamite through the city and see the glare in the sky. One night the hospital laundry burned, and it was due only to a favorable wind that the whole hospital was not destroyed. No other incident disturbed the regular monotony of hospital life, and up to June 15 the patients were charged nothing for room, board or treatment. By June 15 all the civilian patients that could be moved had been taken away, while those that were obliged to remain were charged only the regular forty cents a day that is deducted from a soldier's pay while he is in the hospital. I was fit to be driven home to Alameda on June 25. Therefore my total bill with the hospital was four dollars. I was on crutches until August 15, just four months from the day of the accident.

This tender scene was captured by J.B. Monaco as his wife, Katherine, and son, Dante, rested on Telegraph Hill overlooking the ruins of the Italian quarter in North Beach where the family lived. Monaco managed to save their home by dousing the flames with sheets soaked in water, but his portrait studio on Columbus Avenue (then named Montgomery Avenue) at Pacific Street was completely gutted by fire.

This letter from the California Historical Society archives is one of many there and in research depositories elsewhere for which the writer's full identity is not known. The letter is addressed to "My dear Elise" and signed "Your loving sister Catherine," and is dated April 22, 1906, from 720 Cole Street, San Francisco. A search of the 1910 census reveals that Henry Golcher and his wife lived at that address with their three children: Catherine, Elise, and Bennie. We can also determine that Catherine was 17 in 1906, her sister was 15, and her brother 9. According to the 1905 city directory, the father was vice-president of Clabrough, Golcher & Co., selling guns, ammunition, and sporting goods at 538 Market Street. The census gives the sister's (and mother's) name as "Elsie" rather than "Elise."

"*My dear Elise . . .*"

Before you read this letter through you will surely be saying, Gee, I wish I were there. But we're glad you aren't. Little did we ever expect to see Aline, Mr. Spotorno, and me in line waiting for free food to be given out. Not that we need it, personally, but we never can tell when somebody that we know will apply to us for shelter and so we take all the food that we get, but we have quite a lot of provisions. We got corned beef, a can of sardines and a can of peaches and one of tomatoes and et cetera over at the free food place. All this is fixed up at the Y.M.H.A. There's a narrow passageway through which you go in single file. There you go along in the Gym and people behind a fence deal out things to you and you pass out the next door. You can have all the milk you want, and good milk, too. This we get from behind the fence of the park on Stanyon Street between Waller and Haight. This morning Aline and I got the pink and blue pitcher full. We made biscuits and the oven wasn't quite hot enough and we had a job getting them baked.

You'd die laughing to see the way we cook. Of course, all the chimneys are on the dickey, and so we all have our stoves (they are mostly all laundry stoves) *out on the edge of the street*. Talk about fun. Jiminy, it's a picnic. Spotorno first started it. They put out a small stove, one of those kind that have only two lids, bedroom stoves, you know. Then Eichbaums, Briggs, Schaffers, Joosts, Tanners, Aunt Florence, Maguires, Watsons and everybody have them out on the gutter.

We all divide up our stock of provisions. And all our neighbors are simply lovely to each other. Mr. Watson agitated the Sanitary and

Street Sweeping conditions and of course [they] made him chairman. You ought to have seen him sweeping streets today. And I swear I never saw the streets so clean before. All the ash barrels were emptied and taken over to some place and burnt. Spotorno had some chickens left in their cold storage place and they got a few out here. They got six and they gave us two. We gave one to Uncle Bill. Mr. Wanamaker gave us some elegant fillet of beef so we sent some to Aunt Florence and a good plate full to Sports.

I have to abbreviate everything because I have so much to write and I simply can't compose myself.

All lights are forbidden to be lit after seven, but it's eight now and I'm writing with a candle in the kitchen. Excuse me, but I mean by the light of a candle. If the soldiers should see a light in a house any place, they come and order them out immediately.

It's about time that I got down to my story. But you know how fearfully verbose I am anyway. I'm wondering how many Haywards people will read this letter. It won't last long if you don't typewrite it. Of course, we don't know how exaggerated the stories are that you hear, so Ma says she supposes you'll be showing this letter to everybody. I'm awfelly shamed of it but this is Della's tablet I'm using. Sunday, I couldn't buy even a 5-cent tablet because the stores have been forbidden by the soldiers to sell *anything*. All the saloons are boarded up. Good for Mr. J. He hasn't been drunk since Wednesday.

At first I wasn't frightened a bit but when I heard things start to crash I thought it was time to get up. Just as I got the door open, the chimney crashed in my room. What didn't land in my room went into Della's and a few bricks stayed up in the attic. Oh, Elise, the muss in my room is inconceivable.

The bookcase fell over and the bricks by the tons came in on everything. Of course, the back is all broken. The part with the mirror is all smashed off. The white table and other little one were smashed flat. The whole movable part of the mirror was broken out and bricks, plaster, dust, flats, timbers and everything landed all over the bureau. Dicket's cage was crushed down in the corner by the closet door, but he was still alive. I had to climb over a pile of bricks, 4 or 5 feet high in my bare feet to get to my clothes. Della's room was awful too. The wash basin and pictures were smashed to smithereens and plaster and dirt all over everything. It's a lucky thing that we moved our beds around because one of those heavy rafters came right down and landed where my bed was and all the bricks (mostly all) would have landed on my bed, and I'd have passed to the "Happy Hunting Grounds." Maybe you'll all think that I treat things pretty lightly but we are all the same. We josh each other to pieces.

Sports have a young fellow from the market (a keen kid) staying with them to help out. He is just lovely to Mrs. S. Last night, Saturday, he washed the dishes.

Of course the store's gone. My Father's. It was the last thing to go in that lower part of Market Street. Everything burnt around it, but still it stood. It burnt at 10:30 P.M. Uncle Will stayed until two policemen dragged him away. He was the only man down in the town there. He sneaked back but when he heard the cartridges begin to go, he started home. He got home after one o'clock. Coming out Market Street, he had to ask a man where Haight Street is. You'd never know a street, one from the other, if you were over. It's simply fierce.

All the Bevans speak to me except Dot. Aline says her diamond is a peachy one, and even larger than my pearl ring. She wears it on her engagement finger and things seem pretty serious. He comes over or she goes out. He has brought over quite a few provisions.

MONDAY:

But the funniest thing of all! An immense number of soldiers are encamped in all those three lots at Haight and Cole. This morning I went down for milk at a lot next door to the first white house on the East side of S. Cole Street. There were bugles blowing and all the soldiers getting their breakfast dealt out to them. But, strange to say, I have not seen a single old soldier. They're all young kids and as thick as mush all round.

All lights have to be out by seven. Some women have been shot down for disobeying. Everybody has to be off the streets by nine. The other day Mr. Rosenstein nearly got shot down by a soldier because he wasn't in a hurry to put out his stove when he was told to. This had to be done on account of a high wind.

Everybody talks to everybody else. I've added hundreds to my acquaintance without introductions. Everybody is using Benned's coaster. George Smith's mother's house was ruined by the earthquake and the Smith boys carried loads up to Grant Smith's house up on Ashbury. They took a stove up from the house across the street, Pete's house, upon it. Then the whole neighborhood was in hysterics at Mr. Varney, the father, you know. He coasted all the way down the Frederick Hill from Ashbury, full speed. Then he came down Cole Street, riding on his knee just like the kids. Everybody was roaring.

Friday or Saturday morning, Paul passed here driving one of his father's dirt wagons covered with supplies, grain, etc., from the hill. He stopped about in front of Eichelbaums and Ma saw him and told me. Of course, I flew out. I had on my gray skirt, a mussy white waist with my collar turned in, and my sleeves way up above my elbows. But I didn't care (and I also had on an old apron). He said that the Third Church (Congregational) could have been saved if they had had water.

The Hutchinsons were burnt out, and are out in the Averills' house, although the A's weren't home when they came. They broke down the back door and took possession. They were a funny looking sight when they left their house with their luggage, tied on bicycles and Lock and three or four dogs trudging along behind. (Lock was Chinese servant.)

Of course, all the traveling is done "shanks mare", unless a person gets an automobile or a rig. Our "rig" is one of Sports' small covered delivery wagons.

Girls High School was all shaken to pieces and has to be blown up. Lowell has been condemned. Mission was burned and Poly went down flat between the earthquakes and the rest was finished by the fire. Crocker School has been converted into a place for such as Mrs. Sport and we'll probably take her down there. Grandma [Catherine] Golcher has withstood the fright wonderfully. She thought "her poor heart would burst out of her for good." At first they could get no answer from her but just as Charlie was going to break down the door, she answered.

We got the shock at 15 minutes past five. All the neighbors were out and ever since nearly every body is up and out about six. That part is lots of fun. Wed., Thurs. and Friday nights our neighborhood was almost as light as day. The sky was all bright pink and we expected to flee to the hills. The fire was closing in on us on both sides and Ma and I had everything out on sheets, in pillow cases, and I packed all the silver and cut glass and some china in the clothes hamper. We expected it positively. But we've had it all to put back. Oh, you can't imagine the condition of those things ... everything thrown together. It was awful.

Then all the bricks had to be taken down from the upstairs rooms. Pa got up on the roof and pushed some of Miss Bush's chimney (the remainder) down into the alley ... of course ours in the front was also down, and cleaned all that up. All the dishes were unpacked and put back in the china closet and on the shelf. All our vases and almost all our blue dishes and a great number of the fine ones and pink ones are broken. The vase Pa won with the red glass, the silver one and the little copper one are the only things left besides the brass and bronze things.

All the pictures, nearly, on our walls were knocked down by the earthquake and stripped, and smashed and torn to pieces, by the tons of bricks. The walls just stripped. All the Sports' nice things were broken and their big buffet that takes four men to move, (you know that big one in the upstairs dining room) well, that was moved out 3 or 4 feet. Nobody has anything left, but our house suffered the most from fallen chimneys.

Rita and Mr. Stoupe stayed at the California Hotel that night, of course, after the wedding. Their chimney landed on her bed, all over her beautiful wedding dress and everything. All her presents were broken. If she'd slept home that night she'd have been killed. They had an awfully jolly time. I sat up here with opera glasses and watched the people come to the reception. We didn't go at all.

All our house is straightened up and that's the reason why I haven't written before. I simply couldn't get the time and there was so much to say. I write a little every chance I get and it's taken me since Saturday to write this. This morning ... MONDAY ... Della and I went after food and coming back along Page Street between Shrader and Cole, one of the soldiers came down from his tent and gave me a large tin box. On opening which I found it contained a whole lot of sandwiches. Swell ones, too, made with thin bread. Most of the sandwiches we see are about two inches thick and made for the men who are forced to dig trenches. All the men that pass are grabbed by the soldiers and forced to go to work. So Pa and Mr. Sport are always very busy fixing bricks, sweeping streets and taking our ash barrels out. (Regular scavengers.) All the men are working this way.

Now that we are all fixed up I'm going to help Aline get her house fixed, and when Mrs. Sport is gone, stay in there over nights. I think I will close now, as you must be simply crazy to get a letter and you know I can write all day if I want to, so I will close now, with love to all, and hoping you are all safe. We first got Grandpa's letter a little while ago, but we haven't seen yours.

Alfred, from the store, is out here, waiting for the terrible rain to let up. I'm dying to volunteer to the Red Cross Service but although Mama doesn't object, Papa would be crazy if I asked him.

Your loving sister,
Catherine

The real reason for this letter being this way is that the ink is all disappeared and they won't take very heavy letters. We don't need Postage Stamps over here now. Letters go every place free of charge. Bronson Tufts, I saw on guard over at Shrader and Page. He had a uniform on and when I saw him I burst out laughing. He saw the joke too. The Tufts spent the first night up in the hills. We saw them the next morning coming back with blankets, etc. They looked awfully downcast. If we had known it, Papa would have asked them into our house.

Ed Eichbaum belongs to the National Guard and of course is out on duty in his uniform. He looked perfectly handsome. Maybe Bronson Tufts got out through the Starr King Cadets. The Saunders, Wallace Briggs and the Eichbaums have skipped the country. All rates are free now.

> The above has been taken from a typescript of the letter. Without the original to compare it with, there can be no way of knowing whether passages were edited out or if the writer included the elipses.
>
> The last remark refers to the fact that for several days after the earthquake fares were not required on ferries and trains leaving San Francisco.
>
> Far from being condemned, as Catherine thought, Lowell High School was only minimally damaged by the quake and— located on Sutter Street between Gough and Octavia—was beyond the reach of fire. For a while the building served as the city's police headquarters, with classrooms converted into courthouses, judges' offices, and prison cells.

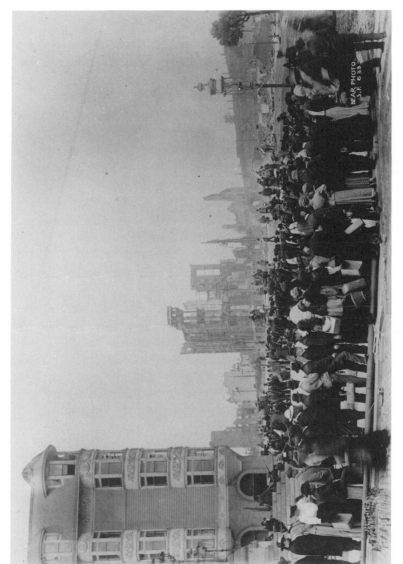

Breadline stretching around the front steps (left) of St. Mary's Cathedral on Van Ness Avenue between Geary and O'Farrell streets.

On May 12, 1906, less than a month after the earthquake, *The Argonaut* published the following excerpts from pieces written by local schoolchildren.

As told by the children

And the people ran to the banks and tried to get their money but they couldn't get it out and the Call building is still standing.

The Palace Hotel was blowed up with dinnimight.

The tides came together and then they broke and many people were cild. Bricks fell on the people also and killed them and then they put the fire out and said San Francisco is going to be larger than it ever was.

The people were aloud to take a bath and eat vegetables.

San Francisco is nothing but a sematery now. When a sick lady in the hospital felt the earthquake she jumped from a six story building and she met death.

The fire burned Hales store but a little place in front which said, "Your credit is good."

A big water main broke and drowned all the people in it.

They said San Fras. was going to be destroyed and so a volcano blew up and cover the city with lather.

They dinamited everybody's house up and we had another big one last night.

Big balls of fire shot out of the ground and started fires all over.

San Francisco was destructed by fire. There was no water because the water front burned first.

People were lined up for bread and water, some being killed by the earthquake.

The fire burned so hard that people came to Napa to live.

The Chronicle building is all hurt in the inside and people are cooking on the outside waiting for their chimneys to be inspected.

They are working hard to get the ruins finished.

There are 400 babies born in San Francisco since the earthquake and people all over the world are making baby clothes.

Children join the line for drinking water at one of the relief camps set up by the army.

For some people, merely having experienced the earthquake and its aftermath was a source of pride bordering on haughtiness. This has been hinted at in some of the accounts in this volume, but the writer of the next piece makes no attempt to conceal these feelings. Rather, she elaborates on the theme, expressing a sentiment probably felt by many but rarely written for publication.

Pauline Jacobson was a staff writer on the San Francisco *Bulletin* and became a favorite for her insightful interviews of contemporary personalities. Later she wrote a series of vignettes about the city's historical characters, some of which were published after her death in a book entitled *City of the Golden 'Fifties*.

This particular piece appeared in the *Bulletin* on Sunday, April 29, 1906, under the heading "How it Feels to be a Refugee and Have Nothing in the World, by Pauline Jacobson, Who is One of Them."

"The most sociable time"

OH, THE JOY OF BEING A TRAMP! When next some irresponsible Weary Willie holds me up for a square meal I shall not feel it my bounden duty to instill into him a wholesome regard for hard work and dull respectability. To have nothing but the clothes on one's back and a hand satchel containing a dozen pocket handkerchiefs, one shirt waist and a linen mesh!

"I missed it all," sighed one man enviously. "Had I your experience I would give $1,000 for it."

Said another: "I've lost everything save what I have on, but it's been worth it all, every cent of it, even the loss of my job."

"Anyhow," retorted one woman consolingly, "if I hadn't the luck to be in the thick of it, I can boast of one refugee," and she bestowed upon her solitary guest the proud possessive look of some prize cow, while the refugee beamed back a benign condescension.

It is truly remarkable the airs that some of these refugees take unto themselves these days. It is no use trying to get ahead, especially of those favored of fortune who escaped in nothing but a dressing gown and slippers. Talk about the earthquake being a common leveler. It is nothing of the sort. It has only turned things upside down. There is as much class distinction as ever, but now-a-days it's your Weary Willie who's on top. It is he who is your mushroom aristocracy, while the under dog is the man so poverty stricken as to know no other experience save the luxurious repose in a brass bedstead on a white curled hair mattress.

And from all this charm of irresponsibility how loath is one to break away. Yesterday I went to Oakland—what a rushing metropolis is this one-time quiet bedroom of San Francisco? I went there with the purpose of laying in a stock of face creams and soap and dresses, and then I weakened. More of this world's goods would mean a trunk, a trunk would imply an expressman, and an expressman a return to at least a partial degree of the old permanency. To go a-gypsying, a foot free nomad yet a day longer. And I slipped my money back into my purse. All too soon would return the halo encircling exclusiveness. All too short would be this reign of inclusiveness. There was plenty of time for petty possessions, plenty of time for the supercilious snubbing of the man or woman not clad according to the latest canons of the fashionable dressmaker or tailor. In the meanwhile how nice to feel no one would take it sadly amiss were you to embrace the scavenger man in an excess of joy at seeing him among the living, or walk the main street with the Chinese cook.

Have you noticed with your merest acquaintance of ten days back how you wring his hand when you encounter him these days, how you hang on to it like grim death as if he were some dearly beloved relative you were afraid the bowels of the earth will swallow up again. It is like a glad gay good holiday—all this reunioning. It is like one vast afternoon tea; like a fete day or a convention. Some take it that we are such "brave, brave women," such "strong, strong men," this holiday mood of ours, this prevalent jocular, chipper strain. Bah! That's spreadeagle, yellow journalist rot! The strain of the woof has not come as yet. To talk of bravery is previous. Wait till this novelty has worn off, this novelty of having been spilled out on the world like so many rats caught in a hole, like so many insignificant ants on the face of the earth, petted objects of charity and of kindness, the focal point of all the world. Wait till we have settled back into the old trying grooves of traditional civilization with the added trying struggles inherited of earthquake and of fire. It is then time to bring out one's adjectives of bravery and of courage. It is not the keynote of the situation now. The chipper mood is not owing to bravery. It is owing in part to the inevitable, nervous reaction—mainly—well—

I remember way back the morning of the earthquake—doesn't it seem ages and ages ago since some vast subterranean force shook and tore this dearly beloved old sea coast of ours with as little abandon as a snarling terrier shaking its prey preparatory to crushing it? I remember back that morning, how one yellow journalist sat over his typewriter, his head buried in his hands helpless for a word to describe it all for the Eastern papers. "I have used 'the greatest disaster' so often," he exclaimed despairingly. "It won't do now. How would you put it?" he finally appealed to me.

"Twenty eight seconds of awful interrogation and then the most sociable time I've ever had in my life."

I still stand by that summing up of that morning, a time long before things were at their worst, long before a red yellow-licking, leaping devil-flame had started on its mad revelry to add the greatest insult to the greatest injury that had yet been done a people. Most of us since then have run the whole gamut of human emotions from glad to sad and back again, but underneath it all a new note is struck, a quiet bubbling joy is felt. It is that note that makes all our loss worth the while. It is the note of a millennial good fellowship.

In all the grand exodus of men, women and children with their poll-parrots and skinny cats, and dogs and pianos and clocks and family pictures, there was little of hysteria manifest, little of excitement. In part it was owing to the pathological calm of a partial emotional paralysis, but in the main it was the healthy calm of this new joy. Everybody was your friend and you in turn everybody's friend. The individual, the isolated self was dead. The social self was regnant. Never even when the four walls of one's own room in a new city shall close around us again shall we sense the old lonesomeness shutting us off from our neighbors. Never again shall we feel singled out by fate for the hardships and ill luck that's going. There will always be that other fellow.

Later after two days of horror, when we had slept on the street and hobnobbed with aristocracy and riff-raff, when we had nothing to eat but bread of the soldiers and the cheese of some kind neighbor, a little Miss Dainty and I, with our hats sadly askew, with cinders and coal dust begriming our hair and eyes and face, traveled at dusk through the burning ruins and melancholy devastation in the wake of a longshoreman we had picked up on the street. We were going towards the bay. On the way a quietly dressed man approached us. "May I walk with you?" he begged. "It's lonesome walking alone." We smiled and nodded and took him in as if we had known him all our lives. Further on, passing the shattered new postoffice, a soldier stood guard over the building.

"Ladies may take the sidewalk," he shouted. "Men must keep to the road." "No velvet then for us," we retorted, and with the longshoreman and the other picked-up acquaintance we stuck to the middle of the road, piled high with burning bricks and treacherously enmeshed telegraph wires.

And when finally across the bay and that great hulking ignorant longshoreman was my vis-a-vis at a steaming, piping hot dinner—my, but didn't he look good to me. And that is the sweetness and the gladness of the earthquake and the fire. Not of bravery, nor of strength, nor of a new city, but of a new inclusiveness.

The joy in the other fellow.

O'Farret & Market Str.   Cook & Frachau
Call & Chronicle Bldg in view   P.C.

This is what Beautiful Market
street looks like now only
the walls left standing, insides
all burned our

Within a few hours of the earthquake, Governor George C. Pardee established his base at the office of Oakland Mayor Frank K. Mott and arranged for a stream of messages to be sent by telegraph around the country pleading for money, food, and other essentials. As a result, relief trains were soon pouring into the Bay Area from all parts of the continent. The following account appeared in the San Francisco *Chronicle* on April 26, 1906, and gives some idea of the generosity of the response. Its headline: "Touching the Heart of the Whole Nation; A Graphic Picture of the Way San Francisco's Disaster Appealed to the Country."

The nation responds

TWO MONTHS AGO I STOOD IN POMPEII and looked up at the smoke of Vesuvius getting ready for eruption. The narrow streets were worn where the chariots had rolled through them 2,000 years before. In one hour I saw all there was worth seeing in the ruins of that city, which history has made a synonym for disaster.

This morning I walked for three hours through the city of San Francisco and then had covered but one side of the area that our age has marked as the scene of man's severest test. There is no comparison. Pompeii is trivial to this.

In the midst of this desolation, where only the physical is hurt, and over which even now the California spirit is rising gloriously supreme, San Franciscans have been too busy to hear just how the world is answering the call of suffering. I am straight through from New York. Let me give you a birdseye view of the hearts that have been touched.

First, is that synonym for all this is not cheerful giving, John D. Rockefeller. He was at his home in Lakewood, N.J., the day of the earthquake. At noon he got the news. He instantly put himself in touch with Clarence Mackay, president of the Postal Telegraph, and thenceforth was among the first in the East to get information. At 5 o'clock that first afternoon he telegraphed his secretary in New York to subscribe $100,000 to the relief fund. The next forenoon he directed that the Standard Oil Company donate another $100,000. The third day H.H. Rogers, his chief of staff, gave a third $100,000.

You have heard how Congress voted $1,000,000 and then another, how the merchants of Chicago got together and in half an hour raised half a million, how Boston sent a million and how New York subscribed a million and three quarters.

But have you heard how the Governor of Arizona, hearing that New Mexico had sent a relief train before Arizona could be heard from, bolted from his office in his shirt sleeves and refused to go back until he could raise two trainloads and $75,000 in cash?

Have you heard how Kansas City subscribed $350,000, and how the Mayor, learning the sum was not round in pronunciation, sent a hurry call at 3:30 o'clock in the afternoon to all members of the Board of Trade and Chamber of Commerce to meet him immediately, and how he would not let them off for dinner until they had brought up the total to $500,000?

You will perhaps hear much of how these mighty of the land responded. But you should also hear how the children of mirth and laughter—the people of the stage—replied.

The day I left every important theater in New York advertised a benefit. Not content with that, the big people got together and arranged a joint benefit. The actors for this were Fritzi Scheff, Otis Skinner, Francis Wilson, Nat Goodwin, Joe Weber, Pete Dailey, Elsie Janis, Blanche Bates and David Warfield.

That afternoon George M. Cohen went into Wall Street and Park Row in a campaign orator's coat, and from the tail of it insulted every stock broker and newspaper man who did not give him a dollar for the San Francisco he said he loved.

The next day the Bernhardt tent,* just from world-renowned service in Texas, was put up on the Lake Shore in Chicago and a benefit announced (seats $1 to $5) in which the magnet was composed of the following names of some repute: Sarah Bernhardt, Leslie Carter, Julia Marlowe, E.H. Sothern, E.S. Willard and Robert Lorraine.

In Boston last Sunday, by special permit from the Governor, the Sunday closing law was broken for the first time in many years by James K. Hackett and Mary Mannering, who put on "The Walls of Jericho," the money to go to the fallen walls of San Francisco.

* See endnote.

In the Angelus Hotel in Los Angeles, two days ago, Blanche Hall, Grace Desmond and other actresses from the local companies sold flowers in the lobby, the proceeds from which went into the common pot, it being whispered that half the money came from a kiss for which Blanche Hall got $100. She threw in the posy.

Yesterday afternoon on Spring Street in Los Angeles there appeared a rambling old spring wagon, drawn by two slouching Percherons and holding about half a ton of oranges. It had to move very slowly, for several thousand people blocked its progress. An hour and a half was consumed in going four blocks. On the front seat Jim Jeffries was driving with one hand, while with the other he frequently leaned over and lit a cigarette from the cob pipe in the mouth of Jack Root. Jeff wore a single suspender, a red sweater, and a torn straw hat and a week-old beard. Back on top of the oranges was Battling Nelson,* getting rid of his golden fruit at $1 apiece. Once in a while someone would give him $5. Then Nelson passed the fellow around and Jeff shook hands with him.

In "The Girl From the Golden West," Belasco's latest hit, Blanche Bates has a final line, when, with her lover, she bids good-by to her home. The line runs: "Farewell, San Francisco! Oh, my California! Oh, my Sierra!" The set is very beautiful, showing the gorgeous dying sun with the dim town hinted in the distance. As she uttered this line the first night of the earthquake Miss Bates' voice failed, and she lurched forward into her lover's arms. He urged her to go on, but she could not, and the curtain was rung down. As they assisted the actress to her dressing-room she exclaimed: "It's my home. I love the town. This is like the going of my best friend. Oh, I can't endure it!"

At Stanley's in New York that same night, after the play, there was a gathering of San Franciscans. Around a table sat David Belasco, Dave Warfield, Blanche Bates, Florence Roberts, James Neill, Daniel Frawley and Edyth Chapman. They tried to order something to eat, but no one seemed hungry. Not a bite passed the lips of anyone. Some wine was ordered and there was a disheartened attempt at drinking. About every five minutes some pair started a conversation, but that also failed. All they could do was to look from one to the other and hope that the newspapers were all yellow. There was that look in the

* See endnote.

eyes of the actors that is to be seen when the company busts in Kansas with no way but by the ties to Broadway.

After a half-hour of this eloquent silence some ill-advised person volunteered to remark:

"It's the end of San Francisco. Seattle'll get it now."

That aroused Tim Frawley. "Never," he said. "They'll not lose an inch. They're good fighters."

Then a quiet, clerical-looking little white-haired man in the corner spoke the only words he uttered that night:

"And bully gamblers," said David Belasco.

At the turn of the century a powerful syndicate tried to take control of all major theaters in strategic cities, forcing traveling companies and managers to pay them exorbitant fees. Rather than comply, Sarah Bernhardt toured the country with her own tent.

James Jeffries was world heavyweight boxing champion from 1899 until his retirement from the ring in 1905. Jack Root won the light-heavyweight boxing title in 1903. "Battling" Nelson won the lightweight boxing title in 1905.

One of many allegorical cartoons that appeared in books, magazines, and
newspapers around the world.

The earthquake and its aftermath provided psychologist and philosopher William James with plenty of first-hand analytical material. At the time, he was teaching at Stanford University, 35 miles south of San Francisco. Although the Palo Alto campus was severely damaged by the quake, James wrote that the mood of people there was one of "joyous excitement." He added, "Here at last was a *real* earthquake after so many years of harmless waggle!" His later observations of how San Franciscans were coping under the circumstances were less flippant.

The following is extracted from James' article "On Some Mental Effects of the Earthquake," published in *Menninger Perspective*, Number 1, 1990, quarterly journal of the Menninger Foundation, Topeka, Kansas.

A "subjective" view

WHEN I DEPARTED FROM HARVARD for Stanford University last December, almost the last good-bye I got was that of my old California friend B. "I hope they'll give you a touch of earthquake while you're there, so that you may also become acquainted with *that* California institution."

Accordingly, when lying awake at about half past five on the morning of April 18th in my little "flat" on the campus of Stanford, I felt the bed begin to waggle. My first consciousness was one of gleeful recognition of the nature of the movement. "By Jove," I said to myself, "here's B's old earthquake after all"; and then, as it went *crescendo*, "and a jolly good one it is too!" I said.

Sitting up involuntarily and taking a kneeling position, I was thrown down on my face as it went *forte*—shaking the room exactly as a terrier shakes a rat; then everything that was on anything else slid off to the floor. As the *fortissimo* was reached, over went the bureau and "chiffonier" with a crash. Plaster cracked, an awful roaring noise seemed to fill the outer air, and in an instant all was still again save the soft babble of human voices from far and near that soon began to make itself heard as the inhabitants, in costumes and negligees in various degrees, sought the greater safety of the street and yielded to the passionate desire for sympathetic communication.

The thing was over, as I understand the Lick Observatory to have declared, in 48 seconds. To me it felt as if about that length of time, though I have heard others say that it seemed to them longer. In my case, sensation and emotion were so strong that little thought and no reflection or volition were possible in the short time consumed by the phenomenon.

The emotion consisted wholly of glee and admiration: glee at the vividness which such an abstract idea or verbal term as "earthquake" could put on when translated into sensible reality and verified concretely, and admiration at the way in which the frail little wooden house could hold itself together in spite of such a shaking. I felt no trace whatever of fear; it was pure delight and welcome.

"Go it," I almost cried aloud, "and go it *stronger!*"

I ran into my wife's room and found that she, although awakened from sound sleep, had felt no fear either. Of all the persons whom I later interrogated, very few had felt any fear while the shaking lasted, though many had had a "turn" as they realized their narrow escapes from bookcases or bricks from chimney breasts falling on their beds and pillows an instant after they had left them.

As soon as I could think, I discerned retrospectively certain peculiar ways in which my consciousness had taken in the phenomenon. These ways were quite spontaneous and, so to speak, inevitable and irresistible.

First, I personified the "earthquake" as a permanent individual entity. It was "*the*" earthquake of my friend B's augury which had been lying low and holding itself back during all the intervening months in order, on that lustrous April morning, to invade my room and energize the move intensely and triumphantly. It came, moreover, directly to *me*. It stole in behind my back and, once inside the room, had me all to itself and could manifest itself convincingly. Animas and intent were never more present in any human action, nor did any human activity ever more definitely point back to a living agent as its source and origin.

All whom I consulted on the point agreed as to this feature in their own experience. "It expressed intention," "it was vicious," "it was bent on destruction," "it wanted to show its power," or what not. To me, it wanted simply to manifest the full meaning of its *name*. But what was this "It"? To some, apparently, a vague demonic power; to me an individualized being, B's "Earthquake" namely. I heard no one say he felt it as coming from the Deity, though one informant had interpreted it as the end of the world and the beginning of the final judgment. This last subject was a lady in a San Francisco hotel who did not think of it being an earthquake till after she had got into the street and someone had explained it to her. She told me that the theological interpretation had kept fear from her mind and made her take the shaking calmly. She probably had sufficient preliminary assurance of her own salvation!

Neither in public nor in private did I hear any ascription of it to God's wrath or any tendency to treat it as His warning or His judgment. This way of taking it must, of course, have existed, especially among the uneducated. But the absence of any expression of it in my hearing has made me feel how thoroughly "science" has done its work for the educated classes in matters geological. The theological stage of explanation is virtually outgrown. Not so the "metaphysical," apparently never ingrained. For in spite of my own "positivistic" *beliefs* about such matters I *reverted*, and reverted overwhelmingly. For "science" when the tensions in the earth's crust reach the breaking point and strata fall into an altered equilibrium, "earthquake" is simply the collective *name* of all the cracks and shakings and disturbances that happen.

They *are* the earthquake; but for me *the* earthquake was the *cause* of the disturbances and the perception of it as a living agent was irresistible. It had an overpowering dramatic convincingness.

I realize now better than ever how inevitable were men's earlier theologic and mythologic versions of such catastrophes and how artificial and against the grain of our spontaneous perceiving are the later habits into which science educates us. It was simply impossible for untutored men to take earthquakes into their minds as anything but supernatural warning or retribution.

.   .   .

Now turn to San Francisco, 35 miles distant, from which an automobile ere long brought us the dire news of a city in ruins, with fires beginning at various points and the water supply interrupted. I was fortunate enough to board the only train of cars (a very small one) that got up to the city; fortunate enough also to escape in the evening by the only train that left it. This gave me and my valiant feminine escort some four hours of observation. My business is with phenomena "subjective" exclusively; so I will say nothing of the material ruin that greeted us on every hand—the daily papers and the weekly journals have done full justice to that topic.

.   .   .

Two things in retrospect struck me especially and are the most emphatical of all my impressions. Both are reassuring as to human nature.

The first of these was the rapidity of the improvisation of order out of chaos. It is clear that just as in every thousand human beings, there will be statistically so many artists, so many athletes, so many thinkers, and so many potentially good soldiers, so then in times of emergency there will be so many potential organizers. In point of fact, not only in the Great City but in the outlying towns, these natural order-makers, whether amateurs or officials, came to the front immediately. There seemed to be no possibility which there was not someone there to think of or which within 24 hours was not in some way provided for.

A good trivial illustration is this: Mr. [William] Keith is the greatest landscape painter of the Pacific slope and his pictures, which are many, are artistically and pecuniarily precious. Two citizens, lovers of his work, early in the day diverted their attention from all other soliciting interests and made it their duty to visit every place which they knew to contain a Keith painting. They cut them from their frames, rolled them up, and in this way got all the more important ones into a place of safety. When they then sought Mr. Keith to convey the joyous news to him, they found him still in his studio, which was remote from the fire, beginning a new painting. Having given up his previous work for lost, he had resolved to lose no time in making what amends he could for the disaster.

The completeness of organization at Palo Alto, a town of 10,000 inhabitants close to Stanford University, was almost comical. People feared exodus on a large scale of the rowdy elements of San Francisco. In point of fact, very few refugees came to Palo Alto. But within 24 hours, rations, clothing, hospital quarantine, disinfection, washing, police, military, quarters in camps and in houses, printed information, employment, all were provided for under the care of so many volunteer committees.

Much of this readiness was American, much of it Californian; but I believe that every country in a similar crisis would have displayed it in a way to astonish the spectators. Like soldiering, it lies always latent in human nature.

The second thing that struck me was the universal equanimity. We soon got letters from the East ringing with anxiety and pathos; but

I now know fully what I have always believed, that the *pathetic* way of feeling great disasters belongs wholly to the point of view of people at a distance. I heard not a single really pathetic or sentimental word in California expressed by anyone. The terms "awful," "dreadful" fell often enough from people's lips, but always with a sort of abstract meaning and with a face that seemed to admire the vastness of the catastrophe rather than suffer from its cuttingness. When talk was not directly practical, I might almost say that it expressed a tendency more toward hilarity than toward grief. The hearts concealed private bitterness enough, no doubt, but the tongue disdained to dwell on the misfortunes of *self* when almost everybody one spoke to had suffered equally.

Surely the cutting edge of all our usual misfortunes comes from their character of loneliness. We lose our health, our wife or children die, our house burns down, or our money is made way with and the world goes on its way rejoicing. In California, *everyone* to some degree was suffering, and one's private miseries were merged in the vast general sum of deprivation and in the practical problem of general recuperation. The cheerfulness, or at any rate the steadfastness of tone, was universal. Not a single whine or plaintive word did I hear from the hundreds of losers whom I spoke to. Instead, there was a temper of helpfulness beyond the counting.

It is easy to glorify this as something characteristically American or especially Californian. Californian education has, of course, made the thought of all possible recuperations easy. In an exhausted country, with no marginal resources, the outlook on the future would perhaps be darker. But I like to think that what I write of is a normal and universal human peculiarity. In our drawing rooms and offices, we wonder how people ever *do* go through battles, sieges, and shipwrecks. We quiver and sicken in imagination and think those heroes superhuman. Physical pain, whether it be suffered alone or in company, is always more or less unnerving and intolerable. But mental pathos and anguish, I fancy, are always effects of distance. At the place of heavy action where all are more or less concerned together, healthy animal insensibility and heartiness take their place.

At San Francisco, there will doubtless be a crop of nervous wrecks before the weeks and months are over; but meanwhile, the commonest men, simply because they *are* men, will keep on singly and collectively showing this admirable fortitude of temper.

This article, which appeared in *Sunset Magazine*, October 1906, under the title "San Francisco at Play," is even more charming when we know the story behind it. Colonel Edwin Emerson was on a lecture tour in the East when the earthquake hit, and he hurried to San Francisco in charge of relief work on behalf of the California Century Clubs of New York City. Before leaving New York he telegraphed a proposal of marriage to Mary Edith Griswold, whose "Three days adrift" appears in this volume. Her letter declining the proposal was delayed in the mail. Unaware of her rejection, Emerson repeated the proposal in person when he arrived in San Francisco, and this time was accepted. The couple were married on May 16 at the home of Mrs. Robert Louis Stevenson, at Hyde and Lombard. These details match the first wedding Emerson refers to in his article, although he does not identify it as his own.

In better times this would have been a grand wedding. The groom had won distinction as a soldier, war correspondent, and lecturer. The bride, who was "given away" by David Starr Jordan, president of Stanford University, was already well-known locally as a writer. Among the congratulatory telegrams was one from President Theodore Roosevelt, with whom Emerson had served in Cuba.

Emerson's delightful description of San Francisco's recovery from the devastation seems an appropriate finale to this volume.

A joyous renaissance

So MANY GLOOMY DESCRIPTIONS have been published of San Francisco's "desolate waste of ruins," and of the discouragement resulting from the fact that certain fire insurance companies failed to do the right thing by their San Franciscan policyholders that outsiders are coming to think that the city is in sackcloth as well as in ashes. Nothing could be farther from the truth.

My own conviction, gained from daily impressions of San Francisco during its period of alleged abasement and dreary reconstruction, is that it is still the gayest city of the Western Hemisphere. In truth I think it would be easier to change the leopard's spots than to shake all the laughter and love of fun out of merry hearted San Francisco. Surely no mere earthquake or fire is going to accomplish it, any more than the rumblings of Vesuvius can make Neapolitans forget their tarantella.

. . .

They say that Nero fiddled on the ruins of Rome. They have said it so long that it has become one of the accepted myths of Christendom. But let it be recorded as a piece of actual contemporary history that during the very first night of the great San Francisco fire, when the homeless thousands fleeing from the flames were huddled together in the open parks and military reservations, there was fiddling and singing and light laughter among the refugees who had lost their all, even while the smoke from their burning homes was overspreading all that was left of the city like a pall.

Can those who pushed and dragged their belongings down Market street, toward the ferry, on the second day of the disaster, ever forget the man who, having grown tired of hauling a heavy trunk along the cable slot, sat down on it and curling his legs up under him, unslung a banjo from his back and sang: "There'll be a hot time in the old town tonight," while the interminable procession of fleeing people surged past him, as a stream swirls around a rock?

About the same time, so they say, another merry soul, coming across an abandoned piano on Van Ness avenue, converted his suit case into a piano stool and entertained the multitude with snatches from "Carmen," as heard but a few nights before at the opening-closing performance of grand opera in San Francisco. So, too, the brazen voices of gramophones were to be heard on all sides during the worst of the trouble.

Later, when the tents of the refugees, and the funny street kitchens, improvised from doors and shutters and pieces of roofing, overspread all the city, such merriment became an accepted thing. Everywhere, during those long moon-lit evenings, one could hear the tinkle of guitars and mandolins, from among the tents. Or, passing by the grotesque rows of curbstone kitchens, one became dimly aware of the low murmurings of couples who had sought refuge in these dark recesses as in bowers of love. It was at this time that the droll signs and inscriptions began to appear on walls and tent flaps, which soon became one of the familiar sights of reconstructing San Francisco.

One of the first of these, which appeared in a conspicuous place on the top of some ruins on Market street, while the embers were still smouldering, it will be remembered, called itself "The San Francisco Spirit." Under this caption was chalked the following doggerel:

The cow is in the hammock
The cat is in the lake,
The baby in the garbage can,
What difference does it make?
There is no water, and still less soap.
We have no city, but lots of hope.

Many took advantage for free advertising on the walls. Thus one firm, which likes to think itself always in the lead, hoisted this placard over its new temporary quarters:

First to shake
First to burn
First to take
Another new turn.

From the tenth story of a ruined skyscraper a lawyer hung out his shingle, with a notice that he had "moved because the elevators were not running."

This was like the broken slab that was to be seen for some time after the fire, standing up on top of a flight of marble steps which no longer led anywhere, doing duty as a directory of the tenants who had been "forced to move on account of alterations on April 18th."

The funniest inscriptions, because the most spontaneous, were those chalked on the curbstone kitchens or smeared on the white canvas of the tents. There were so many that they elude the memory as do most limericks, but some of them made enough of a hit to be remembered. Thus there was the double verse written on the green shutters of an earthquake kitchen, before one of the millionaire's mansions on stylish Pacific avenue:

Out in the cold world,
Out in the street,

To which someone had added:

But what's the use of kicking
When you've got enough to eat?

Many of the street lunch counters in a spirit of fun, affected the high-sounding names of fashionable restaurants that had gone down in the general wreck, such as the Poodle Dog, Marchand's, Delmonico, Zinkand's, Tait's or the Techau Tavern. Others were more original, posting such signs as, "Earthquake shakes, 5¢. a glass," or rival signs like "Wayside Inn," and "Inside Out."

The inscription that afforded most amusement perhaps, was the one saying: "Eat, drink and be merry, for tomorrow we may have to go to Oakland;" but the one that I liked best, was written on the flimsy shutters of a curbstone kitchen by a jealous young husband. All it said was, "Don't kiss the cook!"

Considering all the flirtation and love making that the open-air life in the parks and on the curbstones gave rise to, it is really a wonder that there were not even more of those celebrated earthquake weddings, of which we heard so much. The overworked marriage license clerk has deposed that the fees collected by him for issuing such licenses during April and May, 1906, far exceeded the totals for the same months of any preceding years in San Francisco.

One of these weddings, which was celebrated in a famous San Francisco residence which had barely been saved from the flames and dynamite that reduced all the stylish neighborhood around it to ashes, impressed me as the most joyous wedding I had ever attended. It would have been so, if only for the romantic surroundings and the refreshing lack of formality imposed on all the participants by the incongruous circumstances of the recent earthquake and fire. The guests had been invited by word of mouth only, there being no facilities for issuing wedding cards or for getting them distributed, even if there had been engravers or stationery left in San Francisco. Most of the guests, as well as the principals, had to come on foot, trudging through miles of ashes, since no carriages were to be had then in San Francisco for love or money. Though it was a gathering of some of San Francisco's best society, nobody wore new or formal clothes— not even the bride—nor could any of the men boast of silk hats or gloves. Several gentlemen with a reputation for Beau Brummelism, had to come in outing rig, and even the army officers from the Presidio, usually so punctilious in matters of attire, came in their field uniforms, straight from the line of duty.

By way of wedding presents, many guests brought molten bits of jewelry or plate dug from the ruins of their burned mansions or other earthquake souvenirs. There could have been no other presents, for there were no shops left then in the town, and even if there had been, no one in San Francisco at this time, had any cash to spare, all banks and financial institutions remaining closed. Even the refreshment had to be brought from outside, and the glasses and dishes had to be borrowed, since the soldiers had looted the hostess' wine cellars and pantries, and all the household crockery had been carried off likewise. All these unusual circumstances combined to turn the wedding into a highly entertaining impromptu affair, a welcome change from the customary deadly ceremony which Bernard Shaw has so aptly likened to "funerals of dead hopes."

There was another meeting of kindred spirits in San Francisco during those days of alleged despair which proved no less joyous a gathering. This was the last re-union in the burned city of a well-known coterie of San Francisco artists and writers in Coppa's famous Bohemian resort, now but a place of memory and legend. When they met in the old restaurant in Montgomery Block, the cartoon-covered walls of which were known to be doomed, all the artists had lost their studios and the scribes their typewriters. Incidentally they had lost all their unsold canvasses and rejected manuscripts. It was this riddance of an accumulation of many years of disappointment and neglect, in part, that made this occasion so joyous.

As one of them put it, hilariously: "Gone, gone at last my whole *salon des refusées!* All the musty manuscripts returned with so much chilling politeness, gone to blazes, with no further need to worry where next to send the miserable derelicts! Gone, too, my magnificent collection of printed slips from the editors, announcing the unwelcome return of my poor vagabonds!"

In other respects, the meeting was a memorable one. Outside lay the city in ruins and in total darkness. A squad of soldiers bivouacked around a camp fire among the ashes at the corner, where once a tall bank building had stood. A sentry with carbine in hand lounged at the door. Inside there were only candles to light up the ghostly cartoons of former days overspreading the walls. Even these candles had to be brought by the guests themselves. It was a scene like the famous "Revelry of the Dying:"

> We meet under rumbling rafters,
> While the walls around are bare,
> And amidst our peals of laughter
> It seems though the dead were there.

The wine cellar of the old café having been looted during the fire, and there being no water to be had nearby, the guests had to bring along water bottles and canteens from their places of refuge in Oakland and at the military reservations. Several men appeared who were believed to have perished in the flames, clad in khaki or corduroys, unshaven and unkempt, yet it was a merry reunion, as noisy and as obstreperous as any of former days. "Dance, thumbykin, dance!" was followed by a mock wedding of two members of the party, believed to be constitutionally averse to marriage, amid so much hilarity that the sentinel had to threaten drastic measures. He had been posted there as an extra precaution by the military officer of the district whose permission had to be obtained for the privilege of meeting in a restaurant after nightfall during those troublous times. When the guests dispersed the soldier at the door carefully counted every member of the party as they filed out to make sure that no one remained behind on this forbidden ground.

"If anybody is found inside, after this, who don't belong to your party," he announced as a parting shot, "God help him!"

For once the Bohemians of San Francisco found themselves reduced to the abstemious habits of their favorite proto-types, Henri Murger's "*Buveurs de l'Eau.*"* That an artists' supper with no other beverage than water could prove so jolly a celebration in San Francisco in itself gives the lie to prevalent notion that Bohemianism means degeneracy or that San Francisco's reputation for gaiety was founded on little else but wickedness and debauchery. As one of San Francisco's bards has sung:

> If, as some say, God spanked the town
> For being over frisky—
> Why did He burn the churches down
> And save Hotaling's whisky?

The fact is that throughout the dry period of two and a half months, following the earthquake, when all sale of liquor was forbidden in San Francisco, the town was as gay as ever and the police had nothing to do. I remember, one night, when I was taken all over San Francisco on an automobile tour of observation by a party of friends who had nothing better to do than to find out what was "doing in the old town," we encountered the same gay merry-makers at the Casino, the new Tait's, new Techau Tavern and other reviving resorts, listening to the same old strains of music, as if all the joys of life were as plentiful and easily to be had on all sides as before the disaster.

It has been generally remarked, indeed, that almost the first well-known institutions to revive from the seemingly crushing blow that befell the city were the fashionable restaurants and pleasure resorts. Barely two months after the fire a big public banquet could be held in the midst of the remnants of the Palace Hotel. "Admirable bravado," exclaimed the Eastern press.

On Fillmore street, in little dinky quarters, on Van Ness avenue among former private residences and elsewhere in the unharmed districts

* "Drinkers of water."

of the city, such restaurants as Delmonico's, Tait's, Techau's and the Poodle Dog reappeared. Meanwhile in the Latin quarter the old Bohemian haunts such as Matias's Mexican fonda, or the Buon Gusto, Fior d'Italia, and others of their ilk sprang to life in little wooden shacks arising from the ruins of their former establishments. It was like the clusters of wild lilies and nasturtium that here and there have sprung from the ruins of former gardens in San Francisco, flecking the dismal ashes with gleams of color and fragrance.

At the same time that the restaurants were reopening, the various clubs of San Francisco were getting together in new quarters. Of all the city's clubs only two—the Cosmos and the Officers' Club at the Presidio—had not lost their clubhouses. For a while the members of all the clubs were made welcome at the suburban country clubs or at such well-known clubs in Oakland and Berkeley as the Athenian, the Nile and the Faculty Club of the University of California. But this period of visiting did not last long. Soon certain fortunate club members whose private residences had been saved out of the holocaust opened their houses as a temporary refuge to their comrades. These hospitable homes formed a nucleus for the scattered clubs, while new quarters, occasionally better than before, were being provided. Within an incredibly short period the club life of San Francisco was back on its former lively basis.

Characteristic of San Francisco, as always, was the experience of the Bohemian Club. While the fire was but a few blocks away the old habitués still lounged in the cozy bay-window overhanging the corner of Post street and Grant avenue. When the rush for safety began there was no time to save certain priceless canvasses that hung in the club gallery and a few besides the old cartoons and portraits that enlivened the staircase and bar were rescued. That member of the art committee who saved those precious cartoons knew what he was doing; he knew that the old members cared more for these grotesqueries than for any number of old masters. So he did not even make an attempt to save some of the best products of his own brush which hung in the upper rooms. Now the new quarters of the Bohemian Club, overlooking a refugee camp on Lafayette Square, have been rendered more homelike to the old members by the presence of the accustomed cartoons displayed in position analogous to those of old. As one of the members of the club has expressed it: "Those cartoons meant something to us; but as for old masters the world is full of them."

Thus the club, while it lost some of its priceless treasures, lost none of its membership as a result of the disaster which drove several hundred thousand inhabitants of San Francisco out of town. When the Bohemian Club, a few months later, held its annual midsummer outing in the redwood forest, the attendance was as numerous as ever and the jinks were as lively and debonair as if nothing had happened in the big city by the Golden Gate.

Even the amateur theatricals of the Bohemian Club lacked not for players or for audience, so with the regular theatrical companies of San Francisco, the playhouses of which were destroyed by the earthquake and fire.

The first move, of course, was to shift to the nearest available playhouses in Oakland and out to the Chutes near Golden Gate Park. There the popular Orpheum promptly established itself, playing to crowded houses of refugees larger even than its former audiences in the O'Farrell street playhouse.

It was the same across the bay. A San Francisco manager who had transplanted his stock company to Idora Park and to Ye Liberty Playhouse in Oakland told me that so many people were anxious to seek mental relief from the distressing situation in San Francisco that his playhouses were crowded to capacity from one week's end to the other, and that it was necessary to order seats for Saturdays or Sundays a fortnight ahead.

"The taste for playgoing has become such a rage," he said, "that we can put on any old play, even the oldest chestnuts, and still there is standing room only."

The first new playhouse in San Francisco to arise over its former ruins was the Central Theater, the old home of melodrama and sentimental plays. Here the old stock company had to appear under the shelter of a big circus tent, like the tent theaters in which Sara Bernhardt had to play in Texas and elsewhere last season when the Theater Trust denied her admission to its playhouses. But as was the case with the divine Sara the audiences of the Central Theater did not seem to care whether their favorite plays were presented under a roof or under canvas. The play was the thing, not the accommodations; so the great tent has been crowded night after night ever since it opened.

It is truly a weird sight, after the play is over, to see the throng of playgoers come pushing through the brilliantly lighted entrance to the tent theater,—out into the waste of debris and ashes where there was once the great thoroughfare of Market street. They patter along in couples, chatting merrily on their way to further places of amusement, taking little or no heed of the impressive ruins of the City Hall that stare them in the face.

By the time Madame Bernhardt herself came to the Pacific Coast, a few weeks after the earthquake, there were no more large tents to be had in San Francisco, so she was driven to securing a playhouse. The only one coming up to her unrivaled drawing power was the vast open air-arena of the Greek Theater in Berkeley. There I saw her play "Phèdre" to an audience of fully six thousand persons, an overwhelming majority of whom were women in gay summer dresses, full of flutter and enthusiasm. Yet, as Madame Bernhardt remarked to me in wonder, most of these people had only just lost their homes and all their belongings, so that they could scarcely be expected to enjoy a play.

Yet they did. In the pleasure of the moment they forgot all their misfortunes. Anyone who saw that impressive scene could never doubt the spirit of San Francisco.

To have this conviction borne in upon one, however, there is no need of so elaborate a pageant. To see the pleasure loving people of San Francisco at their best all that is necessary is to take a stroll along the new Van Ness avenue.

This street, which was formerly an avenue set aside for the homes of wealth and fashion, as every San Franciscan knows, now marks the boundary where the greatest fire of history was at last brought to a stop. On one side of it, eastward, lie the ruins of the old city, stretching over miles and miles of ashes, while westward rises the Western Addition of unharmed residences.

No need to compare the new Van Ness with Fifth avenue in New York or Piccadilly—there is no comparison, for its own true gaiety needs none.

As the strong afternoon sun sends long blue shadows slanting across the avenue, and flashes on the new gay dresses of the women as they swish in and out of the shops, or gleams upon the motor cars that dart up and down its broad, smooth pavements, the rush and go of its life makes one think of a Midway Plaisance—a country fair,—or a booming mining town of modern Nevada. The low redwood shops, none over two stories high, hold their freshly painted new fronts to the light, the awnings are new and clean, while flags and variegated banners, bearing well-known merchants' names flutter from every

Maynard Dixon sketched this view of Van Ness Avenue to accompany Emerson's article when it first appeared in *Sunset Magazine* in October 1906.

front and gable. Here and there, where some grim ruin looms gauntly between them, the contrast is made vivid to the point of unreality and illusion.

Some of the more enterprising commercial establishments have encroached upon stately deserted mansions left standing on the avenue with their scorched fronts toward the desolate east, where the ashes lie. Burrowing into their pretentious seclusion they are ousting them bodily.

The bulky old Hobart mansion, for instance, is occupied by a great dry-goods firm, whose trade sign grotesquely overshadows the gothic portal. Up and down its broad steps move the line of shoppers, among them those who come to shop where once they went to call.

Other concerns have crowded in upon what was once quiet lawn and garden. Here the fashionable furrier, the milliner, haberdasher, art-dealer, confectioner and florist are all offering their pretty wares. Look into these places and you will see as vivacious and bright a flutter of femininity as ever at Maskey's [Fine Candies], or at the Peacock or the Golden Pheasant in old days. Everything is new of the newest brand,—the shops, the merchandize in them, the salesmen, even the customers look new,—for there are no shopworn goods or old stock left for the merchant to "work off,"—they were disposed of without his consent.

They say that the fashions of San Francisco are at last abreast of Paris, and London, through that grim "act of Providence." As a friend carefully explained to me:

"You men can't understand what it means not to have to match this year's hat with last year's shoes!" Truly, a vital point, not as easily grasped by a man's mind, as appreciated by his eye.

As the bright throng of women flash in and out of the shops, men hail one another with the hearty interest of those who have plans in common, and the one in the sleek top hat greets his peer in dusty corduroys with the cordial grip of a camp-mate.

All combines in one composite impression,—hurry and hopefulness, gaiety, silken petticoats and starched gowns, corduroys, tramping boots, sombreros, temporary wooden buildings, the flutter of many flags, rush of automobiles, clatter of lumber, banging of hammers and the rumble of drays,—the very sunlit air seems to breathe renaissance.

This is the spirit at the Golden Gate,—the old spirit that still lives—and this is why it is fun to live in the new San Francisco.

Resource notes

It is my practice to identify all relevant sources *within* the body of text, as long as doing so does not interrupt the reader's pace. And I use footnotes only to clarify points within the text. I realize this may not be sufficient for scholars and historians, and so for their benefit I have prepared the following notes keyed to specific pages of text.

For space, names and dates of newspapers and periodicals have been abbreviated. In the case of books, only the author's last name is given along with page numbers, unless the author has more than one title in the Bibliography. These are further defined in the Bibliography.

Example: Levison 120-21 = *Memories for My Family* by Jacob B. Levison, pages 120-121.

War Dept. = War Department Annual Reports for year ended 30 June 1906, Volume 1, Appendix A.

Sunset 17:14 = *Sunset Magazine*, volume 17, page 14.

Page:

27-28 Description of city—*San Francisco and its Environs; San Francisco: The Distribution Point...* (guide books)
29-30 Re faults and plates—USGS Fact Sheet 094-96, 1996; USGS Web page FAQ
30-32 Ruef and Schmitz—Bean; Older; Ruef; Thomas, Lately
31 "French restaurants" defined—Irwin 33-34; Bean 50-51
32-33 Aiken's description—*Sunset* 17:14
33-34 Story of *Wellington*—*Call* 17 May 1906
34 Animals at The Chutes—*Call* 11 May 1906
35 Damage figures—*Sunset* 20:557-58; *Argonaut* 20 Aug. 1927: USGS Web page, "Casualties and damage after the great 1906 San Francisco earthquake."
35 Story of fire chief and his wife—*Argonaut* 16 Jun. 1906, 11 Sep. 1926; 23 Jul. 1927;

Note: The following is offered by archivist Kathleen O'Connor concerning the question whether or not this report was ever classified:
"The report, filed with other documents of the 1906 earthquake and fire, was found among a group of boxes of documents sent by the U.S. Navy to the Archives under the general description, '12th Naval District, Commandant's Office, General Correspondence, 1919-1940.' Some of this documentation was security classified. Along with the above group of records, another set of records was sent in, labeled, '12th Naval District, Commandant's Office, General Correspondence, Classified 1945.' These two distinctly different groups of records boxes were sent in as one set of boxes and put in a secured vault area. Any records released from these boxes were then given 'declassified' status, whether they were originally classified or not. Hence, the 'declassified' status of the Freeman report." (See Bibliography for archive numbers.)

Bibliography

Bancroft, Hubert Howe. *Some Cities and San Francisco and Resurgam.* The Bancroft Publishers, New York. 1907.

Banks, Charles Eugene; Read, Opie. *The History of the San Francisco Disaster and Mount Vesuvius Horror.* Chicago. 1906.

Barrymore, John. *Confessions of an Actor.* The Curtis Publishing Company. 1926. Reprinted by Arno Press Inc. 1980.

Bean, Walton. *Boss Ruef's San Francisco.* University of California Press, Berkeley. 1952.

Blue and Gold: The University of California Annual, 1908. University of California Press, Berkeley. 1907.

Borel, Antoine, Jr. *"San Francisco is No More." The Letters of Antoine Borel Jr. 1905-1906.* Edited by Ronald G. Fick. Menlo Park, California. 1980.

Bronson, William. *The Earth Shook, the Sky Burned.* Doubleday, Garden City. 1959. Reprinted by Chronicle Books, San Francisco. 1986 and 1997.

———. *Still Flying and Nailed to the Mast.* Doubleday & Company, Garden City, New York. 1963.

Burton, Benedict. *The Anthropology of World's Fairs: San Francisco's Panama Pacific International Exposition of 1915.* The Lowie Museum of Anthropology in association with Scolar Press, London and Berkeley. 1983.

Byrne, James W. *Recollections of the Fire.* Privately printed. 1927.

Chinn, Thomas. *Bridging the Pacific: San Francisco Chinatown and Its People.* Chinese Historical Society, San Francisco. 1989.

Cloud, Archibald J. *Lowell High School 1856-1956: A Centennial History of the Oldest Public School in California.* Pacific Books, Palo Alto. 1956.

Coleman, Harry T. *Give Us a Little Smile, Baby.* E.P. Dutton & Co., New York. 1943.

Condon, Emmet; Hansen, Gladys. *Denial of Disaster: The Untold Story and Photographs of the San Francisco Earthquake and Fire of 1906.* Cameron and Company, San Francisco. 1989.

Derleth, Charles, Jr. *The Destructive Extent of the California Earthquake.* San Francisco. 1907.

DeNevi, Don; Saul, Eric. *The Great San Francisco Earthquake and Fire.* Celestial Arts, Millbrae, California. 1981.

Dickson, Samuel. *San Francisco is Your Home.* Stanford University Press. 1947.

Dillon, Richard. *North Beach: The Italian Heart of San Francisco.* The Photographs of J.B. Monaco. Presidio Press, Novato, California. 1985.

Duke, Thomas S. *Celebrated Criminal Cases of America.* San Francisco. 1910.

Everett, Marshall (pseud. of Henry Neil). *Complete Story of the San Francisco Earthquake.* Chicago. 1906.

Eyewitness to Disaster: Five women tell their stories of the 1906 earthquake and fire in San Francisco. The National Society of the Colonial Dames of America in California. 1987.

Field, Charles Kellogg. *The Story of Cheerio by Himself.* Limited edition. New York. 1936.

Genthe, Arnold. *As I Remember.* New York. 1937.

Hall, Carroll D.; Lewis, Oscar. *Bonanza Inn: America's First Luxury Hotel.* Alfred A. Knopf, Inc., New York. 1939. Reprinted by Antler Books, San Francisco. 1983.

Hansen, Gladys. *San Francisco Almanac.* Chronicle Books, San Francisco. 1995.

——; Condon, Emmet. *Denial of Disaster: The Untold Story and Photographs of the San Francisco Earthquake and Fire of 1906.* Cameron and Company, San Francisco. 1989.

Himmelwright, A.L.A. *The San Francisco Earthquake and Fire: A Brief History of the Disaster.* New York. 1906.

Irwin, Will. *The City That Was: A Requiem of Old San Francisco.* New York. 1906.

Jacobson, Pauline. *The City of the Golden 'Fifties.* University of California Press, Berkeley. 1941.

James, William. *Memories and Studies.* Longmans, Green, and Co., New York. 1911. Reprinted by Scholarly Press, Michigan. 1970.

Jordan, David Starr. (Editor) *The California Earthquake of 1906.* San Francisco. 1907.

Keeler, Charles A. *San Francisco Through Earthquake and Fire.* San Francisco. 1906.

Klauber, Laurence M. *Two Days in San Francisco—Year 1906.* Privately printed. 1958.

Kramer, William M. (Editor) *California: Earthquakes and Jews.* Isaac Nathan Publishing Co., Los Angeles. 1995.

Lafler, Henry Anderson. *How the Army Worked to Save San Francisco.* San Francisco. 1906.

Leach, Frank A. *Recollections of a Newspaperman.* San Francisco. 1917.

Levine, Ellen. *If You Lived at the Time of the Great San Francisco Earthquake.* Illustrated by Pat Grant Porter. Scholastic Inc., New York. 1987.

Levison, Jacob B. *Memories For My Family.* John Henry Nash. 1933.

Lewis, Oscar; Hall, Carroll D. *Bonanza Inn: America's First Luxury Hotel.* Alfred A. Knopf, New York. 1939. Reprinted by Antler Books, San Francisco. 1983.

Livingston, Edward, Sr. *A Personal History of the San Francisco Earthquake and Fire in 1906.* The Windsor Press, San Francisco. 1941.

London, Charmian. *The Book of Jack London.* Volume 2. New York. 1921.

Lucey, Paul A. *History of the Oldest Public School in California: Lowell High School, San Francisco.* Lowell Alumni Association, San Francisco. 1989.

Mack, Gerstle. *Surviving San Francisco's Great Earthquake and Fire.* Chronicle Books, San Francisco. 1981.

McAdie, Alexander G. *Alexander McAdie: Scientist and Writer.* Compiled and published by Mary R.B. McAdie, Charlottesville, Virginia. 1949.

Morris, Charles. (Editor) *The San Francisco Calamity by Earthquake and Fire.* Philadelphia. 1906. Reprinted by Citadel Press, New Jersey. 1986.

Muscatine, Doris. *Old San Francisco: From Early Days to the Earthquake.* G.P. Putnam's Sons, New York. 1975.

Narell, Irena. *Our City: The Jews of San Francisco.* Howell-North Books, San Diego. 1981.

O'Brien, Robert. *This is San Francisco: A Classic Portrait of the City.* Whittlesey House, New York. 1949. Reprinted by Chronicle Books, San Francisco. 1994.

Older, Fremont. *My Own Story.* Call Publishing Company, San Francisco. 1919. Reprinted by Post Enquirer Publishing Co. 1925; and The Macmillan Company. 1926.

Olmsted, R.R.; Watkins, T.H. *Mirror of the Dream: An Illustrated History of San Francisco.* The Scrimshaw Press, Oakland. 1976.

Read, Opie; Banks, Charles Eugene. *The History of the San Francisco Disaster and Mount Vesuvius Horror.* Chicago. 1906.

Reedy, William Marion. *'Frisco the Fallen.* San Francisco. 1916. (Reprint of article from *Reedy's Mirror,* 26 April 1906.) Reprinted as *The City That Has Fallen* by The Book Club of California. 1933.

Reid, Constance. *The Search for E.T. Bell, also known as John Taine.* The Mathematical Association of America, Washington, D.C. 1993.

Ross, Ron. *San Francisco's Earthquake and Fire: 75th Anniversary.* San Francisco. 1981.

Ryder, David Warren. *They Wouldn't Take Ashes For an Answer.* Firemen's Fund, San Francisco. 1948.

San Francisco and its Environs. (Guide book.) The California Promotion Committee, San Francisco. 1903.

San Francisco: The Distribution Point for Both Hemispheres. (Guide book.) The Pacific Art Company, San Francisco. 1904-05.

Saul, Eric; DeNevi, Don. *The Great San Francisco Earthquake and Fire.* Celestial Arts, Millbrae, California. 1981.

Searight, Frank Thompson. *The Doomed City: A Thrilling History of San Francisco's Destruction.* Chicago. 1906.

Steele, Rufus. *The City That Is: The Story of the Rebuilding of San Francisco in Three Years.* San Francisco. 1909.

Stetson, James B. *San Francisco During the Eventful Days of April 1906: Personal Recollections.* San Francisco. 1906. Reprinted as *Narrative of My Experiences in the Earthquake and Fire at San Francisco.* Limited edition. Lewis Osborne, Palo Alto, California. 1969.

Thomas, Gordon; Witts, Max Morgan. *The San Francisco Earthquake.* Stein and Day, New York. 1971.

Thomas, Lately. *A Debonair Scoundrel.* Holt, Rinehart and Winston, New York. 1962.

Turner, Patricia. (Editor) *1906 Remembered: Firsthand Accounts of the San Francisco Disaster.* Illustrated by Charlie Aquilina. Prepared by City Guides Oral History Committee. Friends of the San Francisco Public Library, San Francisco. 1981.

Tyler, Sydney. *San Francisco's Great Disaster.* Philadelphia. 1906.

Watkins, T.H.; Olmsted, R.R. *Mirror of a Dream: An Illustrated History of San Francisco.* The Scrimshaw Press, Oakland. 1976.

White, Trumbull. *The Complete Story of the San Francisco Horror.* San Francisco. 1906.

Wiley, Peter Booth. *A Free Library in This City.* Weldon Owen, Inc., San Francisco. 1996.

Wilson, Carol Green. *Chinatown Quest: The Life Adventures of Donaldina Cameron.* Stanford University Press. 1931.

Wilson, James Russel. *San Francisco's Horror of Earthquake and Fire.* Philadelphia. 1906.

Witts, Max Morgan; Thomas, Gordon. *The San Francisco Earthquake.* Stein and Day, New York. 1971.

Young, John P. *Journalism in California.* Chronicle Publishing Company, San Francisco. 1915.

ARTICLES:

Aiken, Charles S. "San Francisco's Plight and Prospect." *Sunset,* June-July 1906.

———. "San Francisco's Upraising." *Sunset,* October 1906.

Atherton, Gertrude. "San Francisco's Tragic Dawn." *Harper's,* 12 May 1906.

Austin, Mary. "Temblor and Fire." *Out West* June 1906. Reprinted in *The Argonaut,* 23 June 1906.

Bacigalupi, Peter. "Mr. Bacigalupi's Own Story." *Edison Phonograph Monthly,* June 1906.

Barry, Richard. "Touching the Heart of the Whole Nation." *Chronicle,* 26 April 1906.

Bell, Eric Temple. "San Francisco Earthquake." *The Eagle* (Magazine of the Bedford Modern School, Bedford, England), July 1906.

Carr, Harry. "The Epic of the Dynamited Metropolis." *Los Angeles Daily Times,* 21 April 1906.

Caruso, Enrico. "Caruso on the Earthquake." *The Sketch* (London). Reprinted in *The Theatre Magazine,* 1 July 1906.

Emerson, Edwin, Jr. "Handling a Crisis." *Sunset,* June-July 1906.

———. "San Francisco at Play." *Sunset,* October 1906.

Fisher, Lucy B. "A Nurse's Earthquake Experience." *The American Journal of Nursing,* November 1906.

Funston, Frederick. "A Letter From General Funston." *The Argonaut,* 7 July 1906.

———. "How the Army Worked to Save San Francisco." *Cosmopolitan,* July 1906.

Griswold, Mary Edith. "Three Days Adrift." *Sunset,* June-July 1906.

Hopper, James. "A Stricken City's Days of Terror." *Harper's,* 12 May 1906.

———. "Our San Francisco." *Everybody's,* June 1906.

Hudson, James J. "The California National Guard in the San Francisco Earthquake and Fire of 1906." *California Historical Quarterly,* Summer 1976.

Jacobson, Pauline. "How it Feels to be a Refugee and Have Nothing in the World." *Bulletin,* 29 April 1906.

James, William. "On Some Mental Effects of the Earthquake." *Menninger Perspective* Number 1, 1990.

Keeler, Charles A. "Children and Their Pets in the San Francisco Fire." *St. Nicholas,* September 1906.

Lafler, Henry Anderson. "My Sixty Sleepless Hours." *McClure's,* July 1906.

———. "The Management of the Fire." *The Argonaut,* 30 June 1906.

Laurie, Annie (pseud. of Winifred Bonfils). "Annie Laurie Tells of the Spectral City." *Examiner,* 22 April 1906.

London, Jack. "The Story of an Eyewitness." *Cosmopolitan*, 5 May 1906. Reprinted as "Jack London Tells of the Fire" in *The Argonaut*, 2 June 1906.

Liang, Hugh Kwong. "The Life Story of Hugh K. Liang. Part 3." *Newsletter*, Chinese Historical Society of San Diego, Spring 1996.

Lincoln, Chester Charles. "My Experience in the Earthquake and Fire of San Francisco." Editor, Harry J. Johnson, Jr. *California History*, March 1986.

McAdie, Alexander G.; Richter, C.M. "Phenomena Connected With the San Francisco Earthquake." *Monthly Weather Review*, November 1907.

Richter, C.M.; McAdie, Alexander G. "Phenomena Connected With the San Francisco Earthquake." *Monthly Weather Review*, November 1907.

Ruef, Abraham. "The Road I Traveled." Serialized in *Bulletin*, 21 May-5 September 1912.

Sedgwick, Charles B. "The Fall of San Francisco: Some Personal Observations." *British-Californian*, May-June 1906.

Stephens, Henry Morse. "How the History of the Disaster is Being Made." *Examiner*, 19 April 1908.

Stevens, Ashton. "Milk of Human Kindness Flows From Bay to Park." *Examiner*, 22 April 1906.

"The Great Fire of 1906." Serialized in *The Argonaut*, 1 May 1926-20 August 1927.

Wall, Louise Herrick. "Heroic San Francisco." *Century*, August 1906.

Watkins, Mrs. James T. "The 1906 San Francisco Earthquake: A Personal Account." *California Geology*, December 1981; *Sacramento Bee*, 17 April 1986. Also included in *Eyewitness to Disaster*, published by National Society of The Colonial Dames of America in California, 1987.

LETTERS AND MANUSCRIPTS:

Berreyesa, Claire Fay. "Growing Up in San Francisco in the 1890's and 1900's." Palo Alto. 1977. Typescript available in some libraries.

"Bertha." Letter to "My Dear Elsa" dated Berkeley, 13 May 1906. Bancroft Library. MSS 98/67C.

Cook, Jesse B. Letter to Captain John B. Martin dated San Francisco, 14 June 1906. Jesse Cook collection.

Coxe, Mabel. Letter to her brother Charles in Manila, dated San Francisco 3 July 1906. *Chronicle*, 13 April 1997. Original in private collection.

"Curt." Letter to Mrs. Walter S. Osborne in Naugatuck, Connecticut, dated San Francisco, 9 May 1907. Bancroft Library. MSS 96/16C.

Enewold, Elmer E. Letter to his father in Omaha dated San Francisco, 3 May 1906. California Historical Society. MS 3474.

Golcher, Catherine. Letter to her sister Elise dated San Francisco, 22 April 1906. California Historical Society. MS 3512.
Mansell(?), Harry. Letter to Miss Maria Mansell in Guildford, England, dated Astoria, Oregon, 8 July 1906, signed "Your loving nephew Harry." British Library. ADD MD 59.652.ff.82-9.
Richter, Clement Max. "Autobiography and Reminiscences written for my children and their children. 1922." Bancroft Library. MSS 71/57C.
Strack, Marilyn JoAnne. "The San Francisco Earthquake and Fire of 1906: An annotated bibliography." (Based on collections at the San Francisco Public Library and California Historical Society.) Author's thesis (MA), San Jose State University, 1976.

REPORTS:

San Francisco Municipal Reports for fiscal years 1905-06 and 1906-07. Excerpts reprinted as *San Francisco Earthquake and Fire 1906* by the office of Mayor Joseph L. Alioto. 1975.
War Department Annual Reports for fiscal year ended 30 June 1906. Volume 1. Appendix A. Includes report of the Secretary of War and report of Major General Adolphus W. Greely, U.S.A., Commanding the Pacific Division. House of Representatives, 59th Congress, 2d Session. Document No. 2. Government Printing Office, Washington, D.C. 1906.
Freeman report. Report by Lieutenant Frederick Newton Freeman (commanding USTBD *Perry* at Mare Island) concerning the U.S. Navy's efforts to save San Francisco waterfront in aftermath of the earthquake. National Archives and Records Administration, Pacific Region, San Bruno, California. RG 181, Records of Naval Districts and Shore Establishments, 12th Naval District, Commandant's Office, "General Correspondence (Formerly Classified) 1919-1927," Accession 181-58-3206; box #S404: folder #280-6. "Navy Participation in San Francisco Disaster of 1906." (See "Resource notes" 54)
USGS. *Probabilities of Large Earthquakes in the San Francisco Bay Region, California.* U.S. Geological Survey Circular 1053. Government Printing Office. 1990.
———. *When Will the Next Great Quake Strike Northern California?* U.S. Geological Survey Fact Sheet 094-96.
———. *The Next Big Earthquake in the Bay Area May Come Sooner Than You Think. Are You Prepared?* U.S. Geological Survey magazine issued 1990.
———. *Seismicity of the United States, 1568-1989 (Revised).* Carl W. Stover and Jerry L. Coffman. USGS Professional Paper 1527. 1993.

Illustration sources

Londonborn Publications acknowledges the following for the loan of illustrations as indicated. Illustrations not listed here are in the author's private collection.

Bancroft Library, University of California: pages 66 (James Hopper
     portrait 2 — cropped); 81 (upper) (1905.7690 — cropped);
     244-245 (1905.17134-589D); 292 (William James portrait 1).
Janet Bell: page 140.
California Historical Society: pages 22 (Luke Fay Collection, FN-10776);
     45 (lower) (FN-13107); 50 (gift of Alma Jones-Demski and Beverley
     Jones Bell on behalf of the Wayland E. and Augusta Jones Family,
     FN-31103 and FN-31104); 145 (FN-31107); 205 (FN-06068);
     229 (FN-31108); 238 (FN-04024); 255 (FN-31106); 275 (Bear Photo
     Service Collection, FN-26707); 279 (George A. Berton Collection,
     FN-14938); back cover (Bear Photo Service, FN-31109 — cropped).
Chinese Historical Society of San Diego (Murray K. Lee): page 118.
Fine Arts Museums of San Francisco: page 239 (Achenbach Foundation for
     Graphic Arts, A046299).
Golden Gate National Recreation Area, pages 81 (lower) (PAM BOX 20);
     93 (PAM BOX 21); 144 (PAM BOX 20); 167 (PAM BOX 18).
Museum of the City of San Francisco: page 98.
National Archives, San Bruno: page 173 (R6181 ND SE MINSY. Historian's
     office. Subject files 1880 circa to 1993. Box 17. Earthquake 1906
     NY9-28412 2-3-56 and NY9-28415 3056).
J.R. Monaco: pages 208 and 267.
Ron Ross: pages 76, 213, 285.
San Francisco Public Library, History Center: pages 65, 100, 110, 218.
Gary Sterling: front cover; title page; pages 36 (upper and lower), 40, 261.
Nancy Weston: page 45 (upper).

Index

Whereas the editorial style throughout this volume has been to retain the spelling of names and words as found in the original pieces, today's standard spelling is employed in this index. The acknowledgments and resource notes are not included. Bold face figures indicate illustrations.

Malcolm E. Barker was born in London, England, and worked as a newspaper reporter in Brighton before traveling extensively as a crewmember on P & O cruise ships. He immigrated to San Francisco in 1961 after first visiting the city on board the s.s. *Iberia.* He became an American citizen in 1983. The following year he founded Londonborn Publications to publish *Bummer & Lazarus: San Francisco's Famous Dogs*—the true story of two stray dogs who roamed the city's streets in the early 1860s. For six years he has been researching, writing, and producing the *San Francisco Memoirs* trilogy, which is completed with the publication of this volume.